The Cambridge Introductic
Chaucer

Geoffrey Chaucer is the best known and most widely read of all
medieval British writers, famous for his scurrilous humour and biting
satire against the vices and absurdities of his age. Yet he was also a poet
of passionate love, sensitive to issues of gender and sexual difference,
fascinated by the ideological differences between the pagan past and the
Christian present, and a man of science, knowledgeable in astronomy,
astrology and alchemy. This concise book is an ideal starting point for
study of all the major poems, particularly *The Canterbury Tales*, to
which two chapters are devoted. It offers close readings of individual
texts, presenting various possibilities for interpretation, and includes
discussion of Chaucer's life, career, historical context and literary
influences. An account of the various ways in which he has been
understood over the centuries leads into an up-to-date, annotated guide
to further reading.

ALASTAIR MINNIS is the Douglas Tracy Smith Professor of English at
Yale University, President of the New Chaucer Society (2012–14), and a
Fellow of the Medieval Academy of America. His most recent books are
Fallible Authors: Chaucer's Pardoner and Wife of Bath (2007) and
*Translations of Authority in Medieval English Literature: Valuing the
Vernacular* (2009).

The Cambridge Introduction to
Chaucer

ALASTAIR MINNIS

 CAMBRIDGE
UNIVERSITY PRESS

CAMBRIDGE
UNIVERSITY PRESS

University Printing House, Cambridge CB2 8BS, United Kingdom

Cambridge University Press is part of the University of Cambridge.

It furthers the University's mission by disseminating knowledge in the pursuit of education, learning and research at the highest international levels of excellence.

www.cambridge.org
Information on this title: www.cambridge.org/9781107699908

© Alastair Minnis 2014

First published 2014

Printed in the United Kingdom by Clays, St Ives plc

A catalogue record for this publication is available from the British Library

Library of Congress Cataloguing in Publication data
Minnis, A. J. (Alastair J.)
The Cambridge Introduction to Chaucer / Alastair Minnis.
    pages   cm. – (Cambridge introductions to literature)
Includes bibliographical references and index.
ISBN 978-1-107-06486-7 (hardback) – ISBN 978-1-107-69990-8 (paperback)
1. Chaucer, Geoffrey, –1400 – Criticism and interpretation.   I. Title.
PR1924.M466   2014
821′.1 – dc23   2014034913

ISBN 978-1-107-06486-7 Hardback
ISBN 978-1-107-69990-8 Paperback

Contents

Chapter 4 *The Canterbury Tales*, II: experience and authority

Illustrations

Abbreviations

The Riverside Chaucer	*The Riverside Chaucer*, general ed. Larry D. Benson, 3rd edn with a new foreword by Christopher Cannon (Oxford: Oxford University Press, 2008) (All Chaucer references are to this edition.)
Boethius, *Consolatio*	Boethius, *De consolatione philosophiae*, in *The Theological Tractates and The Consolation of Philosophy*, ed. and tr. E. F. Stewart, E. K. Rand and S. J. Tester (Cambridge, Mass.: Harvard University Press, 1973), pp. 130–435
ChR	*The Chaucer Review*
Dante, *Comedy*	Dante Alighieri, *The Divine Comedy*, tr. Charles S. Singleton, 3 vols. (Princeton, N.J.: Princeton University Press, 1970–5)
DNB	*Oxford Dictionary of National Biography* (Oxford University Press); online edn at www.oxforddnb.com
Gower, *Confessio Amantis*	John Gower, *Confessio Amantis*, ed. Russell A. Peck and Andrew Galloway, 3 vols. (Kalamazoo, Mich.: TEAMS, 2000–4)
Havely, tr., *Chaucer's Boccaccio*	N. R. Havely, tr., *Chaucer's Boccaccio: Sources of Troilus and the Knight's and Franklin's Tales* (Woodbridge: Boydell and Brewer, 1980)
MED	*Middle English Dictionary*, ed. Hans Kurath et al. (Ann Arbor: University of Michigan Press, 1952–2001); online edn at www.hti.umich.edu/mec
Roman de la Rose	Guillaume de Lorris and Jean de Meun, *Le Roman de la Rose*, ed. Félix Lecoy, 3 vols. (Paris: Champion, 1965–70)

S&A	Robert M. Correale and Mary Hamel, eds., *Sources and Analogues of the Canterbury Tales*, 2 vols. (Cambridge: D. S. Brewer, 2002–5)
SAC	*Studies in the Age of Chaucer*
Windeatt, tr., *Chaucer's Dream Poetry*	Barry A. Windeatt, tr., *Chaucer's Dream Poetry: Sources and Analogues* (Cambridge: D. S. Brewer, 1982)

Life and historical contexts

Geoffrey Chaucer was born in London, probably shortly after 1340, into a family of prosperous merchants. The Chaucers were upwardly mobile. Geoffrey's great-grandfather Andrew may have kept a tavern in Ipswich, but his son Thomas became a distinguished parliamentarian and rich landowner, while his granddaughter Alice married particularly well, first to Thomas Montagu, Earl of Salisbury, and subsequently to William de la Pole, Earl of Suffolk. Alice gained some notoriety as an astute wheeler-dealer, who accumulated an extraordinary number of wealthy estates, enjoyed a lavish lifestyle, and shifted her political allegiances when necessary. She sounds like an upmarket version of the Wife of Bath.

Would that we had so much information about the doings of Alice's grandfather Geoffrey. His life records are sparse, insubstantial, tantalizing.[1] Our first scrap of evidence (dated 1357) names Geoffrey Chaucer as the recipient of a minor benefaction from Elizabeth de Burgh, Countess of Ulster and wife of Prince Lionel, the second surviving son of King Edward III (1312–77). Chaucer was involved in the English invasion of France in September 1359, probably serving in Prince Lionel's company. He was captured but soon released; King Edward made a modest contribution to his ransom. During the peace negotiations at Calais in October 1360, Chaucer carried letters back to England. Perhaps this marks the beginning of his career as an international emissary.

We lose track of Chaucer until 1366, evidently an important year for the family. His father died, and his mother married again, to another London vintner. A grant made on 12 September to one Philippa Chaucer, of the queen's household, indicates that by this time Geoffrey Chaucer was her husband, although we have no idea of when the nuptials had taken place. This Philippa is usually identified with the 'Philippa Pan' named in the earlier records as being in the service of the Countess of Ulster (where, presumably, she had met Chaucer) and believed to be the same person as Philippa Roelt, daughter of Sir Payn Roelt, a knight of Hainault, who had come to England with Edward's Queen Philippa. Philippa Roelt was the sister of Katherine Swynford, the mistress and later the wife of John of Gaunt, King Edward's fourth son. Chaucer's first major

1

poem, *The Book of the Duchess*, commemorates the death of Gaunt's first wife, Blanche of Lancaster. The love affair between Gaunt and Katherine Swynford is often assumed to have begun after Blanche's death in 1368, and early during his second marriage, to Constance of Castille, but we have no way of knowing. Neither can we know if the family association benefitted Chaucer's career. But surely it cannot have harmed it.

Yet another record from 1366 names Chaucer as the recipient of a safe conduct permitting him to travel through Navarre, probably on some diplomatic mission. Other enigmatic references to his travels follow. In 1368 Chaucer was given a royal warrant to pass through Dover; in 1369 he may have accompanied John of Gaunt on an ineffectual military campaign in Picardy; in 1370 he was sent to 'parts beyond the sea', those 'parts' and indeed the purpose of the mission being unspecified. In 1372 Chaucer visited Italy to participate in negotiations with the doge of Genoa concerning the expansion of trade with England. It is unclear which other areas of the country he included on this trip, which lasted the best part of six months, but Florence was certainly one of them. Dante Alighieri (d.1321) had been born in Florence, and his fame there was assured. There is no evidence that Chaucer met Giovanni Boccaccio (d.1375) during his stay in the city or that his itinerary included Padua or Arquà, where he might have met Francis Petrarch (d.1374), the writer he was to laud as the 'lauriat' who had 'Enlumyned al Ytalie of poetrie' (*CT* IV.33). In 1378 Chaucer made a second Italian visit, this time to Lombardy. Was his knowledge of the *tre corone* due to those visits, or had he heard tidings of them at home, from Italian merchants in London? That is the most likely explanation for Chaucer's knowledge of the Italian language. Whatever the success of his commercial and political enterprises in Italy may have been, there is no doubt that the time he spent with its literature was of the first importance for his own creative development. Chaucer amassed a rich treasure trove of sources that were little, if at all, known in fourteenth-century England. Thus he was uniquely well placed to bring Italian confidence concerning the 'illustrious vernacular' to bear on his own vulgar tongue. But he did this in his own, highly individualistic if not plain eccentric, way.

On 8 June 1374 Chaucer's circumstances changed dramatically. He was appointed to an administrative position of considerable status, the comptrollership of the customs for the port of London. This entailed a return to the city of his birth, where he resided in a rent-free dwelling over Aldgate Bridge and a significant shift from a life centred on the royal court (a mobile and amorphous entity in itself), although Chaucer remained an esquire of the king's household, a position he had held since at least 1367. It was in London that Chaucer wrote *The House of Fame*, *The Parliament of Fowls* and at least part of *Troilus and Criseyde*. In recent criticism the impact of the city on Chaucer's cultural formation has been afforded more significance than hitherto. With mixed results. London's slander-filled space may indeed be reflected by the chaotic confusion of truth and falsehood that characterizes *The House of Fame*. But the poet did not need to have lived in London to have created those textual conditions, and, indeed, specific reference to the place is notably absent from his work.

What research on 'urban Chaucer' does particularly well, however, is to challenge long-established, although often misleading, distinctions between court and conurbation, region and capital, centre and periphery, mainstream and marginal – and indeed between town and gown. Take for instance the fascinating case of Ralph Strode, the 'philosophical Strode' respectfully named at the end of *Troilus and Criseyde* (V.1857), along with the poet John Gower (d.1408). Strode's early career was as an Oxford don. By 1359 he had become a fellow of Merton College, and we know that he debated with that most turbulent of priests, John Wyclif (d.1384), on the vexing subjects of necessity, contingency, and the freedom of the human will (subjects addressed by Chaucer himself in the fourth book of *Troilus and Criseyde*). On 25 November 1373 Strode was elected as common serjeant or pleader of the city of London, an office he held until 1382. It seems that he had left Oxford for London, having chosen to pursue a secular career; we know that he got married because a wife and at least one child survived him when he died in 1387. Some have wondered whether we are dealing with one and the same man, but the combination of professional interests indicated here was by no means uncommon in Chaucer's day. This was a period in which many of the brightest and best students were choosing a career in law rather than in theology. Strode lived at Aldersgate from 1375 until 1386. In 1381 he stood surety for John Hende, a merchant who became mayor of London in 1391 (and served as the leading royal financier during Henry IV's reign). Geoffrey Chaucer's name appears on the same document, as another surety. All Londoners together.

And yet in 1386 Chaucer left London, giving up his jobs and the Aldgate house, to move to Kent, possibly Greenwich. Why? As a government employee, Chaucer was in the service of King Richard II (who had ascended the throne in 1377), and this was not a good time for the king's servants. The deteriorating relations between Richard and parliament came to a head in November 1387, when he was presented with an indictment of treason against several of his supporters; executions followed the next year. Those who perished included three men whom Chaucer must have known well, by dint of one or more of his appointments: Sir Nicholas Brembre, who had served three terms as mayor of London; Chief Justice Sir Robert Tresilian; and Sir Simon Burley, constable of Dover and Warden of the Cinque Ports since 1384. (Tresilian and Burley served with Chaucer on the commission of the peace for Kent, to which he had been appointed in 1385.) Yet another victim of the 'Merciless Parliament' was the best documented of all of Chaucer's early readers, Thomas Usk, who had shifted his allegiance to Brembre at the worst possible time. In his prose allegory *The Testament of Love*, Usk praises Chaucer as 'the noble philosophical poete in English'[2] and displays extensive knowledge of *The House of Fame, Boece* and *Troilus and Criseyde.* Usk was hanged and brutally beheaded at Tyburn in 1388.

Meanwhile 'the noble philosophical poete' himself may have been lying low in Kent. It is tempting to speculate that the bookish and bumbling persona that he sometimes presents in his poetry concealed a man with a fine instinct for survival. This hypothesis is strengthened by the fact that when Richard II regained his royal authority in 1389, Chaucer's fortunes also rose. On 12 July of that year he was appointed clerk of the king's works, with responsibility for the accounts relating to building and maintenance at Westminster, the Tower of London and several other castles along with seven manors (including Eltham and Sheen). A supplementary position followed in 1390 when Chaucer was made clerk of the works for St George's Chapel, Windsor. He was now a man of some power and influence in 'Greater London' (if that anachronism may be allowed), having gained entry into the higher echelons of the new profession of 'civil servant' that had emerged as secular bureaucrats took over the administration of government from the clerics who previously had performed this function.

But in 1391 something seems to have gone wrong. Chaucer's clerkship of the works was transferred to one John Gedeney. Was Chaucer removed because of a lack of zeal or efficiency, or was this a voluntary retirement? On 3 September 1390 he had been robbed by highwaymen, presumably while he was on official business; perhaps the stresses and strains of the job were proving too much for a man of declining years. (Assuming he was born *c.*1340, Chaucer would have been around fifty by this time – old by medieval standards.) What is clear is that certain (albeit relatively minor) marks of royal favour continued. At some point during the 1390s Chaucer was appointed as deputy manager of the royal forest of North Petherton in Somerset (a typical sinecure for good service). In 1393 Richard II awarded him a gift of £10; an annuity of £20 followed in 1394, and, in 1397, the grant of a tun of wine (252 gallons) annually. More puzzling is a two-year warrant of royal protection, issued in 1398, for going on the king's 'arduous and urgent business' in diverse parts of England. Was Chaucer still performing important administrative or diplomatic services, or was this a general protection against lawsuits lingering from the time when he had held high public office?

In December 1399 Chaucer, aged around sixty, leased a house near Westminster Abbey, although he may well have moved back to the metropolis before that date (and his work as clerk of the king's works would have necessitated some sort of base there). A month earlier, King Richard II had been deposed, and Henry Bolingbroke claimed the throne. These tumultuous events probably made little difference to the writer's then-current circumstances. For a large part of his life Chaucer had enjoyed powerful political connections with the house of Lancaster, as did his highly successful son Thomas, who managed to retain Henry IV's favour during all the king's political machinations – no small feat. King Henry renewed various grants that Richard II had made to Chaucer and even added an extra annuity. Unfortunately, the payments seem to have been slow in coming, and it has been suggested that at this time Chaucer wrote (or adapted) a begging poem (the *Complaint to his Purse*), to be presented to the king. However, there is no way of knowing whether the poem was a conventional witticism or prompted by genuine need. Whatever the state of Chaucer's finances may have been, given Thomas Chaucer's secure social and financial situation around 1400, it seems highly unlikely that his father spent his last months in genteel poverty.

After June 1400 the records of payments of Chaucer's royal grants cease; according to a sixteenth-century tradition he died on 25 October of that year. Chaucer's burial in Westminster Abbey, initially at the entrance to St Benedict's chapel, was for reasons quite unconnected with his poetry, although in 1556 his remains were moved to a new tomb, in a part of the abbey that subsequently became known as Poets' Corner.

Public honour for the poet Chaucer's mortal body came rather late; what may be said about the recognition and reputation his literary corpus enjoyed during his lifetime? The attempt to answer that question takes us into difficult territory. In the first instance, we are faced with general problems of determining the extent and cultural significance of the courtly patronage of learning and literature in late-medieval Europe, together with a specific scholarly controversy concerning the part that Richard II played, or failed to play, as a patron of literature and the arts.

The English court of his predecessor, Edward III, seems to have been a stimulating place for an aspirant poet. The king and his inner circle were familiar with a wide range of figures from *chansons de geste* and romances, as well as devotional and encyclopaedic works. Edward's queen, Philippa of Hainault, had brought her family's sophisticated cultural tastes to England and was regarded as an enthusiastic recipient of poems. Jean Froissart (*c.*1337– after 1404), who was working as Philippa's secretary at the time of her death, celebrated a splendid court presided over by a feared king and a noble queen whom he served with beautiful songs and treatises of love. Philippa was the addressee of *Li Regret Guillaume* (a lament on the death of her father), which was composed by another writer who enjoyed some favour at Edward's court, Jean de la Mote, praised as one of the greatest 'makers' (*faiseurs*) of the day. Although there is no evidence that Jean was still alive when Chaucer entered the outer fringes of Edward's court in the late 1350s, it seems reasonable to assume that some of his poetry still circulated in that milieu. We are on safer ground in the case of Oton de Graunson (*c.*1340–97), praised as the 'flour of hem that make in Fraunce' at the end of Chaucer's *Complaint of Venus*, which is an adaptation of three ballades by the French knight-poet. Graunson was a retainer of John of Gaunt's, and his name, like Chaucer's, appears on several occasions in Gaunt's register; on two occasions they appear together in records of gifts. They may have known each other personally.

How does the court of Richard II compare with this? Not very well. Such patronage as may be associated with the king himself is largely confined to the sphere of architecture, the extensive rebuilding of Westminster Hall (undertaken during Chaucer's tenure of the clerkship of the king's works) being the grandest project. John Gower's 'book for King Richard's sake', the Middle English *Confessio Amantis*, seems to have been the consequence of a chance encounter on the River Thames rather than a formal royal commission (however much Gower tried to exalt the occasion). According to a colophon to one of the items included in Oxford, Bodleian Library MS Bodley 581, it was prepared for the 'consolation' of the most noble king in 1391; alongside is what seems to be a portrait of Richard II. However, there is no evidence that he had commissioned it or any of the other texts in this manuscript.

If we move from the king himself to his circle of associates, a more positive picture emerges. Two of Richard II's chamber-knights, Sir John Clanvowe (*c.*1341–91) and Sir John Montagu (Third Earl of Salisbury, *c.*1350–1400), were poets. None of Montagu's poems – written in French – have survived, but they were praised by Christine de Pizan (d. *c.*1430), a precociously proto-feminist author whose writings were popular at Charles VI's court and who met the earl in Paris in 1398. Another French member of the Montagu household was Jean Creton, who went on to write a metrical history of Richard II's deposition. A poem by Clanvowe, *The Book of Cupid*, has survived, and a devotional prose treatise, *The Two Ways*, has been attributed to him. The former text displays parallels with at least three of Chaucer's poems. Of their friendship there is no doubt: Clanvowe is on record as having supported Chaucer in a mysterious legal case involving one Cecily Champain, who in 1380 brought the charge of *raptus* against him. (The term may mean either abduction or physical rape.)

Another of Chaucer's supporters on that occasion was Sir William Neville, also a knight of the king's chamber.

It may be assumed that Chaucer knew the chamber-knight Richard Sturry because the two men were part of the negotiating team sent by Edward III to pursue peace talks with the French at Montreuil-sur-Mer in 1376. Sturry was involved in arranging an audience at which Froissart presented Richard II with an anthology of his love poems. Yet another chamber-knight, Lewis Clifford, brought from France a poem by Eustache Deschamps (*c.*1346–1406) which praises Chaucer as a 'Grant translateur'; Clifford himself is mentioned in it. Elsewhere Deschamps gives Clifford the epithet 'amorous', which we may take to mean that he was well versed in the fashions of *fin' amors*, a reader of fashionable love poetry. Clifford's son-in-law, Sir Philip de la Vache, seems to have been the addressee of one version of Chaucer's ballade *Truth*.

All of this evidence takes us to the very centre of the court, the *camera regis*, and to position Chaucer within or at least near it. This is not, of course, to claim that the cultural interests of some of Richard's familiars were encouraged by the king himself. But at the very least it can be supposed that he shared some of them. Perhaps King Richard should be seen as a typical, if somewhat unadventurous, aristocratic consumer of courtly culture who shared, in how-ever basic a form, the interests of his more intellectual courtiers but did little if anything to reward them.

Higher estimations of the king's role have been put forward. But even the most generous valuation pales into insignificance when compared to the enter-prise of the French king Charles V (d.1380), who commissioned more than thirty French translations of authoritative works, including several by Aristo-tle. The scale of Charles' patronage is extraordinary, yet he was following in the footsteps of several regal predecessors who also had promoted the produc-tion of works deemed to serve the public good (as the self-promoting rhetoric had it). Special mention may be made of two books dedicated to the ruth-lessly brilliant King Philip IV 'the Fair' (d.1314), Giles of Rome's *De regimine principum* (written originally in Latin but soon translated into French) and Jean de Meun's *Livres de confort*, a French translation of Boethius' *Consolatio philosophiae* which is of special interest to readers of Chaucer because it formed the basis of the *Boece*.

How exactly does Chaucer's *Boece* fit in to his career? Its lack of a preface is intriguing – particularly given that his primary source, Jean de Meun's *Livres de confort*, had provided him with a nicely up-to-date model (complete with a prestigious initial citation of Aristotle) which he could easily have adapted. The French preface addresses King Philip IV. Could it be that Chaucer had written a similar dedication, perhaps to John of Gaunt or even King Richard II himself, which had to be excised due to political expediency, and hence the entire prologue was lost? What is quite clear is that the *Boece* meets the highest standards of its time with regard to academic-style translation of authoritative texts – texts which for generations had been studied in medieval schools and universities. A literal translation is provided, together with explanatory glosses for the reader's benefit. By including them, Chaucer was proceeding in the best academic manner of his age – and acknowledging, indeed respecting, the abilities of an audience that was not narrowly academic and may have been predominantly lay.

We should also appreciate the masterly way in which Chaucer, in his *Treatise on the Astrolabe*, rendered in English the Latin version of an Arabic work by Messahalla (Masha'allah ibn Atharī, an eighth-century Persian Jewish astrologer), which he supplemented with material from John of Holywood's *De sphaera*. The *Astrolabe* treatise is as much of a public text as the *Boece*, intended for an audience far wider than the mysterious 'Lyte [little] Lowys my sone' to whom it is addressed. It was here that Chaucer chose to invoke the concept of *translatio studii*: knowledge has been transmitted from one culture to another and translated from one language to another, and therefore English people should have 'trewe conclusions' made available to them 'in her owne tunge [tongue]'.[3] (Charles V's translators had frequently cited this concept, in commending their French renderings.) The fact that this work has survived, wholly or partially, in thirty-one manuscripts (in contrast with the sixteen extant manuscripts of *Troilus and Criseyde*) is telling.

Chaucer would have fitted in well at Charles V's court, where there were many intellectuals who shared his interests in literature and what then counted as science. In comparison, Richard II's court may seem rather dull, even parochial, despite the king's love of the more ephemeral aspects of French fashion – clothes, cuisine and ceremonial. But the poet had some people to talk to; the 'Chaucer Circle' was fairly extensive. Several of its members have already been named (the knights John Clanvowe, William Neville, Richard Sturry, Lewis Clifford and Philip de la Vache); the literary interests of Sir John Montagu have also been noted. Which brings us to a historical fact of considerable importance: several of those personages were accused of being adherents of heretical doctrines (known as 'Lollardy') deriving from the radical thought of the Oxford theologian John Wyclif. This raises the question of Chaucer's own attitude to Lollardy.

In 1395 the so-called *Twelve Conclusions of the Lollards* was nailed to the doors of Westminster Abbey and St Paul's Cathedral, an action which, according to the chronicler Thomas Walsingham, was made possible by the support of Sturry, Clifford and Montagu, along with Sir Thomas Latimer.[4] This extraordinary document allows us some insight into what Wycliffite teaching meant for learned laymen. It begins with the claim that the English Catholic Church, following the example of 'her stepmother, the great Church of Rome', has fallen into the dotage of 'temporality', a major symptom of which is the maintenance – at great cost to the people of England – of a 'proud prelacy' for which there is no precedent in the New Testament. The imposition of celibacy on men and women who are unable to cope with it allegedly results in a horrifying range of sins, including homosexuality. Priestly powers are denigrated, particularly those relating to the confection of the Eucharist and confession, and suspicion is expressed concerning such practices as paying for indulgences (on which see pp. 105–6 below), saying special prayers for the dead, and making offerings to crosses and other material images.

On one level, this manifesto expresses a desire for a simpler, more authentically New Testament, form of worship, free from the ostentation, materialism and decadence its authors saw in religious practices of their time. On another, it evinces lay unease concerning the activities of a vast ecclesiastical establishment, which uses 'feigned' powers and miracles to assert its authority, extorts money from the people of England and encourages rather than controls sin by imposing on men and women vows of celibacy which they find impossible to keep. The 'temporality' into which the church has fallen has resulted in confusion between the relative powers of church and state.

Many of these attitudes can be traced back to Wyclif himself, who during the 1370s was acting as a sort of spin doctor on behalf of the English ruling élite. Temporal lords had the right to use church property in time of need, he argued, and the state should police the church, acting to curb its excesses and punish its transgressions. Little wonder that temporal lords, including the Lollard knights, approved of this theologian. John of Gaunt enlisted Wyclif as an ally in his own disputes with the church, and when (in February 1377) this prompted a summons for Wyclif to appear before Archbishop Simon Sudbury at St Paul's, Gaunt accompanied him and became involved in a heated argument with Sudbury. Later that same year, Wyclif defended his view that in time of national crisis, taxes due to the pope could be withheld. In the early spring of 1378 Wyclif's views were investigated once again, this time at Lambeth. And once again a secular lord stepped up to defend Wyclif, ordering the prelates not to pass any formal decision against him. This time it was Sir Lewis Clifford, Lollard Knight and friend of Chaucer.

It would seem, then, that in the 1370s at least some aspects of Wycliffite thought were seen as supportive of the state's best interests. But that situation did not last. Richard II bit the hand that sought to feed him, having decided that a tough line with Lollardy was necessary for the maintenance of royal power. Following his return from Ireland in 1395, he made it quite clear that anyone who gave aid or comfort to the Lollards would suffer dire consequences. Sir Richard Sturry was threatened with a most shameful death if he failed to renounce his heterodox views.

Where did Chaucer stand in relation to all of this? His extant works contain only one direct allusion to Lollardy. When Chaucer's idealized 'povre Persoun of a toun' (*CT* I.478–9) takes Harry Bailly to task for his virulent swearing, Harry retorts, 'I smelle a Lollere in the wynd' and warns the Canterbury pilgrims that this 'Lollere' is going to 'prechen us somwhat' (II.1173–7). This is said in jest. Harry is not claiming that the Parson *is* an actual Lollard, merely that he sounds like one (given Lollard aversion to oaths of any kind, including blasphemy). The Shipman then fantasizes that the Parson will preach exclusively from biblical quotations and introduce 'difficulte' (hard and/or controversial material), thereby sowing cockle (a weed) 'in our clene corn' (1180–3), the implied comparison being with the way in which the clean corn of orthodoxy was infiltrated by the weeds of Lollardy. Here two inveterate swearers have joined forces to ridicule what they regard as extreme religiosity. It might be concluded that, for Chaucer, Lollardy was a bad thing to be accused of, rather than a movement with which he wished to be associated.

Attempts to move beyond Chaucer's Lollard joke to uncover a measure of sympathy with Lollard doctrine have met with limited or highly quali-fied success. The counter-argument has been that Lollardy never gained a monopoly on, for example, attacks on church corruption and systemic failure; so Chaucer's attacks on money-grubbing friars and pardoners did not make him a follower of Wyclif. A poet can be radical, abrasive, contentious, in ways which ultimately manage to be supportive of the prevailing religious and social orthodoxies.

There we must leave the debate. It may be a cliché of literary criticism to term Chaucer 'elusive', but that is no more than the simple truth, evident in both his life and his writings. 'He was a townsman and yet a courtier, a Londoner and yet a country gentleman. . . . He frequented court, but managed to distance himself from court politics'.[5] Of bourgeois origins, he served the most powerful aristocrats in the land and enjoyed the friendship of some of the most ideologically radical among them. He had seen military service during the Hundred Years War with France, yet his most extensive treatment of warfare, *The Knight's Tale*, is heavily dependent on an Italian source, which in its turn had described military mores supposedly characteristic of ancient Greece. Pagan antiquity held a special fascination for him, and he allowed his virtuous heathen a considerable degree of moral probity and philosophical insight, while withholding comment on the issue of their salvation. In a time of religious ferment and heresy-hunting he kept his innermost thoughts on religion to himself.

> I wot myself best how y stonde;
> For what I drye, or what I thynke,   *suffer*
> I wol myselven al hyt drynke,
> Certeyn, for the more part,
> As fer forth as I kan myn art.   *I have knowledge of*
>   (*House of Fame*, 1878–82)

That statement of extraordinary self-sufficiency and self-containment, which hides more than it reveals, is as close as we can get to Chaucer.

Chapter 1

Love and lore: the shorter poems

Some twenty-two short poems have been attributed to Chaucer. In general they reflect the influence of French courtly verse, and it is reasonable to assume that Chaucer may have composed some courtly verse in French that is no longer extant. An impression that much more was written (in whichever language) than has survived is conveyed by the statement in *The Legend of Good Women* that Chaucer made: 'many an ympe [hymn] . . . | That highten balades, roundels, virelayes' for the God of Love (F Pro 422–3; cf. G Pro 410–11). A measure of rhetorical exaggeration is obviously involved here, and the short poems we do have range far beyond the context of *fyn lovynge*, as Chaucer terms the aristocratic way of love (*LGW* F 544). Yet the strong possibility remains that the present corpus is only a small fraction of what once existed.

Setting apart the intercalated lyrics – self-contained texts that feature within longer, narrative works – Chaucer's short poems can be classified only in rather broad and sometimes shifting terms, and many of them may be placed in more than one group. First may be listed a number of 'complaint' poems, which lament 'some loss incurred or injustice suffered or grief experienced':[1] *The Complaint of Venus, The Complaint of Mars, The Complaint unto Pity, Anelida and Arcite, A Complaint to his Lady, Compleynt d'amours,* and *A Balade of Complaint. The Complaint of Chaucer to his Purse,* in which Chaucer appeals to King Henry IV to pay him the annuity he is owed, could also be included here, but it is usually thought of as a 'begging' poem, as is the *Lenvoy* to the well-placed Henry Scogan, whose support and patronage the poet seeks. Furthermore, the *balade* to Fortune ends with Fortune herself asking 'princes' to help this petitioner to 'som beter estat', so that he will stop crying out and complaining to her. Returning to the earlier-mentioned complaints: all of them are amatory laments, wherein pagans gods or first-person narrators express the sufferings they are enduring for love. Another group of love poems, *Womanly Noblesse, To Rosemounde, Merciles Beaute* and *Against Women Inconstant,* are in either ballade or roundel form. Among them, *To Rosemounde* is distinctive for its bathetic comparison of the passion-tossed lover to a pike steeped in sauce – either a *reductio ad absurdum* of the usually hyper-inflated language of courtly desire or a graphic illustration of how love can make fools of men.

Then there are the lyrics on philosophical topics: *Gentilesse, The Former Age, Lak of Stedfastness, Truth* and *Proverbs; Fortune* also merits inclusion in this group. More specifically, *Fortune, Gentilesse* and *The Former Age* could be termed 'Boethian' poems because they address, briefly but densely, major themes from *De consolatione philosophiae.* Fortune and her ever-turning wheel are treated at greater length in *Troilus and Criseyde, The Knight's Tale* and *The Monk's Tale,* while gentility or nobility features prominently in *The Franklin's Tale* and *The Wife of Bath's Tale. Truth* includes a punning reference to 'Vache' – Sir Philip de la Vache, Sir Lewis Clifford's son-in-law. (The common noun *vache* means 'cow', the point here being that man, in the wilderness of the present world, is but a mere beast; he should look up to his true home, heaven, and keep on the secure road to salvation.) Therefore it may be set alongside the lenvoys to Bukton (probably Sir Peter Bukton of Holderness) and Scogan as poems directed at named individuals who were Chaucer's friends at court.

A couple of short poems stand alone, resistant to being part of any group. In *Chaucer's Wordes unto Adam, His Owne Scriveyn,* the poet berates his scribe for careless copying of the *Boece* and *Troilus and Criseyde.* It has been suggested that the *scriveyn* in question here is Adam Pinkhurst, who produced documents for the London Guildhall and the Mercers' Company, but this has not met with universal acceptance. Comparable difficulties of historical contextualization surround *An ABC,* a translation in alphabetical form of a prayer to the Virgin Mary from Guillaume de Deguilleville's *Le Pèlerinage de la vie humaine.* In his 1602 edition, Thomas Speght notes that 'some say' this was made 'at the request of Blanche Duchesse of Lancaster, as praier for her privat use, being a woman in her religion very devout'.[2] But no earlier version of this claim exists, and so it must be treated with suspicion.

However, there is no doubt whatever of the association of another of Chaucer's poems with Blanche: *The Book of the Duchess* was written in her memory, probably shortly after her death on 12 September 1368. This appears to be Chaucer's first attempt at a dream-vision poem, a genre he developed with considerable originality during the next few decades, and which is the main subject of the present chapter. The issue of whether dreams were a reliable guide to truths that underpinned waking reality and/or a trustworthy means of predicting the future was hotly debated in Chaucer's day. The literary fictions that drew on the resultant theory – the thirteenth-century *Roman de la Rose* of Guillaume de Lorris and Jean de Meun being the prime example – could veer from valorization through citation of biblical prophetic dreams to subversion through warnings against putting one's trust in dreams, or recourse to the medical belief that they were symptoms of illnesses, and hence of natural rather than supernatural origin. Among the literary forms of the later Middle Ages, the dream-vision is remarkable for its generation of ambiguity and resistance to closure. Little wonder that Chaucer found it so appealing.

Remembrance and consolation: *The Book of the Duchess*

Blanche of Lancaster, one of the wealthiest heiresses of the time, had married John of Gaunt in 1359, thereby providing a firm basis for the financial and political fortunes of this fourth son of Edward III. Line 1318 of Chaucer's commemorative poem punningly links 'white' of 'long castel' (= Lancaster) with 'Johan' of 'ryche hil' (= Richmond; Gaunt held the title of Earl of Richmond until 1372). The Man in Black, the poem's dominant speaker, may be taken as an idealized personification of the sorrow felt by Gaunt at the death of his wife of nine years. Such allusion to historical personages is a common feature of the French *dits amoureux*, to which *The Book of the Duchess* is heavily indebted. In Guillaume de Machaut's *Remede de Fortune* (*c.*1360) the lady who governs the action is identified as Bonne, daughter of King Jean of Bohemia, through a wordplay on her name (54–6).[3] In other examples of the genre, including Machaut's *Jugement dou Roy de Behaigne* and *Jugement dou Roy de Navarre*, the author names directly the personage who is the object of his ostentatious flattery; the first of these poems is the main source of Chaucer's *Book of the Duchess*.

However, the English text takes some time to reach the point at which the Man in Black's exquisite emotions of love and loss are admiringly presented. First we hear a re-telling of a tale of love and loss that derives from Ovid's *Metamorphoses*, XI.410–750: the gods make it known to Queen Alcione that her beloved husband King Seys has perished at sea, whereupon she dies of grief. (Here Chaucer may be incorporating, with less than total success, a poem he had written previously, as a separate and self-contained unit.) Then, after the dreamer finally starts dreaming, comes the description of a brightly lit chamber decorated with the imagery of love's pains and pleasures, which leads into an account of a deer hunt. Finally a small dog (presumably a hunting dog) leads the first-person narrator to his encounter with 'A wonder wel-farynge knyght | . . . clothed al in blak' (452–7).

At the outset the narrator is introduced as a man who has been suffering for eight years from what looks like unrequited love (although we are never told this plainly). Despite the length of time he has been afflicted by this 'sicknesse', his 'boote' (remedy) is no nearer; there is 'phisicien but oon | That may me hele', the implication being that only his beloved lady can cure him (37–40). 'But that is don', he remarks curtly; that's enough of that. And he proceeds to speak of his effort to cope with his insomnia by reading a book 'of fables' about the lives of queens and kings, which clerks of long ago had 'put in rime' to read and remember (52–8). Those opening lines draw on the beginning of Froissart's *Paradys d'amours* in which the narrator laments the long period of time that 'sad thoughts and melancholy' have tormented him, because of his recollections of 'the fair one, for love of whom I entered into this torment and suffer such sleeplessness' (7–12).[4] Although the narrator of *The Book of the Duchess* does not specify a 'fair one' as the source of his pain, I see no reason to doubt this explanation. Chaucer is usually thought of as a poet who creates personae who 'knowe nat Love in dede', and speak of love 'unfelyngly' (*PF* 8; *T&C* II.19), yet on certain occasions he does speak in the voice of a suffering lover, as in many of the short love poems mentioned above.

The intimate relationship between lovesickness and melancholy was discussed extensively in medieval medicine. Constantine the African (d.1087), a Benedictine monk well versed in Arabic lore, explains that 'if erotic lovers are not helped so that their thought is lifted and their spirit lightened, they inevitably fall into a melancholic disease. . . . [They fall] into melancholy from labor of the soul'.[5] Evrart de Conty, physician to King Charles V of France, describes in similar terms the melancholy that is caused 'by loving excessively *par amours*, which malady is called in medicine *amor hereos*'.[6] Chaucer himself speaks of erotic/heroic love (the terms *eros* and *heroes* were commonly confused) in *The Knight's Tale*, where Arcite is depicted as suffering not only 'the loveris maladye | Of Hereos' but also a 'manye' (frenzy) | 'Engendred of humour melencolik' (I.1373–6). In this case, melancholy is regarded as the direct outcome of lovesickness; what is a quite distressing condition in itself has induced in him an even worse, and possibly terminal, disease. One of its regular symptoms is of special significance for *The Book of the Duchess*. The melancholic condition was generally believed to cause the sufferer to dream of black things, due to the large amount of black bile that it caused to collect.

> . . . the humour of malencolie
> Causeth ful many a man in sleep to crie
> For feere of blake beres, or boles blake,   *bears, bulls*
> Or elles blake develes wole hem take.
>   (*NPT*; *CT* VI.2933–6)

Hence it need not surprise us that a person suffering from unrequited love should dream of a Man in Black; this image is utterly appropriate to the dreamer's psychic condition.

But this particular 'sorwful ymagynacioun' (14) takes on a life of its own, moving far beyond the dreamer's mental ownership. The Man in Black is deferred to, addressed in terms of the greatest respect, as befits a man from the highest social echelon. Having heard him pour his heart out in a most pitiful 'compleynte' (464), the dreamer moves to stand before the lamenting lord, doffing his hat as politeness demands and greeting him with all due decorum. Whereupon his interlocutor apologizes to *him* – for not realizing that someone else was present. This is quite unnecessary, of course. If anyone should apologize, it is the dreamer, for having intruded on this high-ranking person's privacy and hearing a profession of grief that was meant for no one's ears apart from those of the Man in Black 'hymselve'. *Noblesse oblige*; such a gratuitous but *gentil* act affirms the agent's good breeding, further evidence of which is given by the fact that the Man in Black's emotions are now under firm control, so much so that (as the dreamer admiringly declares) it is as if he were talking to a different man (529–31). The poem proceeds to fictionalize the class-determined power and privilege of Gaunt's social position in terms of a superiority of sentiment and emotional capacity. Such is its discourse of deference and flattery, the manner of the service that the dreamer performs to the Man in Black – a reflex of the service the young courtier Chaucer is willing and able to perform to John of Gaunt. In that sense, it could be said that the poem has more to do with the living Gaunt than with his dead duchess.

Having found his cryptic companion 'tretable [affable], | Ryght wonder skylful [discerning] and resonable', despite 'al hys bale [torment]' (533–5), the dreamer offers to do all he can to help restore him to health.

> ... certes, sire, yif that yee
> Wolde ought discure me your woo,   *reveal to*
> I wolde, as wys god help me soo,
> Amende hyt, yif I kan or may.
> Ye mowe preve hyt by assay;   *prove it by trying it out*
> For, by my trouthe, to make yow hool
> I wol do al my power hool ... (548–54)

Far from being a pact between equals (as in the *Behaigne*, where a knight and a lady readily agree to hear about each other's sorrow), the help offered here proceeds in one direction – is rendered by the lower to the higher. The Man in Black makes no request to hear about the dreamer's suffering; indeed, the dreamer does not even mention his own psychic state during their extensive conversation. In the *Behaigne* no less a judge than Jean of Luxembourg is invited to adjudicate on whose pain is the worse. In *The Book of the Duchess* there is no need for such a judge because there is no formal competition of fine emotions; the Man in Black's sorry plight is given exclusive attention and articulation. If there is any implicit competition between his distress and the dreamer's, the dreamer is definitely the loser – as befits his lower social position, which is related to an inferior ability to experience intense emotion. The logic here is circular: because the Man in Black is a high-ranking aristocrat, he feels things more intensely than lesser mortals possibly can; because the Man in Black feels things more intensely than lesser mortals possibly can, he must be a high-ranking aristocrat.

Little wonder, then, that the Man in Black is skeptical about his companion's ability to grasp the true nature of his grief. 'Hooly, with al thy wyt, | Doo thyn entent to herkene hit' (751–2), he admonishes the dreamer: listen carefully, and try to understand. When the dreamer apparently fails to do so, the Man in Black, in some exasperation, exclaims,

> 'Thou wost ful lytel what thou menest;
> I have lost more than thow wenest'.
>
> (743–4)

This couplet is reiterated in lines 1137–8 and 1305–6. On the first of these three occasions, the dreamer asks, why make such a fuss about a chess piece? (741); a decoding of the allegory of amatory chess is clearly needed. A second question, how did you first declare your love to her? (1130–5), is quickly followed up with two more: did she not love you? Or did you do something wrong that made her leave you? (1139–43). Finally, the dreamer asks, where is she now? (1298), which prompts – at last – the poem's confrontation of Blanche's death.

On all these occasions the dreamer is seeking a 'tale' – meaning a pretext – whereby he may gain 'more knowynge' of the Man in Black's 'thought' (536–8). Reports of the dreamer's naivety and obtuseness are greatly exaggerated. It may be accepted that the dreamer has registered his interlocutor's early declaration that his lady 'Is fro me ded and ys agoon' (479). He has *some* 'knowynge' of the Man in Black's thought but wants 'more'. Furthermore – and quite crucially – if his companion would honour him with the whole story,

> 'Peraunter hyt may ese youre herte,   *Perhaps*
> That semeth ful sek under your syde'.   *sick*
>
> (556–7)

Here is what is meant by making the Man in Black 'hool' (to return to the idiom of lines 553–4). The implicit medical mechanism may be that thoughts of pleasant things (in this case, a successful courtship and the achievement of a loving relationship) are a means of guarding against *melancholia*. If the dreamer is suffering from this disease, how much more, and how much more dangerously, is his superior, a man of finely tuned emotional sensibility?

This brings us to the most important difference between *The Book of the Duchess* and Machaut's *Behaigne*. In the French poem, the central dialogue is between a knight who is an unrequited lover inasmuch as he has been jilted by his faithless mistress, and a noblewoman whose husband has died. Whose sorrow is the worse? The knight wins the case. Chaucer systematically reverses that judgment by showing that the meagre fantasies of unrequited love cannot possibly compete with either the heights of joy first experienced by the requited lover or the depths of grief subsequently experienced by the bereaved lover.

At the centre of this radical rewriting of Machaut's *Behaigne* is a refusal to accept its blunt assertion that love dies with the body. Reason (as personified in the poem) claims that because 'Love comes from carnal affection' it cannot survive the grave (1709–11). 'As soon as the soul leaves the body, love withdraws and sets off'; therefore both the love and the sorrow of the bereaved lady is 'constantly diminishing from day to day' (1717–23). Out of sight is out of mind: 'Since she will not see him again, it happens that I [= Reason] will make her forget him; for the heart will never love anything so much that it won't forget it after separation' (1677–81). This chimes with the view expressed earlier by the jilted knight, to the effect that 'when the soul has left the body and the body is interred beneath the gravestone, it is soon forgotten' (1109–22).

A far more positive view of memory and reminiscence concerning past life and love is implied in *The Book of the Duchess*. In one of the English poem's most compelling statements, the Man in Black declares,

> '...while I am alyve her,   *alive*
> I nyl foryete hir nevere moo'.   *forget*
>   (1124–5)

John of Gaunt's humble servant, Geoffrey Chaucer, has written a poem that not only supports this view but also functions as a powerful aid to such recollection. If 'olde bokes' did not exist, as Chaucer says elsewhere, 'Yloren [lost] were of remembraunce the keye' (*LGW* F and G Pro 25–6). In his new book, *The Book of the Duchess*, Chaucer has provided Gaunt and his household a key that will unlock remembrance of Blanche. (Of course, whether Gaunt actually read or heard the poem is beyond our knowledge.) *Pace* the voice of Reason in the *Behaigne*, human love does *not* die with the body and is more than a matter of carnal affection and fleshly delight. Out of sight is *not* out of mind; the image of 'faire White' will remain in the memory of the Man in Black, just as the image of Blanche will remain in the memory of John of Gaunt. And Chaucer's poem will ensure that same image will survive far into the future. Such is the consolation it offers.

This is consolation of a strikingly secular kind. One can readily imagine Chaucer offering consolation of an explicitly religious kind, concluding his poem with a confident assumption of Blanche's heavenly reward and an invitation for prayers for the repose of her soul. Indeed, Chaucer could have found the inspiration for such a manoeuvre in the version of the story of Ceyx and Alycone included in the *Ovide moralisé*, an extensive moralization of the entire *Metamorphoses* by a Franciscan friar writing in the early fourteenth century. Here the ship in which Ceyx traveled is interpreted as the human body, the sea as mortal life, the storm as sin. Alcyone is reduced to worldly vanity, the story as a whole being read as a warning against putting one's trust in earthly things; the pleasures of this world are fleeting, like those very seabirds into which, in the original narrative, Ceyx and Alcyone were metamorphosed.[7] From this Chaucer could easily have devised an ending for *The Book of the Duchess* in which Gaunt was tactfully counseled to recognize that ephemeral things, however beautiful they may be, are ultimately of little worth, especially in view of the joys of heaven, which Blanche could have been envisioned as enjoying.

But Chaucer did not go down that route. The rigour with which he avoids any form of religious counseling is remarkable; the materialism of his conclusion to the Ovidian narrative surprising. Morpheus manages to take up the corpse of Seys and bear it to Alicone (in Ovid only a simulacrum is involved). This body offers no hope to the grieving woman who loved it in life.

> 'Let be your sorwful lyf,
> For in your sorwe there lyth no red;   *remedy*
> For certes, swete, I am but ded.
> Ye shul me never on lyve yse'.   *alive*
>
>   (202–5)

All Alcione can do is bury that same body, which now she will find washed ashore for that purpose. Dead is dead. And a similar bluntness marks the end of Chaucer's entire poem, where an expression of pity is the only conclusion offered – it cannot be called closure.

> 'She ys deed!' 'Nay!' 'Yis, be my trouthe!'
> 'Is that your los? Be God, hyt ys routhe!'   *a pitiful situation*
>
>   (1309–10)

Despite the fact that, many lines back, we heard the Man in Black declare that his 'lady bryght' is dead and gone (477–9), this still comes as a shock. It is as if the dreamer and the Man in Black have, between them, managed to keep the fact of Blanche's death hidden from the poem. Now it impacts, and suddenly

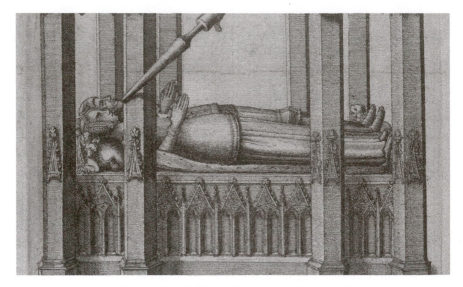

Figure 1. The tomb of John of Gaunt and Blanche of Lancaster in old St Paul's Cathedral, the work of Henry Yevele (destroyed in the Great Fire of London, 1666). From an etching by Wenceslaus Hollar.

there is no more to be said. But what more could be said? Chaucer allows silence to speak louder than words.

Yet the Man in Black (and by inference, John of Gaunt) can value the transformative experience he had with his white lady, during her time on earth; his early courtship, as described for the narrator's benefit and thereby made a matter of record, may be a source of comfort to him. And here is no small thing. Secular remembrance and consolation rarely, if ever, get better than this, given the high rank of the lovers and the rich rhetoric in which their 'designer emotion' (so to speak) has been presented. It is intriguing to note that the real-life John of Gaunt commanded that he should be buried beside Blanche (see figure 1), rather than either of his two subsequent wives. To see this as an expression of his genuine love for her is tempting, but he may merely have been following social convention. Political ambition and obligation alone demanded that this powerful aristocrat should not remain unmarried for long. Within a few months of Blanche's death, negotiations to find a replacement were well under way.

A comic cacophony: *The House of Fame*

Could it be that *The House of Fame* (usually dated *c.*1379–80, and hence positioned as Chaucer's second major poem) also had aristocratic courtship and marriage as its overriding theme – a theme that would have become quite clear had Chaucer completed this work? (Or, to assume that Chaucer did complete this work, if its ending had survived, and his purpose had been explained therein?) Perhaps it was intended to celebrate the news in late 1380 of the betrothal of Anne of Bohemia to Richard II, or indeed an announcement in the following year of Anne's imminent arrival in England. Are those the *tydynges* that the narrator initially lacks (644, 675) but which would have been revealed at the poem's climax? An alternative suggestion is that Chaucer had in mind the expected betrothal of John of Gaunt's daughter Philippa to Charles VI of France (which, in the event, did not happen). So, then, was the 'man of gret auctorite' mentioned in the last line of the poem as it has survived (2158) going to be identified as John of Gaunt, or even King Richard himself?

Such speculations fail to convince. For a start, Chaucer's I-persona is vague about the sort of news he hopes to hear. In the House of Rumour, he merely says that he has come in search of 'Tydynges . . . | Of love or such thynges glade' (1888–9). So the eagerly sought news is not necessarily about love; it could concern some other happy circumstance. Even more crucially, it is difficult if not impossible to find the makings of a prothalamium in a poem that has as its point of origin the passage in Virgil's *Aeneid* (IV.173–97) wherein the vile goddess rumour (*fama*) flies around swiftly, filling the ears of the nations with incessant gossip about the 'shameless passion' of Dido and Aeneas – a character assassination in which truth and falsity are blurred together (cf. Chaucer's reference to 'tydynges . . . of fals and soth compouned', 1027–9). If that may have been insufficiently obvious to some, Chaucer's reductions of 'pious Aeneas' to a philanderer and Dido to an easy conquest (286–8) are hardly subtle. It is difficult to imagine any aristocratic couple being thrilled with such a means of announcing their nuptials.

If no specific amatory event was in the offing, might Chaucer have been thinking about love poetry, particularly his own? In Book II the eagle explains that Jupiter has sent him to reward the poet's service to love and to provide him with the 'tydynges | Of Loves folk' that he lacks, material for future poems (644–5). This theory has much to commend it, given that *The House of Fame* begins with an account of the temple of Venus (119ff.) and goes on to pronounce 'Geffrey' (as the narrator is named at line 729) the servant of her son, Cupid (605–40, 661–71). It would seem, then, that Venus has some claim to be declared the work's presiding deity. Her presence is less obvious in Book III, although 'Venus clerk Ovide' has his own special pillar, because he has spread wonderfully wide 'The grete god of Loves name' (1486–91), and Love's folk comprise the sixth company who seek the approval of Fame. The narrator declares to an anonymous figure who greets him that, thus far, in seeking fresh information about love or some such happy thing

(1886–9, quoted above), he has been disappointed. Finally, in a corner of the House of Rumour, 'Geffrey' hears men telling of 'love-tydynges' (2141–4). There is considerable commotion among them – some major piece of news seems imminent. Then a 'man of gret auctorite' appears: can he be the bearer of such information? We will never know, for here the poem, as we have it, stops.

Was that man to have been Virgil, author of the tragic love story of Aeneas and Dido, as featured in the first book of the poem, together with the related account of the gossip-generating goddess *fama*? Or is Ovid a more plausible identification? Apart from being, in general terms, 'Venus clerk', Ovid was the specific source of a contra-Virgilian account of Dido and Aeneas, which aggressively takes the side of betrayed Dido against false Aeneas (*Heroides*, VII, an obvious influence on both Book I of *The House of Fame*, and the subsequent *Legend of Dido*). He also had constructed a House of Rumour (*Metamorphoses*, XII.39–63), in language echoed in Chaucer's poem. There is no doubt that Ovid's *œuvre* contributed many of the strands that interweave in this torn tapestry of a text.

However, it is difficult to argue that the *auctorite* borne by Chaucer's mystery man relates to love exclusively, for in the poem's final book the issues fan out with a speed and scope that is at once bewildering and exhilarating; the particularities of individual lives and loves are subsumed under larger categories. One of the structuring devices on offer is the abovementioned scene in which Fame announces her judgments to various groups of supplicants, nine in all. The members of the first group deserve good fame but do not get it. Those in the second group, who are equally worthy, suffer slander and undeserved shame, whereas the third group will have their good works lauded beyond what they deserve. The fourth and fifth companies have performed good works for the love of God, for which they want no reward, yet the fifth will actually be rewarded, whereas the fourth will not. The sixth and seventh groups consist of indolent lovers; equally unworthy, the former will enjoy a reputation for great success, whereas the latter will be known as the 'ydel wrechches' they are (1777). The eighth and ninth companies are bad lots indeed – respectively, traitors who have done greater 'wikkednesse' than any heart could guess, and shrews who 'delyt in wikkednesse' (1811–14, 1830–1). The eighth group wants the evil deeds of its members to be obliterated with 'good renoun' (1817), but Fame refuses to perpetrate what even she deems an injustice. Uniquely among all the companies, the ninth and last supplicants ask for their evil deeds to be broadcast widely – and the goddess agrees. In short, this entire excursus emphasizes the lack of any secure connection between personal merit (or demerit) and the response of posterity.

Which makes it a fitting continuation of at least some of the things said earlier in Book III, when another structuring device was offered – the three major subject matters of literature (about the Jews, about Troy, and about Rome). Given the unreliability of our memories (men are forgetful, and what they do remember will die with them), writing is an indispensable 'keye' of 'remembraunce' (cf. *LGW* F and G Pro 25–6). In the detailed description of the House of Fame provided at the beginning of Book III, it is said that the letters inscribed on the side of the ice-mountain, which is unprotected by the shade of Fame's castle, are fading away (1136–46). By contrast, the inscriptions on the side that Fame shades are as fresh as if men had written them that very day or hour (1151–8). As Isidore of Seville (d.636) explained in his widely disseminated *Etymologiae*, 'the practice of letters was invented for the memory of things. Things would vanish into oblivion unless they were bound by letters'.[8] John of Salisbury (d.1180) asked the rhetorical question, 'Who would know of Alexander or Caesar, or would respect the Stoics or the Peripatetics, unless they had been distinguished by the memorial of writers? . . . How many powerful kings have there been of whom there is nowhere a word or thought?' It is literature's job to preserve past glories. We cannot learn anything from 'the excellence' of the 'conduct' of great men unless we read about them; 'the light of letters' necessarily keeps illuminated what otherwise would be enveloped in the 'perpetual darkness' of oblivion.[9]

But can one believe what one reads? Can we be sure that a person's fame or infamy is rightly assigned and that virtue is appropriately commended, and vice condemned, by future generations? Chaucer's account of the matter of Troy does not inspire confidence in this regard and is of a piece with his subsequent description of the unreliable judgments of Fame.

> Oon seyde that Omer made lyes,
> Feynynge in hys poetries,   *Feigning/fictionalizing*
> And was to Grekes favorable;
> Therfor held he hyt but fable.
>
>   (1477–80)

Indeed, not just one but several writers had criticized Homer in these terms, including two on Chaucer's list of the supporters of the fame of Troy, 'Dares' and 'Guydo' (1467, 1469): Dares Phrygius, allegedly a Trojan eyewitness of the Trojan War but actually a writer of much later vintage, and Guido delle Colonne, author of the *Historia destructionis Troiae*. Guido had complained that 'Homer, of greatest authority among the Greeks in his day, turned the pure and simple truth of his story into deceiving paths, inventing many things which did not happen and altering those which did happen'.[10] Homer was not alone. 'Even Virgil' was 'in some things unwilling to depart from the fictions of Homer', Guido continues, and at the end of his *Historia*, 'that highest of poets, Virgil, whom nothing obscures' is coupled with Homer and Ovid as writers who were deficient 'in describing the truth about the fall of Troy', whether 'according to the histories of the ancients or according to fables'.[11]

Here Guido (and Chaucer in the passage just quoted) allude to a medieval tradition about the unreliability of poetic fiction, as set in opposition to the transmission of accurate reporting expected of history, *historia*. 'The fables (*fabulae*) of the poets are named from *fando* [speaking], because they are not true things but only spoken fictions', to quote a definition from Isidore of Seville. *Fama* is also derived from *fando*, says Isidore, noting that it refers to good and bad things.[12] Writers have the fame of those they write about in their hands, the opportunity to inscribe things both good and bad, and indeed to compound the true and the false. They are the makers (and the breakers) of reputation. In creating both fiction and fame, sound is crucial: both take their name from *fando*, both involve speech acts.

Medieval grammarians saw speech first and foremost as spoken utterance; writing followed after as a secondary activity, a material recording of sound. Priscian had defined spoken utterance (*vox*) as 'very thin struck air or its property perceptible to hearing, that is, what property strikes the ears', and according to Macrobius 'sound is produced only by the percussion of air'.[13] Chaucer's amusingly erudite eagle seems to know all about this.

> 'Soun ys noght but eyr ybroken;   *broken air*
> And every speche that ys spoken,
> Lowd or pryvee, foul or fair,   *private*
> In his substaunce ys but air;   *substance*
> For as flaumbe ys but lyghted smoke,   *flame*
> Ryght soo soun ys air ybroke'.
>
> (765–70)

Some grammar teachers worried about the notion that the 'substaunce' of sound 'ys but air'. If this were true, could not human speech be considered simply as mere sound, and writing as its servile reporter? Chaucer takes that question a stage further. If everything that human beings say and write has this same substance, how can some utterances be deemed superior to others? Could it be that the most profound reasonings of the philosophers, the most acute descriptions of human virtue and vice within the framework of exemplary history, and the most affective effusions of poetry, are on a par with the squeak of a mouse (785) or the dubious speech and sounds of wizards, magicians, tricksters, witches, enchantresses, and sorceresses, with all their sinister 'exorsisacions' and 'fumygacions' (invocations and ritual censings; 1259–64)? It seems unlikely that Virgil, Ovid, Lucan, Claudian and the other *auctores* who grandly rest atop their pillars would wish to keep company with such riff-raff.

Yet they have no choice in the matter. Irrespective of who or where it came from, 'everych ayr' (817), 'every speche, or noyse, or soun' (783) produced in the sublunary world causes a ripple effect or 'multiplicacioun', which ascends to Fame's house – just as, when a stone is dropped into water, it causes a series of waves that eventually reach the riverbank (787–822). In Fame's domain those noises are blended together in a way that strips them of their proper values and renders impossible any secure distinctions between truth and falsity, poetic fiction and historical fact. 'We wil medle us ech with other!' the competing sounds gleefully exclaim; no man will get the one without the other (2102–5). 'Thus saugh I fals and soth compouned | Togeder fle for oo [fly as one] tydynge', ruefully remarks 'Geffrey', who, in seeking 'tydynges', has found only confusion.

What is fame? A lot of broken air. Here, then, is a quite extraordinary *reductio ad absurdum* of the desire for reputation and celebrity, a robust revelation of the vanity of human wishes. Chaucer is certainly not sermonizing; instead he makes his point through the creation of a comic cacophony that never loses its humour. Indeed, humour remains the dominant note. And that note, above all else, separates this poem from the predecessor that is never far from Chaucer's mind throughout his narrative. Although the *Comedy* is by no means a major source, its presence is felt again and again, as Chaucer borrows lines and ideas from the Italian text, or alludes to it, in ways that indicate a confident command of its design. This is the first Middle English poem in which the Muses are invoked;[14] Chaucer does this on two occasions (520–8, 1091–1109), and both follow passages in the *Comedy*. However, Chaucer's self-construction 'Geffrey' could hardly be more different from Dante's authoritative I-persona. Here is no anxiety of influence, but rather a desire to affirm difference and independence.

Above all other vernacular poets of the later Middle Ages, Dante was the one who most assiduously sought the accolade of *auctor* – who wanted to be honoured not only as a poet but also as an authority figure, comparable in status with the great poets of the past who were reverently studied in medieval grammar schools, writers who were celebrated for their sententious sayings as much as for their fine verse forms. Medieval grammarians identified one of the main constituents of the etymology of *auctor* as the Greek noun *autentim*, denoting authenticity and authority. A literary *auctor* was a figure whose writings were worthy of belief, implementation and imitation, which enjoyed great respect in terms of their pedagogic and doctrinal content. Dante proceeded to construct himself as such a figure. His self-authorizing moves include an audacious moment in the *Comedy* where he writes himself into a distinguished company of poets that includes Virgil ('my master and my author'), 'Homer, sovereign poet', Horace, Ovid, and Lucan (*Inferno*, IV.88–90, cf. I.85). Indeed, the Dante-persona goes so far as to pronounce himself 'sixth amid so much wisdom' (IV.101–2), implying that he possesses sagacity of a kind that justifies his membership in this exclusive club.

In sharp contrast stands 'Geffrey's' self-isolating statement that he himself will drink everything in, and from, his own cup (1880): apparently he will share this beverage with no one else, or there is no one with whom he can share it. How should we interpret this stance? As aloofness or as an acute version of the standard medieval 'modesty topos'? Are we meant to feel that, unlike the better (self-)positioned Dante-persona, 'Geffrey' has no club to join? If the men of great authority can disagree so irresolvably (as for example in their conflicting versions of the story of Dido and Aeneas), if they are the purveyors of lies and half-truths (the lies of lovers being only a small part of a greater malaise), how can – why should? – one associate with them? If no common core of truth, no universal reservoir of *auctoritas*, unites them, they lack any secure basis for community. Furthermore, if there is nothing secure to share there is nothing secure to pass on, so the prospect of a 'translation' of textual authority into the vernacular seems bleak – or at least it would be bleak, were Chaucer not so concerned to keep the tone light. The English poet has caused the pillars of textual authority to tremble and invited us to enjoy the spectacle.

What, then, of that authority figure announced in line 2158? Can he bring some order to this comic chaos? It seems unlikely – *seems* being the operative word. 'He *semed* for to be | A man of gret auctoritee' (2157–8). In other words, he looks the part, but the reality may be quite different. Here, yet again, Chaucer seems to be echoing the *Comedy*, and, yet again, the contrast between the two texts is telling. In Dante's account of the dead poets' society that he (although alive, Christian and a vernacular writer) is eager to join, the merit of its pagan worthies is emphasized; their 'honoured fame' resounds through human existence and even wins 'grace in Heaven' (*Inferno*, IV.76–8). Apparently they occupy a Castle of Fame, full of people with 'looks of great authority' (112–13). This community includes the souls of virtuous heathen warriors (including Aeneas) and exemplary women, along with those of the great pagan philosophers, with Aristotle as their master. Poets and philosophers are obviously happy in each others' company: indeed, the poets are referred to as 'sages' (*savi;* IV.110). Clearly, these figures do not just look authoritative, they *are* authoritative: authentic men (and women) of great authority. No such confidence can be placed in the figure who fails to appear at the end of *The House of Fame* as we have it, missing his big entrance.

At the beginning of the *Paradiso*, Dante had invoked Apollo as his muse in elevated terms: 'make me such a vessel of your worth as you require for granting your beloved laurel, ... Enter into my breast and breathe there' (I.13–36). Chaucer's echo of this passage in *The House of Fame* involves the Chaucer-persona declaring that, if only Apollo will help him, he will go up to the very next laurel, 'And kysse yt, for hyt is thy tree'(1106–8). A supplication for the infusion of divine power (Apollo being the god of music, poetry and prophecy) has been reduced to a promise to kiss a plant. Humour rarely gets as pervasive as this. And with it Chaucer exorcises the spectre of Dante; with wit that sharp, he needs no 'exorsisacion' or 'fumygacion'. Yet the *omage* he is paying to his predecessor is highly evident.

This is writing of extraordinary self-confidence and maturity. Can *The House of Fame* really be as early as *c.*1379–80, as is widely assumed? There is no compelling reason in favour of that dating, and I myself feel that this comic cacophony just might have been composed after *Troilus and Criseyde* and 'the love of Palamon and Arcite l Of Thebes'.[15] On that reckoning, it represents a crucial stage in Chaucer's intensive engagement with Italian literature, when he moved from Boccaccio to Dante, and away from the *roman antique* genre, to confront, in his own contrarian way, the *Comedy* and all it implied for vernacular poetics.

Concordia discors? The Parliament of Fowls

The *Parliament of Fowls* brings to English poetry, for the first time, the rhyme royal stanza (using the rhyme scheme ababbcc). Another major innovation is the introduction of material from Boccaccio's *Teseida* (*c.*1339–41) to the world of the *dit amoureux*, where it interweaves with discourse from the *De planctu naturae* of Alan of Lille (d.1202/3) and Cicero's *Somnium Scipionis* as interpreted in Macrobius' fifth-century commentary. The poem is usually assigned to the period between the late 1370s and the early 1380s. (Chaucer returned from his first Italian visit in 1373, but nowadays critics are quite willing to countenance the idea that he may have read manuscripts of Italian texts imported at London, before he set foot in the country of their origin.) Efforts at more precise dating fix on the distinctive astronomical reference at lines 117–18, where Venus is said to be in an extreme northern position ('north-north-west'), and/or the statement that the bird parliament was held on St Valentine's Day (309, cf. 683).

Venus had such an aspect during April and May of 1374, 1377 and 1382, but of course a poet can easily refer back to some striking event that occurred some time before he was writing. The Valentine's Day references are even more perplexing because there were several Saint Valentines, most relevantly the third-century Roman saint who is commemorated on 14 February (this being the lovers' saint of popular culture) and Valentine of Genoa, whose feast day was on 2 May – the latter being a more appropriate time for a celebration of love long associated with the coming of spring. Indeed, it has been suggested that the two saints got confused, hence producing the rather unseasonable location of Valentine's Day in the dead of winter.[16] Against that, it should be noted that long-standing traditions placed the beginning of spring on days in either February (as with the Roman Lupercalia) or March. Any part Chaucer may have played in this creative confusion is hard to determine, as is the extent to which he was responsible for the assimilation of the discourses of *fyn lovynge* to the cult of some Saint Valentine or other. However, one can risk the claim that this cultural development probably occurred during his lifetime and maybe even within his literary circle (broadly understood), for Valentine poems were written by Oton de Graunson, Deschamps, Clanvowe and Gower; Christine de Pizan and Charles d'Orléans would elaborate the conventions further. Chaucer, then, definitely played a significant role in this process of innovation.

But why should he decide to write a Valentine's poem at this particular time? Here we must return to the circumstances of the marriage of Richard II and Anne of Bohemia, which some have sought to link (with greater difficulty) to *The House of Fame*. The couple were married in Westminster Abbey on 22 January 1382, and perhaps that was the year of the poem's composition (we may recall that Venus was 'north-north-west' in the spring of that year). However, their marriage treaty was concluded on 2 May 1381, which gives us another date to play with, given that this coincided with the feast day of St Valentine of Genoa. All this is, of course, pure speculation. But it adds an extra edge to the question, why should a poem that begins by revealing the insignificance of 'lytel erthe' (57) within the immense reaches of the universe, and emphasizing the paramount importance of one's immortal soul (73), go on to celebrate the earthy pleasures of a raucous mating festival? The sobriety of the initial stanzas, filled with Macrobian rigour, gives way to a quotidian humour that arises from the dissonant voices of the bickering birds, each expressing the characteristics assigned to it in beast-fables and sometimes mimicking the sounds made by its model in nature.

The goos, the cokkow, and the doke also
So cryede, 'Kek kek! kokkow! quek, quek!' hye,
That thourgh myne eres the noyse wente tho.

(498–500)

One superior species of birds, the noble eagles (prominent among the birds of prey), is set apart from the rest. Three of the males love one and the same female, and the poem ends with this beautiful creature insisting that on this occasion she will serve neither Venus nor Cupid and not accept any of her suitors. The other birds happily pair off, leaving the lovelorn eagles to return the following year, to try their luck then, and an avian choir performs a roundel to welcome summer and honour Saint Valentine. A poem that ends with no marriage between aristocrats (albeit aristocrats of the bird world) seems a strange means of celebrating a royal wedding, and the refusal of the formel (female eagle) stands in sharp contrast to Anne of Bohemia's acceptance.

This point gains even more force when the intertextual valence of Alan of Lille's 'Pleynt of Kynde' (316) – the source of the parliament's presiding figure, Dame Nature – is considered. In a rhetorical tour de force Alan had described the phantasmagoric garments worn by this goddess of Christian Neoclassicism, including a robe of state decorated with an animated picture of a parliament of birds, a mantle with images of aquatic animals which in its folds shows the colour of water, and a multi-coloured tunic impressed with a 'kind of magic picture' of land animals.[17] All nature functions in accord with Nature's laws, ranging from the obediently revolving firmament to the birds who, 'stamped with their various natural qualities', 'look with heartfelt longing' to her 'instructions'.[18] Prominent among those instructions is the order to procreate. Nature has a 'priest' called Genius (a figure subsequently developed in Jean de Meun's part of the *Roman de la Rose* and in Gower's *Confessio Amantis*) who derives from the pagan god of generation and here is enlisted in support of the Christian imperative to 'be fruitful and multiply, and fill the earth' (Genesis 1:28). The Earth never ceases in tireless generation to bring the various species of creatures to birth, says Dame Nature. However, one creature, and one alone, refuses to obey her universal law, dares to stir up strife against his queen's dignity. This is man – the ungrateful wretch who engages in deviant sexual practices, particularly homosexuality, which is the cause of Nature's complaint. Of course, there is no suggestion of homosexuality in the *Parliament*, where the entire natural world seems simplistically straight. But one species, it could be argued, is going against the order to pair off and procreate – the eagles, representatives of the nobility with their special (might they be called deviant?) way of pursuing love.

There is not much by way of explicit reference to procreation in Chaucer's poem, but that is to be expected given that the purpose of the parliament is to enable the birds to choose their mates; procreation will come later. (Besides, the poetry of *fyn lovynge* is generally concerned with the pursuit of love rather than with its fruits.) However, and even before Dame Nature makes her entrance, the dreamer does see some birds getting on with the business of producing their young: 'Some besyede hem here bryddes forth to brynge' (192). Given the extraordinary natural opulence of the beautiful garden in which this dream-vision is set, it is hard not to see it as a procreant cradle (in Shakespearean phrase). John Gower has his Genius figure wonder why maidens should waste any time in hastening to the feast of 'honeste' married love, which involves the begetting of children – essential if the world is to survive (*Confessio Amantis*, IV.1480–97). This statement follows a tale of hesitation or slothfulness in love, featuring a princess, Rosiphelee, who desires neither marriage nor indeed the love of paramours, despite being physically and emotionally ready for love (IV.1266–71). In a bizarre vision of an afterlife wherein amatory achievement is rewarded, Rosiphelee finds herself in a beautiful garden, replete with vivid greenery, singing birds, and mating animals. Here she encounters a company of beautiful ladies on fine horses, attended by a distressed woman who is forced to carry horse halters for her better-favoured companions (IV.1305–442). Her crime, for which she is enduring Cupid's punishment, was to be slow to love. Having been shown the error of her ways, Rosiphelee vows that this will never happen to her. But might it happen to the formel?

That is highly unlikely. The creature is well aware of her social role and future destiny. Rather than totally refusing to participate in the mating game, she requests a period of one year's delay, so she can consider the issue: 'I axe respit for to avise me' (*PF* 648). Which must mean, to consider which of the three suitors she will pick. That is the – quite specific – end to which her 'choys al fre' (649) shall be directed. Dame Nature immediately accepts this decision, which is in fact a mere deferral. A few moments earlier she had remarked that, if she were Reason, she would advise choosing the royal tercel (the most noble and most worthy eagle). But she does not insist on that choice. Being Nature, she is well aware that factors apart from high rank sometimes affect a person's choice of sexual and marital partner. Being a fictional character, she colludes in the consoling fiction that, in the marriage negotiations of prominent aristocrats, such factors can prove decisive. In any case, at the end of the one-year postponement, Nature's purposes will be served, the heterosexual norms observed; this *grand dame* will have no need to complain in the manner of her Latin predecessor. For her part, the formel will never be punished like Rosiphelee's interlocutor. Her somewhat curt expression ('Ye gete no more',

651) should not mask the fact that she is displaying ladylike reluctance of a kind quite appropriate to (and which is a marker of) her superior position, in humorous but socially significant contrast to the haste with which the lower-order birds have picked their partners. Aristocrats take longer in love, engage in more elaborate rituals, than the common flock.

The *Parliament* has much of the debate poem about it, and it may be presenting for discussion an implicit yet compelling *demande d'amour*, a 'love question' of a kind then fashionable as a noble entertainment. Such a *demande* is made explicit in *The Knight's Tale*. Arcite is a free man but cannot see his lady, whereas Palamon is a prisoner but can see his lady every day, through the window of his prison. Which lover is the worse off, Arcite or Palamon? (*CT* I.1347–54). No obvious answer is forthcoming; this is the stuff of courtly debate. Similarly, in the *Parliament*, the question tacitly arises, which type of love is better, that pursued by the birds of the three lower classes (waterfowl, seed-eaters and worm-eaters), who can choose their mates right here and now on this Valentine's Day, or that pursued by the birds of prey, wherein desire is deferred – but, one might argue, is all the more exquisite and pleasurable for that? The turtle dove, spokeswoman for the seed-eaters, complicates things nicely, by offering an idealistic view of love that would do credit to any aristocrat (582–8). No doubt Chaucer's noble readers would side with the eagles, while enjoying the hurly-burly just as much as their avian equivalents seem to ('The laughter aros of gentil foules alle', 575).

Real-life frustrations may be in play here, having been rendered as play; the long wait the tercels must endure no doubt reflects those marriage negotiations that, in the highest echelons of society, could drag on for a long time (as they had in the case of King Richard and Anne of Bohemia, and also that of John of Gaunt and Blanche of Lancaster). But, of course, no eagle would want to be a duck or a cuckoo. What true courtly lover could accept the principle, 'But she wol love hym, lat hym love another!' (567), or exclaim that, as long as he can gain his own mate without hindrance, he doesn't care what happens to anyone else (605–6)? Yet such a lover could nevertheless laugh at those vulgar remarks. So, then, this poem's appeal to aristocrats seems to be considerable: their sense of their own superiority is being confirmed (through flattery a lot more subtle than that directed at John of Gaunt in *The Book of the Duchess*), and respectful notice taken of the many tiresome procedures and conventions that come with their elevated position.

Some have found acute social antagonisms and irresolvable class division in the *Parliament*, while others optimistically believe that a *concordia discors* emerges from the narrative: just as all the discord in nature is resolved ultimately within a harmonious universe, so too within human society an overriding orderliness prevails; a controlling structure is kept in place by the pressure of those very antagonisms and divisions. The root of such thinking is found in the ancient belief that the four elements in nature (air, earth, fire and water) are inevitably in conflict, but that very conflict creates an overall harmony and is essential for the proper functioning of the system as a whole. Hence Boethius (in a metre Chaucer was to adapt in *Troilus and Criseyde*, III.1744–72) celebrates the way divine love keeps all things in regular balance and harmony, ensuring that the sea and the land do not extend beyond their 'fixed bounds' (*De consolatione philosophiae*, II, met. viii, 1–15). Expanding on this, Alan of Lille's Dame Nature explains how she formed man as a microcosm or little world, to mirror the vast universe. 'For just as concord in discord, unity in plurality, harmony in disharmony, agreement in disagreement of the four elements unite the parts of the structure of the royal palace of the universe, so too, similarity in dissimilarity, equality in inequality, like in unlike, identity in diversity of four combinations [meaning the four humours] bind together the house of the human body'.[19]

All of this sounds very reassuring. But does it really apply to the interactions of human beings in society, as depicted through the avian analogues of Chaucer's poem? Sometimes discord, plurality, disharmony, dissimilarity, and inequality may spill over the boundaries that contain them and normally ensure their positive contribution to the total structure – an effect less easily rationalized in social theory than it is in metaphysics. Then there are the many discords that similarly trouble the little world of the individual. Alan's Dame Nature is far from sanguine when she addresses the disharmony that exists within man between 'the movement of reason' and the 'movements of sensuality',[20] even as Boethius had expressed the hope (*only* the hope) that 'the love that rules the stars' should also rule the hearts of men (II, met. viii, 28–30). Similarly, Cicero, as expounded by Macrobius and summarized by Chaucer, denounces 'brekers of the lawe' and 'likerous folk', who are destined to 'whirle aboute th'erthe alwey in peyne', because they failed to know themselves 'first immortal' and to work towards the common good (71–84). In human behaviour, *concordia* is a goal that must be striven towards, attained through proper moral choices and actions; sometimes, however, all we have is the chaos of *discordia*.

Those *auctores* speak with one voice – unsurprisingly, for we are dealing with several iterations of a single body of doctrine, a Neoplatonism comprising the belief that 'oure present worldes lyves space | Nis but a maner deth' (53–4), and therefore one should not 'in the world delyte' (66). Given those animadversions, it should be emphasized that 'the noble philosophical poet in English' (see p. 4 above) was no hard-line Neoplatonist, although he was attracted by the poetic possibilities afforded by Neoplatonic discourse, as his constant use of Boethius makes quite clear. The secularism that pervades so much of Chaucer's work was a source of resistance, and in any case his visionary poems all profess to be love-visions, hence their tendency to take 'delyte' in the present world is par for the course. When Scipio the Elder (here called 'Affrycan', Africanus) appears in the narrator's dream it is not to berate him for his sins but rather to direct him to a garden of Venus (where the goddess herself appears wearing the medieval equivalent of sexually provocative lingerie, 267–73).

The relationship between this embodiment of eroticism and Dame Nature, who appears later and presides over the bird-parliament, has exercised much criticism of the poem, although both are appropriate figures in a narrative in which lovers select their partners. A man of great authority has come down from his high pillar to act in a way so uncharacteristic that it is quite ridiculous and hence hilarious, on the amusingly implausible pretext that he must reward the poet for having perused his torn old book (110). This move may be compared to the way in which, in other love-visions, Chaucer had Morpheus, in Ovid a fearsome son of the god of sleep, and Jove's eagle's, the grave messenger bird of the most powerful pagan god, appear in contexts that are quite beneath their original dignity.

In *The Parliament of Fowls*, as elsewhere, Chaucer's narrators leave abstruse disputation concerning 'hevene and helle I And erthe, and soules that therinne dwelle' (32–3) to the professional theologians. Love, in all its 'wonderful werkynge' (5), is what this poem is about – to judge by its opening lines. That is the context in which we find the resonant affirmation that 'al this newe science [expert knowledge] that men lere [learn]' comes 'out of olde bokes' (24–5). After having read Macrobius the I-persona feels that

> ... bothe I hadde thyng which that I nolde,
> And ek I ne hadde that thyng that I wolde.
>
> (90–1)

What does he have that he did not want? Macrobius' sombre teaching, perhaps? And what does he want that he does not have? More understanding of the astonishing power of love, perhaps? If such an interpretation is accepted, a moralistic response would hold that the narrator should be acutely aware of what he read in Macrobius and less concerned with Love's spurious 'myrakles' and 'crewel yre' (11). But surely that is to read the poem in too binaristic a way. Alan of Lille did not condemn human love out of hand, only the type that hindered the ongoing propagation of the species. Further, the bad behaviour condemned by Macrobius consists of the failure to serve the 'commune profit': Cicero's Africanus had urged his grandson to protect the commonwealth (a political system beloved by the supreme ruler of the universe), by assuring him that a special reward is reserved in heaven for those who have 'saved, aided, or enlarged' that state.[21]

Here, then, is no advocacy of the contemplative life, of withdrawal from social exchange, but rather an exhortation to work effectively within the active life. Many writers of Chaucer's age followed Aristotle rather than Plato in asserting that man is a social animal, and regarded marriage and family life as obvious outcomes of that sociability. According to Giles of Rome's *De regimine principum* (*c.*1285), Aristotle taught that great love and friendship should exist between husband and wife,[22] and Nicole Oresme (Charles V's most impressive scholar-translator) attributed to him the belief that nature bestowed sexual pleasure on the human species 'not only for reproduction of its kind but also to enhance and maintain friendship between man and woman'.[23] Human love can indeed serve the common good; the relationship between a man and a woman is the primal social unit, and happy marriage is conducive to a harmonious society.

In such doctrine we may detect something of the tone of the *Parliament*, wherein the possibilities for genuine social subversion are scarcely explored. Class distinctions and stereotypes have been made the object of mirth, but that does not make them any less stable; the poem can easily be read as a celebration of the status quo. Chaucer the rich vintner's son and public man occupies an excellent vantage point from which to regard all the birds on their respective perches. But he does little to shake the tree. A beautiful love-garden, filled with laughter and joie de vivre, has been created, but only the aristocrats, and those aspirants who seek to share their values (and some of their privileges), have the full measure of that pleasure.

In both *The Book of the Duchess* and the *Parliament*, he who pays the piper calls the tune, but fortunately the tune is played superlatively well. *The House of Fame* is tantalizingly different. Its concern is with textual rather than socio-political authority, an area in which Chaucer is supremely confident, quite willing to admit, and indeed to create, *discordia*. Among the dream-visions, here is the work that reveals just how high the poet's thought can fly, how 'fer forth' his art poetical can reach.

Chapter 2

Fictions of antiquity: *Troilus and Criseyde* and *The Legend of Good Women*

Troilus and Criseyde was probably composed during the early and middle years of the 1380s and completed no later than 1387, which places it after the *Boece* and certainly before the earliest version of the prologue to the *Legend of Good Women*, where it is cited. In five books of rhyme royal stanzas the 'double sorrow' of Troilus is charted as he loves, wins and loses Criseyde, the story being set within the context of the Trojan War, which Chaucer embellishes with extensive use (and to some extent creation) of appropriately pagan history, philosophy and religion. Chaucer took the relatively straightforward account of an amatory love triangle from Giovanni Boccaccio's *Il Filostrato* (1336–8?) and reworked it with occasional recourse to two sources Boccaccio himself had used, Benoît de Sainte-Maure's *Roman de Troie* (of the mid-twelfth century) and the Latin prose rendering of that French poem that Guido delle Colonne completed in 1287, the *Historia destructionis Troiae*. Guido had introduced heavily moralistic comments about the evils of pagan love and lore, but this is quite different in tenor from Chaucer's transformation of Boccaccio, which is marked by a desire to find virtue in his heathen characters and to endow Troilus (thanks to material derived from Boethius' *Consolatio philosophiae*) with the ability to engage in intricate philosophical analysis, as he suffers the slings and arrows of outrageous fortune. Here is an 'historical novel' conceived on a grand scale; featuring a distinctive and internally consistent heathen imaginary which manifests distance, difference and otherness. A world all of its own.

Other worlds: pagan philosophy and desire

In Chaucer's day, it was widely recognized that many worlds existed within the present one, inasmuch as it accommodated different peoples and races, many of which followed creeds that were quite different from Christianity. Several hundred years of crusades (with Jerusalem, the place of Christ's death, as the great prize) had prompted some awareness, however crude and miscomprehending, of the tenets of Islam, and in 1243–5, approximately two decades before Marco Polo began his travels in Asia, Persia, China and Indonesia, Friar William of Rubruck had made an arduous journey to meet the fourth Great Khan of the Mongol Empire, Möngke (1209–59).

Möngke's grandfather Genghis Khan (d.1227), the founder and first Great Khan of the Mongol Empire, may be the 'noble kyng' commended at the beginning of *The Squire's Tale* for having kept the 'lay' (law) of the religion into which he was born to such a superlative extent that he exemplifies all the regal and knightly virtues.[1] 'So excellent a lord in alle thyng',

> Hym lakked noght that longeth to a kyng.
> As of the secte of which that he was born
> He kepte his lay, to which that he was sworn;   *law*
> And therto he was hardy, wys, and riche,
> And pitous and just, alwey yliche;   *always in equal measure*
> Sooth of his word, benigne, and honurable;
> Of his corage as any centre stable;
> Yong, fressh, and strong, in armes desirous   *filled with desire for arms*
> As any bacheler of al his hous.   (V.15–24)

Here we may detect an echo of a controversial theological doctrine of the later Middle Ages – that 'by doing what is in him' a righteous non-Christian, a person who has not been baptized into the church, may nevertheless have done enough to receive God's grace. Thus salvation can be attained by a 'virtuous pagan' or heathen – someone born in the wrong place and/or at the wrong time and hence unaware of the supreme religion (not having been blessed by a visit from the likes of William of Rubruck).

To make this claim is not to attribute to Chaucer the layman (however learned) privileged knowledge of doctrine so recherché that it was the prerogative of professional theologians. The doctrine in question had escaped over the walls of the schools, enjoying sufficient currency to trouble the Augustinian canon Walter Hilton (d.1396), who – writing in the vernacular– attacks certain men who grievously err by saying that Jews, Muslims and pagans, all of whom lack the Christian faith, may nevertheless be saved. According to this unacceptable argument, if infidels keep their own law, believing it is secure and sufficient for salvation, they may perform many good and righteous deeds – and perhaps if they knew that the faith of Christ was better than theirs, they would leave their own faith and follow it. But, Hilton retorts, Christ is the sole mediator between God and man, and no one can be reconciled with God or come to heavenly bliss except through Him.[2]

Chaucer's viewpoint seems to have been a lot more tolerant than Hilton's. Yet the poet does not stray far into such contested territory, because he is silent on Cambyuskan's prospects for salvation, even as he withholds comment on the final destination of the soul of Troilus. We are simply told that, after being killed by Achilles, Troilus went forth 'Ther as Mercurye sorted [allotted] hym to dwelle' (*Troilus and Criseyde*, V.1826–7), without any specification of where that actually was. (A similar reticence marks Chaucer's reference, near the end of *The Knight's Tale*, to the ultimate destination of the soul of Arcite; I.2809–14.) This is consonant with the way in which Chaucer's pagan characters disclaim expert knowledge of matters relating to fate, providence and ultimate destiny. Dorigen leaves to 'clerkes' all 'disputison' (disputation) concerning why God should make such an 'ydel' (useless) thing as the black rocks that she imagines will destroy her husband's homecoming ship (*Franklin's Tale*, V.890). In similar vein, Palamon leaves to 'dyvynys' (theologians) the problem of what sort of governance could possibly exist in a divine foreknowledge that seems to torment the guiltless (*Knight's Tale*, I.1323). And Troilus declares that 'Almyghty Jove' alone knows the true answer to a question that has long perplexed many 'grete clerkes': the relationship between the 'forsight of divine purveyaunce [providence]' and 'fre chois' (*Troilus and Criseyde*, IV.961, 968–71, 1079–82).

That said, the large number of virtuous pagans that the poet depicts, with obvious sympathy and respect, is truly remarkable – not only the protagonists of *Troilus and Criseyde* and *The Legend of Good Women* but also those of the Canterbury tales recounted by the Squire (of course), the Knight, the Franklin, and the Physician; the Monk adds a few more. To concentrate on Troilus, it is quite clear that he, like Cambyuskan, is 'pitous and just', true to his word, benign, honourable, courageous and eager to engage 'in armes' – witness his brave exploits against the Greeks, together with his honourable courtship of Criseyde, wherein he goes to great lengths to protect her honour. Furthermore, Troilus experiences a moment of high enlightenment at the end of the third book of *Troilus*, where he sings a hymn in praise of 'Love, that of erthe and se hath governaunce' (III.1744). Chaucer moves away from Boccaccio's *Filostrato* here, using as his source Book II, metrum 8, of the *Consolatio philosophiae*, a celebration of the 'regular harmony' that governs the many changes through which the world moves, ending with a prayer that 'the love that rules the stars' may also rule the hearts of men (1–4, 28–30). According to the Dominican Nicholas Trevet (d. *c.*1334), the commentator who was Chaucer's main guide to the meaning of Boethius' intricate text, this is to be interpreted as referring to the divine love that causes concord in celestial things and can cause the concord of friendship in men's hearts. Chaucer refers all of this back to the will of a benevolent God, the author of nature, who wished to encircle every heart with his great bond of love, so that not a single creature might escape. Troilus prays that this same God may force all cold hearts to love, so they may always take pity on hearts in pain and look after true lovers (III.1765–71). Presumably Jupiter is the all-powerful deity in question here.

The monotheistic import of the hymn places Troilus in the good company of Socrates and the Platonists, who, in the eyes of some medieval thinkers, had believed that the plurality of gentile gods could be reduced to one alone. For example, St Augustine of Hippo (d.430) had praised Plato and his followers for belief in 'the true God' who is 'the author of all created things, the light by which things are known, and the good for the sake of which things are done'. Due to their 'ingenuity and zeal in seeking the causes of things and the right way to learn and to live', these philosophers, 'by knowing God, have discovered where to find the cause by which the universe was established, and the light by which truth is to be perceived, and the fount at which we may drink of happiness'.[3] For his part, Aristotle was commended for his theory of a primary, unmoved mover and first cause that was the source of all motion and being in the universe ('The Firste Moevere of the cause above', as *The Knight's Tale* terms it; I.2987). This ultimate force was easily identified with the Christian God. It could be said, then, that by rationalizing from his own experience and 'doing what was in him', Troilus has transcended the polytheism and fatalism (the conviction that future events are predetermined and inevitable) that he espouses elsewhere in the poem. Such enlightened paganism has much to commend it to medieval Christians; here is a significant intersection of belief systems.

But is there not a problem in the fact that the particular experience that prompted Troilus' vision was one of sexual consummation? Augustine would not have approved, and, according to Christian norms, one would expect such transcendence to occur only after a rigorous process of ascetic self-denial and corporeal abnegation. Against that may be set Chaucer's vigorous insistence that the past of his poem is a foreign country, and they did things differently there (see II.27–8). In any case, this moment of fulfilled desire and philosophical breakthrough is fleeting, and within *Troilus and Criseyde* as a whole, it stands out as a rare instance of peace and rest. Polytheism and fatalism are rife throughout the poem, with capricious Fortune being seen as a cruel foe (I.836–40) and the influence (often perceived as malevolent) of the planets and stars exerting a constant pressure.

Chaucer's understanding of the relationship between natural forces and divine omnipotence is well illustrated by his account of how inclement weather prevents Criseyde from leaving Pandarus' house. A dreadful rainstorm has been produced by the conjunction of 'The bente moone' with 'Saturne, and Jove' in the zodiacal sign of Cancer (III.624–8). So it might seem that the stars have brought Troilus and Criseyde together for their first night of love. However, this follows a stanza which emphasizes that Fortune and the stars are mere secondary causes subject to the all-controlling first cause, God:

> But O Fortune, executrice of wierdes,   *fates*
> O influences of thise hevenes hye!
> Soth is, that under God ye ben oure hierdes,
> Though to us bestes ben the causez wrie.
>
> (III.617–20)

Such 'influences' may be our 'hierdes' (shepherds, guides), inasmuch as they do affect our behaviour – but they do not determine it. The freedom of the human will cannot be denied, for one can chose to accept or reject those same 'influences'. Whatever the alignment of the heavenly bodies, it is up to Pandarus and Troilus to exploit the situation – which they proceed to do.

Venus was 'not al a foo | To Troilus in his nativitee' (II.684–5). To rephrase that elegant understatement, he was born with a good chance of future success in love.

> . . . blisful Venus, wel arrayed,
> Sat in hire seventhe hous of hevene tho,
> Disposed wel, and with aspectes payed,   *made propitious*
> To helpe sely Troilus of his woo.   *wretched*
>
> (II.680–4)

Because the seventh heavenly house is the house of marriage, this is good news indeed for Troilus. But, were he not to act – or, rather, were his friend Pandarus not to galvanize him into action – his love for Criseyde would come to nothing. Thus, Troilus gets to display an acute emotional sensitivity exceeding even that of the Man in Black in *The Book of the Duchess*, while his more practical friend helps ensure that something physical actually happens.

When the going gets tough, Criseyde blames her horoscope:

> 'Allas', quod she, 'out of this regioun
> I, woful wrecche and infortuned wight,   *unfortunate creature*
> And born in corsed constellacioun,
> Moot goon and thus departen fro my knyght!'
>
> (IV.743–6)

But Chaucer carefully describes the long process through which she came to love Troilus as a series of free choices on her part. Initially she inclined to like him, and subsequently, 'by proces and by good servyse | He gat hire love, and in no sodeyn wyse' (II.673–9). In bed with Troilus, Criseyde confidently tells her lover that had she not wanted this, she wouldn't be here (III.1210–11). In coming to love Troilus she took her time and exercised her free will; the stars did not force her into anything.

All of this is consonant with standard late-medieval attitudes to astrology (interwoven with astronomy, the break between the two not yet having occurred). When, in his *Treatise on the Astrolabe*, Chaucer comes to discuss the practice of making 'particular predictions' concerning the fate of an individual, he identifies this as a pagan belief that he, as a Christian, cannot accept: 'Natheles these ben observaunces of judicial matere and rytes of payens, in whiche my spirit hath no feith, ne knowing of her *horoscopum*'.[4] This bears comparison with Chaucer's general castigation of 'payens corsed olde rites' at the end of *Troilus* (V.1849–53), although at that point he has particularly in mind the misplaced worship by humans of rascally pagan gods. In brief, the practice of making specific predictions concerning the destinies of individuals from the configuration of the stars at their births was deemed a risky practice, as uncertain as it was unlawful (for a good Christian).[5] The ancient heathen were frequently criticized for having followed this practice, which sometimes was associated with devil worship; according to a common narrative of their origin, the pagan gods were identified with the rebellious angels who had been banished from heaven. Here was a crucial aspect of their fatalism – whatever will be will be, and no human being can escape his or her allotted fate, which is written in the stars. Such views constitute the pagan Other as presented in *Troilus and Criseyde*.

They find their fullest, and most pessimistic, expression in the fourth book of the poem, when Troilus, in deep 'despeir' as he faces the prospect of Criseyde's departure from Troy, concludes that human lives are governed by absolute necessity: 'al that comth, comth by necessitee: | Thus to ben lorn [lost/dispossessed], it is my destinee' (IV.958–9). On this argument, from eternity God has predetermined all future events, and individual destiny must be accepted as irrevocable. No human action can alter the necessary course of events; there is no freedom of the will (IV.1048–59). The source of this long disquisition (occupying some 120 lines – quite a tour de force) is Boethius' *De consolatione philosophiae*, V, prosa 3. Dame Philosophy had proceeded to refute its claims, by proving that fate and divine providence are one (from below, providence is seen as fate, while from above, fate is seen as providence) and that free will is utterly compatible with divine omniscience. But in Troilus' disputation with himself (cf. IV.1084), there is no such resolution. He breaks off with a prayer to 'Almyghty Jove in trone [throne]': may the high god intervene, either killing him promptly or freeing him and his beloved from this distress (IV.1079–82). Here Troilus' desires obstruct any philosophical progression, in marked contrast to what we witnessed at the end of Book III, that vision of 'Love, that of erthe and se hath governaunce' (1744ff.) which was so replete with promise and possibility. Troilus fails as a philosopher long before he is bested in battle by the fierce Achilles (V.1806). His older and wiser alter ego in *The Knight's Tale*, Duke Theseus the philosopher king, will achieve much more.

Chaucer's most overt criticism of pagan religion centres on the character and role of Calkas – a 'lord of gret auctorite', 'gret devyn' (I.65–6), priest of Apollo, defector from the Greek camp, and the father of Criseyde. This is a matter of some significance, given that in Guido's *Historia destructionis Troiae* he is presented as a pious man (who acts in obedience to the divine will) and the caring father of Briseida (as Criseyde was named before Boccaccio), although his traitorous actions are acknowledged. In *Il Filostrato*, Criseida vociferously denigrates her father as an old miser.[6] Chaucer parallels the priest's untrustworthy character with the untrustworthiness of the god he worships, 'Daun Phebus or Appollo Delphicus' (I.70). Calkas does have other sources of information, being described as an expert in 'calkulynge' and 'astronomye' (I.71, IV.115). So he is a man of *science* (cf. the Latin *scientia*; I use the term in the medieval sense of a body of secure technical knowledge). But in his decision making the 'answer of this Appollo' is paramount (I.72, IV.114). Calkas is devalued further by Criseyde's claim that her father's avarice is stronger than either his faith in oracles or his *science* (IV.1397–400). Hence the plan with which she tries to set Troilus' mind at rest. Once in the Greek camp, she intends to tell her father that certain Trojans want her to manage the movement of a huge quantity of personal possessions from Troy into his 'safe' keeping. His eagerness to get his hands on those 'moebles' will, she is convinced, ensure his support for her trips to town, thereby enabling her to see Troilus. If Calkas is still unconvinced, Criseyde continues, she will persuade him that he misunderstood the answer of the gods because of fear:

> 'For goddes speken in amphibologies,   *ambiguities*
> And for o soth they tellen twenty lyes.
> Ek, "Drede fond first goddes, I suppose" –
> Thus shal I seyn – and that his coward herte
> Made hym amys the goddes text to glose,   *interpret*
> Whan he for fered out of Delphos sterte'.   *for fear*
>   (IV.1406–11)

The statement that 'Fear first created gods in the world' may be an echo of Statius, *Thebaid*, III.661; here they are put in the mouth of one Capaneus, a madman and blasphemer, who doubts if prayers can 'really coax from the void of heaven the causes and hidden names of things'. In Chaucer's reiteration they become a more substantial castigation of paganism; for a moment Criseyde talks in a way that takes her far beyond her historical location, even anticipating the poem's final condemnation of 'payens corsed olde rites' (V.1849).

The gods originated in human fear, and humans then feared them – and with good reason. Speaking in 'amphibologies' (using ambiguous language), they tell twenty lies instead of a single truth, Criseyde declares. In his *Speculum doctrinale*, Vincent of Beauvais (d.1264?) explains that the term *amphibolia* denotes 'dubious meaning', and as an example cites Apollo's response to Pyrrhus: 'I say that you . . . the Romans can defeat'. Here it is unclear as to who will be defeated and who will win – the Romans or Pyrrhus.[7] This is a typical piece of heathen doublespeak, according to the usual medieval argument, deployed by a false god (a devil in disguise) who seeks to lead credulous humans astray.

Likewise, Nicole Oresme warns that 'the words of the diviners are sometimes of double meaning, *amphibolic*, two-faced':[8] discourse comparable with Diomede's phrase 'a word with two visages', which he uses to gloss his term 'ambages' when expressing his suspicion that Calkas is leading on the Greeks 'with double wordes slye' (V.897–9). The clear implication is that Calkas may be telling lies. Maybe he is just passing on the oracles of a deceptive god, but it seems more likely that he himself intends to deceive. Like god, like worshipper: neither Apollo nor Calkas can be trusted. In sum, Chaucer's Calkas is an unscrupulous traitor with a 'coward herte', and Troilus' description of him as an 'oold, unholsom, and myslyved man' (IV.330) seems quite appropriate. His vices throw into sharp relief those moments of ethical virtue and philosophical enlightenment that lighten the darkness of the poem's benighted pagans.

Fearful Criseyde

At the beginning of Book IV of *Troilus* we read of how Antenor, 'oon the grettest' of Troy (IV.192), is taken prisoner by the Greeks, and of how this prompts Calkas to propose a deal through which he can get his daughter back. (Given that Calkas' earlier desertion of Criseyde had put her social status in Troy, and indeed her very life, at risk, this belated action hardly redeems him as a father.) The Greek offer to exchange Antenor for Criseyde having been put to a Trojan parliament, Prince Hector – who after Calkas' defection had vowed to protect this hapless woman – is outraged. Criseyde is no prisoner and hence should not be used in this demeaning way. 'We usen here no women for to selle', Hector exclaims; we Trojans are not in the habit of selling or bartering women, treating them as mere chattels (IV.179–84). But the populace shout him down. Antenor is judged to be of far more importance to besieged Troy than the mere woman Hector is trying to shield: he should let his 'fantasies be', get real (183–96). Thus Criseyde is forfeited. The irony is that Antenor will prove to be a traitor to the town. (The further irony is that one traitor is exchanged for another; Antenor will be untrue to Troy just as Criseyde will be untrue to Troilus.)

So then, it would seem that the Trojans are willing to 'selle' women after all, to engage in a 'traffic in women' reminiscent of the sociopolitical practice described so well by the cultural anthropologist Gayle Rubin.[9] For our purposes, the important argument is that 'women are taught to be', and used as, 'feminine products for exchange within a masculine economy'. Men function as the powerful 'givers' and women as the passive 'gifts' they exchange, these gifts being a means through which men gain and maintain power (as when they make political alliances through marriage, for instance). In this manner, Criseyde is reduced to collateral, a major asset in a negotiation in which her own wishes are set at naught, a victim of male hegemony. One man – her father – wants her back, and the Trojans value another man, Antenor, far more highly than her. Her fate is sealed, particularly since no Trojan male is powerful enough to countermand the process, Hector having tried but failed and Troilus not having tried at all, on the grounds that he cannot publicly reveal his love for Criseyde without her permission (IV.162–8). Here, it might be said, is one situation in which the principle of secrecy enjoined by *fyn lovynge* looks very flimsy indeed, in light of the political realities.

Just before Diomede begins his courtship of Criseyde in earnest, Chaucer describes her as 'slydynge [sliding] of corage' (V.825), meaning that she is changeable in disposition, temperament, desire. A generous interpretation would take this as meaning that she is easily moved, this being consonant with her pitying and tender-hearted nature, qualities attributed to her in this same passage (823–4). But if a more moralistic overtone is detected here, she stands accused of wavering in courage, of having an inconstant disposition (the Middle English phrase *of litel corage* means 'of little faith or fidelity', 'fearful').[10] That more negative valuation has been emphasized by many of Criseyde's modern interpreters, who have proceeded to ask, who or what is responsible for such *slydynge*? In the societies she is describing, Rubin discovers a strong preference for women to be passive sexually, because the girl who is exchanged will have little if any agency in the matter of whom she has sex with. Criseyde's case may intimate that the *slydynge* nature of women is essential for the purposes of the men who traffic in them.

On this argument, beyond the walls of Troy and far away both from Hector her champion and Troilus her lover, Criseyde is obliged to accept the advances of the alpha male who comes for her; she needs a new protector, and Diomede fulfils that role. Here, and indeed at every significant point in the poem, Criseyde's 'fear is justified and has specific grounds, her weakness is a genuine aspect of a social reality in which women are a subordinate group, and her feelings of isolation are a subjective registering of both the particular crisis she faces and a more general vulnerability and precariousness in the position of woman'. That is the opinion of David Aers, who, in discussing the scene in Book II where Criseyde is termed 'the ferfulleste wight | That myghte be' (II.450–1), claims that at this point, as elsewhere, 'her fear has . . . been given a thoroughly sufficient social basis and there is no reason to treat it as a peculiar flaw'.[11] The designation of Criseyde's fear as a 'fatal flaw' derives from C. S. Lewis, who placed her within a group of women who, as he puts it, always have 'some male relative to stand between them and the terrifying world of affairs'. 'If fate had so willed, men would have known this flaw only as a pardonable, perhaps an endearing, weakness; but fate threw her upon difficulties which convert it into a tragic fault, and Cryseide is ruined'.[12] Lewis is speaking in the terms of Aristotelian theory of tragedy – quite anachronistically, because, although the later Middle Ages did indeed have a version of Aristotle's *Poetics*, it was rather different from the one Lewis knew. Furthermore, as a man of his time, Chaucer's own understanding of 'tragedye' (the generic term he applies to *Troilus* at V.1786) in the original, classical sense of the term was decidedly hazy.

In any case, it is quite possible to read Criseyde's characterization as 'the ferfulleste wight that myghte be' in a positive manner and as a major departure on Chaucer's part from his sources.[13] Benoît, who first fleshed out the character of Briseida/Criseyde, briefly mentions that she is 'very timid' (5287) but concentrates on the related themes of temporary female power (as enjoyed by the courtly love-object) and perennial female shame. At the outset we are told that the heroine's 'heart was not constant' ('sis corages li chanjot'; *Roman de Troie*, 5286. Presumably this is the specific source of Chaucer's phrase 'slydynge of corage'). Her future behaviour lives up to this prediction. When she is obliged to live in the Greek camp, soon Briseida 'ensnares' Diomede. Condemnation comes swiftly. Troilus, when sparing Diomede in battle, berates Briseida for 'her lack of constancy, her treachery and wrongdoing'. Briseida herself seems to acquiesce in this condemnation: 'I was false, fickle and foolish'. These vices are, for Benoît, symptomatic of the universal untrustworthiness of the female sex: women's 'minds are indeed quickly changed and lack both sincerity and constancy, and their hearts are most vain and fickle'.[14] Guido, ever the phobic misogynist, goes even further: 'It is clearly implanted in all women by nature not to have any steady inconstancy.... There is truly no hope so false as that which resides in women and proceeds from them'.[15]

In this regard, Boccaccio's *Filostrato* bears the imprint of Guido. Troiolo becomes an exemplum of the foolish man who has been led astray by a young woman, young women being 'inconstant and eager for many lovers'. Criseida is very much the urban sophisticate who is fully aware of the behaviour of her social peer group ('I know of no woman in the city who does not have a lover') and embarks on her affair with eagerness and utter confidence: 'welcome this sweet love', she advises herself, 'and satisfy his burning desire'. Her discourse is essentially that of the Ovidian merry widow who is keen to gather rosebuds while she may. She thinks briefly of marriage but brushes the idea aside: there's a war on, and so this isn't the time to take a husband. Besides, and probably more important, 'to keep one's freedom is much the wiser course.... Water gained by stealth is a much sweeter thing than wine that can be taken freely– and so in love the pleasure that remains secret far excels that of constantly embracing a husband'.[16] Given these attitudes, her defection to Diomede can hardly be deemed a surprise. Boccaccio has deployed discourses that pave the way for the ultimate condemnation of his unworthy heroine on the charge of inconstancy.

Chaucer changed all of this quite radically, as he did the episode in which Criseida strives to make Troiolo see in the best possible light her imminent departure to the Greek camp. Gone is one of Criseida's weighty arguments against elopement, namely that their love will last only if it can be enjoyed 'rarely and by means of stealth'[17] – Chaucer may have felt that this statement indicated a demeaning interest in snatched physical gratification that was inappropriate to the figure he was reconstructing, however much it fitted the inconstant character that Boccaccio was building up for a fall. Even more crucially, Chaucer associated her with feminine fear. Occasions for fear are shown to surround his Criseyde; fearfulness is used as a major defining characteristic. And there is nothing necessarily or self-evidently negative about those emphases.

In Book I, Criseyde has no warning of her father's desertion, and, believing that she may be held accountable for his actions, justifiably fears for her own life. Chaucer accentuates her vulnerability by declaring that she is a widow and 'allone | Of any frend to whom she dorste hir mone' (I.97–8): the friends and ladies-in-waiting who surround her in Book II are carefully kept out of the picture here, as is Uncle Pandarus. Criseyde does not choose to fear wilfully, but does so instinctively in response to her abrupt change of circumstances.

In Book II, she becomes the 'ferfulleste wight' because here a number of specific, and very real, fears merge. She is unsure what to expect from a relationship with Troilus and worried about doing anything that might disturb her already precarious position within Trojan society. Then perhaps there is her fear of death, this time not her own but Troilus' and Pandarus'. (I say 'perhaps' because soon she is spiritedly assuring Pandarus that threats of male death will not force her into acting against her own volition; II.484–9.) Criseyde is also fearful of shame, anxious about being held responsible for any extreme action which the two males in question might undertake (II.454–5). All of this helps to convince her – the 'sorwful ernest of the knyght' (453) plays its part too, of course – that she should at least explore the possibility of a relationship with Troilus. Once she resolves to accept Troilus' affection, her dread substantially lessens. In Book III, we are assured that Troilus has become to her a wall of steel and a shield from every disturbance; hence 'she was namore afered' (III.479–82).

All of the dread that Chaucer has thus far attributed to Criseyde seems to reflect the standard medieval definition of 'natural fear' (*timor naturalis*), an emotion that in itself bore no moral opprobrium. Further, it may be noted that, in Chaucer's day, *timor naturalis* was an emotion frequently attributed to women, but not necessarily with some negative valence. On the contrary, fear could be seen as an emotion that made a woman womanly, functioned as a defining characteristic of her true nature, in contrast with the steadfast *corage* associated with the male of the species. Indeed, Christine de Pizan polemically suggested that fear was one of the many virtues that made women better than men.[18] A woman does not kill, wound or mutilate, foster any treasonous misdeeds, steal gold or silver, cheat others out of their inheritance through bogus contracts, and the like; her greatest fault can cause but little harm. If someone were to say that female traits and qualities (*condicions et taches femenines*) are not inclined towards activities like making war and murdering, and therefore women deserve no special credit for refraining from them, Christine would utterly agree with them. Such a claim would in fact reinforce her own view, which is that the essential nature of woman involves the qualities of gentleness, compassion – and fear.

> For woman's nature is but sweet and mild,
> Compassionate and fearful (*paoureuse*), timorous
> And humble, gentle, sweet, and generous,
> And pleasant, pious, meek in time of peace.
> (*Epistre au dieu d'amours*, 668–71)

Without these qualities, a woman cannot satisfy the promptings of her true nature.

Because Chaucer's heroine excels in so many of the virtues traditionally associated with the courtly lady, it is appropriate that she should also exhibit, in large part, the *condicion* of *paoureuse*. (Indeed, she is a theoretician of that emotion – as already noted, the insight that pagan religion originated in fear is put in her mouth.) Chaucer goes even further, presenting Criseyde's *taches femenines* as complementary to those of men. Normative female behaviour acts in accord with, and in some cases prompts, normative male behaviour, as when she secures Hector's support (I.108–25). 'Wel neigh out of hir wit for sorwe and fere', Criseyde kneels before him in her widow's garment, asking for his 'mercy', 'with pitous vois, and tendrely wepynge'. Seeing that she is in a sorrowful situation – and, it must be added, noting her beauty – Hector responds in the appropriate manner; he is 'pitous of nature', as a gentleman should be.

A similar pattern is evident in a social exchange of a very different kind, namely the first sexual encounter of Troilus and Criseyde, as described in Book III.1093–323. As Troilus swoons, Pandarus exclaims, 'Is this a mannes herte?' A few minutes later, when Troilus recovers and Criseyde confronts his self-torment, she expresses the same attitude in the remark, 'Is this a mannes game?' and appeals to his sense of shame to make him snap out of it. Such behaviour on Troilus' part is not damagingly effeminate; rather, his swoon manifests his highly strung aristocratic sensitivity – providing of course that he does not indulge it too long. There is no risk of that here. Soon he is displaying his manly vigour by demanding of Criseyde, 'Now yeldeth [yield] yow!' – somewhat incongruously, given that a few minutes ago she was the active partner, working hard (with Pandarus) to help him recover his senses. Any possible doubts are soon dispelled. The force of Troilus' male desire is emphasized when Chaucer likens him to a sparrow-hawk that has caught a lark in its claws (1191–2). Such aggression, it would seem, is understood as being at once erotically potent and socially acceptable. For her part, Criseyde is all a-tremble –

> Right as an aspes leef she gan to quake,   *aspen leaf*
> Whan she hym felte hire in his armes folde . . .
>
> (III.1200–1)

– as she accepts the ardour of her entrapping and enfolding lover. She is now playing a passive role, performing a version of fear that conforms to normative female sexuality as understood in Chaucer's time and that clearly is attractive to her sexual partner. Required female behaviour provokes passion in Troilus just as, on a previous occasion, it provoked pity in Hector. In both instances Criseyde is the 'wommanliche wif' (III.106, 1296) par excellence.

So, then, Chaucer may have engaged in an attempt to reclaim and revalue Criseyde, by way of reaction against, and critique of, the fickle women he had found in his sources. It is hardly surprising that so much attention should be paid to Criseyde's fear in Book II, given that this is the section of Chaucer's poem in which her interiority is explored in extraordinary detail. In the public, militaristic male world of Book V, we are given little access to Criseyde's mind. She becomes unrecognizable, is rendered unknowable, as the narrator reminds us that she is a widow (and therefore had a sexual relationship before her affair with Troilus), notes that she has a physical flaw (her eyebrows are joined together, a feature sometimes taken as the sign of a lecherous woman) and admits that he does not even know her age (V.813–26). This distancing, occluding effect may seem somewhat strange, given that now she is living among the very Greeks she professed (in Book II) to fear so much and is being assailed by Diomede's love entreaties on the one hand and, on the other, by his – and her father's – bleak view of the future of Troy. Thus many motives for fear are present here; many opportunities for psychological analysis available. All we get, however, is a passage in which Criseyde briefly expresses her 'drede' of what might happen if she were caught trying to return to Troy under cover of darkness; she could be deemed a spy or assaulted by some lowlife (V.701–6). The 'ferfulleste wight that myghte be' of Book II fails to rematerialize.

Why is this? Perhaps because, for Chaucer, Criseyde's fear was a vital part of her rehabilitation in Books I through III, wherein a positive discourse of fear as an aspect of true womanhood is deployed – a discourse that has no place as the poem nears its end. For in Book V the narrator is obliged to recognize that 'Criseyde was untrewe' (V.1774); all the compassion in the world cannot alter that fact. She was 'slydynge of corage' (V.825). But only at this late stage does that phrase occur, in contrast with its early appearance in Benoît's narrative, where (as already noted) it is clearly condemnatory. It is not to be found in Book II of *Troilus*; it is, so to speak, being kept well away from the language of Criseydan fear. There is no reason to follow Lewis' linking of fear and 'slydynge of corage' in terms of cause and effect, as the dynamic of a fatal flaw.

Chaucer's condemnation of Criseyde is thus deferred – and, when it comes, it is surprisingly gentle. 'Al shal passe; and thus take I my leve' (V.1085). She slips back into the mists of antiquity, attempting to preserve some modicum of dignity ('To Diomede algate [at any rate] I wol be trewe', 1071). Her fate is unknown (whereas Troilus' death is reported), and she is unpunished – in sharp contrast to the continuation of the story by Robert Henryson (*fl. c.*1460–1500) wherein Criseyde is deserted by Diomede, and (some men say) becomes a common prostitute. When she cries out in protest against the gods, they inflict leprosy (here understood as a venereal disease) upon her. Chaucer's reaction to Criseyde's behaviour could hardly be more different. Pity ('routhe') would be a sufficient reason to excuse her, if all else failed (V.1097–9). Besides, he refuses to scold this 'sely' (unfortunate) woman 'Forther than the storye wol devyse', more than his sources permit (1093–4). But Chaucer has done a lot more than that. He has gone far beyond what his sources permit in the extent to which he has enabled Criseyde to be viewed sympathetically, right up to Book V (and even there, the criticism is muted). His attribution of fearfulness to her may be regarded a part and parcel of that recuperative strategy.

The *makynge* of good pagan women

'Thou hast translated the Romaunce of the Rose,
That is an heresye ayeins my lawe,   *heresy*
And makest wise folk fro me withdrawe;
And of Creseyde thou hast seyd as the lyste,
That maketh men to wommen lasse triste,   *women less trusted*
That ben as trewe as ever was any steel'.
(F Pro 329–34, cf. G Pro 255–66)

Here, in the prologue to *The Legend of Good Women*, the God of Love takes (a particularly deferential and self-denigrating version of) the Chaucerian I-persona to task for having written ill of women, thereby causing men to distrust them. Jean de Meun's part of the *Roman de la Rose* was seen by some as an Ovidian *remedium amoris*, a warning against love, and that seems to be the line followed here. As far as Criseyde is concerned, gone is the subtlety of her depiction in *Troilus*. The God of Love has reduced her to a faithless woman, impure and simple. The favour-currying poet goes along with that, without protest. No true lover should blame him for having spoken 'som shame' of 'a fals lovere' (F Pro 467, G Pro 457); whatever his sources may have meant, his own intention was

To forthren trouthe in love and yt cheryce,   *respect it*
And to ben war fro falsnesse and fro vice
By swich ensample...
(F Pro 472–4; cf. G Pro 462–4)

Feeble excuses. This defendant is sorely in need of the intercession graciously provided by Alceste of Thessaly, the embodiment of *fyn lovynge* and virtuous womanhood (F Pro 544–5, cf. G Pro 534–5), who has accompanied the God of Love on this visionary visitation. The dull-witted poet is pardoned on condition that, in the future, year after year, he will devote most of his time to 'making' (*makynge* in the sense of literary construction) a 'glorious Legende' of Cupid's Saints, an anthology of the life-stories of noble pagan women who were 'trewe in lovyng al hire lyves' (F Pro 485; cf. G Pro 475). Quite a long-term commission – but there is plenty of material to work on, given that the proportion of good women to bad is a hundred to one (G Pro 277), and Cupid knows of twenty thousand more than the writer will find in all his books (F Pro 559–61). They were 'hethene, al the pak' (G Pro 299), and the *pak* (a bundle or assembly) was apparently a large one.

How much time did Chaucer actually spend on this enterprise? Only nine legends are extant, the last of which breaks off in mid-sentence. However, when the Man of Law gives the *Legend* a good review, he calls it a large volume and mentions several women who do not appear in the text as we have it (*CT* II.60–76). In Chaucer's *Retraction* it is titled 'the book of the XXV. Ladies'.[19] So, then, we may have lost a large part of what Chaucer originally wrote. There is no reason to believe (as has sometimes been suggested) that he set aside this work on becoming preoccupied with that more ambitious collection of stories, *The Canterbury Tales*. Whatever may have happened to fracture the *Legend*, it is unlikely that boredom was to blame.

Chaucer's revision of the original (the F prologue)[20] may be dated after 7 June 1394, when Richard II's queen, Anne of Bohemia, died; she is designated as a future recipient of the book at F Pro 496–71, lines excised from the G Prologue. This would mean that Chaucer was working on it during the period in which he wrote some of the most innovative parts of *The Canterbury Tales*. It is no accident that the God of Love's account of the 'sixty bokes olde and newe' wherein the poet may find many 'storyes grete . . . | Of sundry wemen' (G Pro 273–307) should bear such a striking resemblance to the 'book of wikked wyves' described in *The Wife of Bath's Prologue* (III.685). That may seem ironic in the extreme. However, in the books in question, good women often keep company with wicked ones, and in at least some cases, the issue of what makes feminine goodness is to the fore – as it is in Chaucer's *makynge* of good pagan women.

Among all those books, Chaucer was most attentive to several of Ovid's – the *auctor* with whom, according to the Man of Law's account, he was in direct competition. The English poet is said to have

> . . . toold of loveris up and doun
> Mo than Ovide made of mencioun
> In his Episteles, that been ful olde.
> (*IntroMlT* II.53–5)

The 'Episteles' (= the *Heroides*) were a primary source for the legends of Phyllis and Hypermnestra and drawn on for the endings of those of Dido, Ariadne, and Hypsipyle. Chaucer turned to the *Metamorphoses* and/or the *Ovide moralisé* in the cases of Thisbe, Ariadne, Hypsipyle and Philomela, and perhaps also that of Medea, although there the influence of Guido delle Colonne's *Historia destructionis Troiae* is dominant. Another of Ovid's works, the *Fasti*, is the direct source of the *Legend of Lucrece*. The major exception is the mini-saga of Cleopatra (who was not known to Ovid and little-known in the Middle Ages), which Chaucer found in the *Speculum historiale* of Vincent of Beauvais, the text referred to at G Pro 308.

As candidates for amatory sainthood, this is a problematic *pak*. Two of those women, Medea and Philomela, could easily be (and often were) described as indubitably bad. The sorceress Medea had robbed her father and killed her brother, the children she had with Jason, and Jason's new wife. Philomela, having been raped and mutilated by Tereus (the husband of her sister Procne), exacted a terrible revenge, with Procne's help, by killing and cooking Itys (the son of Procne and Tereus), and serving this horrendous dish to his father. Ariadne, out of love for Theseus, betrayed her father and her half-brother, the Minotaur, whom Theseus killed. Hypsipyle spared her father's life, thus refusing to take part in a female plot to murder all the menfolk in her country. The other women had no such qualms. Hypermnestra's father Danaus ordered his fifty daughters to kill their husbands on their wedding nights; she alone refused. It might seem, then, that Chaucer's God of Love has got totally wrong the proportion of bad women to good. Moving beyond Ovid, Virgil's depiction of Dido is primarily that of a woman crazed by love, and Vincent of Beauvais regarded Cleopatra as a faithless woman who was responsible for the death of her lover Anthony; when he realized that she was trying to abandon him and form an alliance with his enemy Augustus, he committed suicide.

Against all of this, however, may be set the powerful precedent of Ovid's *Heroides*, where women cry out in protest against the men who wronged them – performances of virtue rendered possible by systematic excision of many of the problematic aspects of the stories. It should be recalled that Christine de Pizan was quite comfortable about including flattering portraits of Dido and Medea in her *Book of the City of Ladies*.[21] It is all a matter of perspective. Ovid had shown ambitious male poets how they could ventriloquize intense female emotions, and when an ambitious female writer got into the act, she deployed the same rhetorical and editorial techniques (while, uniquely, claiming the authenticity her gender conferred). Therefore the practice of radical selectivity in narration does not, in itself, support the theory that Chaucer's

Legend is some sort of satire or parody which, under the veil of panegyric, is actually ridiculing female characters who really are far from good, and hence a target for condescending male laughter.

The extent of Anne of Bohemia's knowledge of English is a matter of controversy, as is the extent to which women readers and listeners were part of Chaucer's initial audience. But whatever the social realities may have been, surely a poem that declares itself fit for presentation to the queen of England can hardly have been intended as an exposé of the frailties of women. Perhaps we should, as in the case of *The Parliament of Fowls*, postulate for *The Legend of Good Women* a milieu of courtly debate, in which the matters raised by the poem would have been discussed, in a manner that combined earnest and game, within the context of sophisticated courtly entertainment. At F Pro 72, Chaucer alludes to lovers who side with either 'the leef [leaf] or with the flour', those being the emblems of two aristocratic companies or 'orders' who would pit their wits against each other. Deschamps wrote several poems about such a debating society, one of which declares the poet's own preference for the flower and goes on to identify John of Gaunt's daughter, Philippa of Lancaster, as another flower-follower. The Chaucer-persona's eulogy for the daisy-lady Alceste in the F Prologue (where the influence of French *marguerite* or 'daisy' poetry is strong) indicates that he too wanted to take that side.

A comparison with another source for the *Legend*, Machaut's *Jugement dou Roy de Navarre*, is helpful here, particularly in view of the way it brings together the ideas of poetic repentance and commendation of women. A lady named Bonneürté takes the Machaut-persona to task for having 'sinned against women' in the attitudes expressed in his *Jugement dou Roy de Behaigne*; thus a 'severe penance is called for' (811, 918–20).[22] In response to the way in which the earlier poem had privileged the sufferings of a jilted male lover over those of a bereaved woman (see pp. 18–19 above), she provides a series of *exempla* designed to prove that women love better and more loyally than men, and suffer worse. The narrator welcomes the idea of a full debate and the ultimate judgment of some wise individual (who, of course, turns out to be the king of Navarre), as providing joyful entertainment: 'It will be a pleasant task | To hear the arguments rehearsed | And the parties dispute | With subtlety, with pretty distinctions' (*biaus argumens*; 1084–7). His opponent laughingly agrees to engage in disputation with him, 'however it might turn out' (1089–93). Her name literally means 'good fortune, happiness'; a debate with Bonneürté is inevitably a source of pleasure and joy. This could also be true of a discussion of the issues concerning female virtue and sacrifice that are posed by the

Legend, following the precedent of the *Navarre*. Those topics are scarcely trivial, but the rules of the game are clear; the arguments must be both subtle and *biaus*, affording ample occasion for the elegant performance of aristocratic sensitivity. There is no need to think of a grand occasion of the kind illustrated by Cambridge, Corpus Christi College, MS 61, fol. 1v (figure 2), an utterly fictional depiction of Chaucer reading aloud *Troilus and Criseyde* to a courtly audience. Where two or three, of whatever sex, were gathered together, there could have been a 'Court of Love'.

Much material for debate is provided by the way in which Chaucer turns the world upside down by providing neo-stereotypes of false men and true women – or, more accurately, by subjecting men to the kind of stereotyping that women had long endured. The heathen antiheroes of the *Legend* are being placed in a subject-position, as traditionally occupied by women, which bespeaks inferiority and untrustworthiness. Where, asked the purveyors of antifeminist clichés, is the virtuous woman to be found? Where, asks contrarian Chaucer, is the faithful man to be found? Piramus is a rare specimen: 'Of trewe men I fynde but fewe mo | In alle my bokes, save this Piramus' (917–18). It is not simply that women can be as good as men – 'God forbede but a woman can | Ben as trewe in lovynge as a man!' (910–11) – but rather that they are much better, a point previously emphasized by Machaut's Bonneürté. At the end of *Troilus*, Criseyde became both an example and a symbol of 'false worldes brotelnesse', the brittleness and mutability of our present existence (V.1832). But, in the *Legend*, male characters bear that stigma. Phyllis learns to her cost just 'how brotel and how fals' Demophon really is (2556), and *The Legend of Lucrece* ends with the admonition that the 'trewest' of men 'ys ful brotel for to triste' (1883–5).

As fashioned here, Chaucer's stereotypical male is a betrayer of women. Anthony deserts his first wife; Aeneas is false to Dido, Theseus to Ariadne, Demophon to Phyllis and Jason to both Hypsipyle and Medea ('There othere falsen oon, thow falsest two!', exclaims the excited narrator, 1377). Tereus mutilates his wife's sister. So selfish is Lyno that he runs away (with almost farcical haste), leaving Hypermnestra – whose warning has saved his life – to be captured and imprisoned. This figure is often a 'traytour'; Chaucer applies that epithet to Aeneas (1328), Jason (1656) and Tereus (2324). Another recurrent theme is that of the romantic seafaring stranger who has, and leaves, a girl in every port; Aeneas, Jason, Theseus and Demophon are all cast in that role. Whereas, in Ovid's *Ars amatoria* (II.645) and the *Roman de la Rose* (13235–8, 18102–16), women were castigated as liars and deceivers, in the *Legend*, it is men who act like that, saying and doing anything to get what they want, then wantonly breaking any oath or promise they may have made. The great wit

Figure 2. A fictional portrait of Chaucer reading aloud to an audience. Cambridge, Corpus Christi College, MS 61, fol. 1v.

and subtlety they bring to the deception of women receives much attention, as when Aeneas, Jason and Theseus unscrupulously pretend to be in love (1264–76, 2114–22, 1376, 1548–56), and Tereus feigns sorrow at the alleged death of Philomela (2352–5).

There is a 'conduct manual' aspect to all this. English women may feel far removed in time and place from the *hethene pak* of unfortunate women, and it is highly unlikely that men will ever be as cruel to them as Tereus was to Philomela. Nevertheless, the narrator continues, they should learn from those ancient stories, and 'be war' of smooth-talking men who profess to be enamored of them (2387–91).

Chaucer takes great pains to protect the reputations of the *Legend*'s good pagan women. A 'legendary' was a collection of saints' lives. In this pagan equivalent, Chaucer replaces the mystical marriage of the female saint to Christ the Bridegroom, of central importance in the hagiography of holy women, with material marriage, with the *Legend*'s false men taking the place of the tormentors who try and test Christian sanctity. In Cupid's martyrology, marriage, rather than virginity or chastity, is the overall imperative, the motivating force and object of desire, the factor that legitimates behaviour that normally would be deemed extreme. (Chaucer shows no interest in pagan virginity cults.) Thereby Cleopatra's spectacular suicide in the snake pit is valorized. Always 'unreprovable unto my wyfhod', she keeps her 'covenaunt' with Anthony – going beyond her wifely duty even as she affirms it – by joining him in death (688–95; cf. the similar discourse in *The Legend of Thisbe*, 896–9). In Middle English, *wyf* can mean simply 'woman', but in the *Legend*, Chaucer uses it predominantly to designate a married woman. The cause of true 'wifehood' explains Thisbe's rash departure from the protective city into the fields 'so brode and wide' (782), where a lioness lurks. Why Piramus, Thisbe, Medea and Hypermnestra should reject the authority of their fathers. And why Dido, rather than begging Aeneas not to depart, should ask him to take her as his truly legal wife, so she can die in that worthy state (1319–20).

Chaucer's heroines are married, or believe themselves to be married, or believe that soon they will be married; there is no promiscuous leaping into bed with their lovers. Jason 'wedded' Hypsipyle and 'upon her begat . . . children two' (1559–60) before deserting her. Demophon swears to marry Phyllis and solemnly plights his troth, before she allows him to do 'what so that hym leste' (2469). Similarly, Jason and Medea reach a full accord that 'Jasoun shal hire wedde, as trewe knyght' (270). Having come to her chamber at night and made there 'his oth', 'Upon the goddes' . . . | To ben her husbonde whil he lyve may' (1635–41), Jason then 'goth with hire to bedde'; the morning after, 'he hym spedde [hastened away]' (1644–5). Hypermnestra warns her husband about the plot to kill him, preferring to be 'ded in wifly honeste | Than ben a traytour lyvynge in my shame' (2701–2).

Here, as in so many other respects, the *Legend of Philomela* stands somewhat apart, although marriage is implicated inasmuch as Tereus violates his marital bond with Procne even as he violates Philomela's body. Furthermore, 'humblesse of wifhood' is related to sisterly love, making clear the store Procne sets by family ties and responsibilities (2260–9). Most bizarre of all is the extent to which Chaucer wrenched the story of Lucrece to suit his all-controlling purpose. Surely here is a case of superlative female goodness that required no special pleading, her story no heavy editing. Yet, to be part of Chaucer's legendary of Cupid's saints, it certainly does.

Ovid located the cause of Lucrece's suicide in her feelings of personal disgrace. For Augustine, it exemplified that excessive desire for praise that compromised the virtue of so many good pagans: 'she feared that, if she remained alive, she would be thought to have enjoyed suffering the violence' that Tarquinius Collatinus inflicted on her. It is not that Lucrece actually *did* experience lustful feelings – Augustine (infamously) raised that as an argument ploy but soon rejected it. It is all a matter of how things appear in the public eye, what people may think of her.[23] Likewise, Chaucer's Lucrece is totally blameless; indeed, during the rape, she is described as being in a swoon, and 'feleth no thing, neyther foul ne fayr' (1818). But it is concern for her husband's reputation rather than for her own which motivates her actions.

> She sayde that, for hir gylt ne for hir blame,   *guilt*
> Hir husbonde shulde nat have the foule name,
> That wolde she nat suffer by no wey.   *allow*
>
> (1844–6)

That same husband stands before her, together with her father, mother and all her friends, assuring her that there was no 'gylt' whatever on her part; 'it lay not in hir myght' (1849). But to no avail.

> 'Be as be may', quod she, 'of forgyvyng,
> I wol not have noo forgyft for nothing'.   *forgiveness*
> But pryvely she kaughte forth a knyf,
> And therwithal she rafte hirself hir lyf . . .
>
> (1852–5)

The principle of not giving her husband a 'foule name' has been raised to a level of abstraction that transcends the norms of family life. Secular marriage has been apotheosized, taken above and beyond the social status and power of any actual husband. In particular, it has been honoured as a valid reason for suicide.

Augustine had used the story of the rape of Lucrece to affirm the superiority of the virtue of Christian women who, in such a case, would not wish to make matters much worse by committing 'murder on themselves out of shame'.[24] On the contrary, the legend's narrator sees here an illustration of the 'gret feyth' that, in all the land of Israel, Christ found only in a woman (1879–82). That passage garbles the faithful Canaanite woman of Matthew 15:28 with the faithful gentile centurion of Matthew 8:10, a reflex of Chaucer's desire to create an image of specifically female *hethen* goodness. His conceptual difficulties here are all too obvious; reconciling the values of the traditional Lucrece (public opinion is everything) with those of the God of Love (love conquers all) is no easy task. In *The Legend of Lucrece* Chaucer struggles to present *wyfhod* in its purest form, as maintained by the most perfect of his virtuous pagan women. A formidable figure, to be admired from afar rather than imitated.

'He was evir . . . all womanis frend'.[25] Thus the Scots poet Gavin Douglas (who completed his translation of the *Aeneid* in 1513) sought to explain the offence that, he claims, Chaucer had given to Virgil by writing *The Legend of Dido*. To call Aeneas false, brand him as a traitor, was to question Virgil's entire edifice, render worthless his twelve years' labour. Douglas could have made a similar accusation against Ovid's treatment of Virgil in *Heroides*, VII. But his interest is in Chaucer, and particularly in the impression the poet gives of being a friend to all women. That impression has never ceased to fascinate Chaucer's readers. Was he capable of making at least some proto-feminist gestures? (Maybe gestures are all they are – but what else could they have been, given Chaucer's ideological milieu?) Or were his concerns predominantly, inevitably, literary: are we dealing with a poet eager to propagate 'newe corn' from 'olde feldes' (*PF* 22–5), who delighted in reversing the polarities of his narratives, in turning tales inside-out, as he sought fresh perspectives?

Whatever the truth of this may be, it is pleasant to enter into the spirit of Chaucerian fiction by imagining 'Geffrey' as having returned to the House of Fame, where 'tydynges . . . of fals and soth' are 'compouned', to do some compounding of his own. There he found materials that enabled him to create good pagan women, creatures fit to be in the company of manly Troilus and Theseus, as they experienced their moments of greatest enlightenment. But is that *makynge* convincing? That, I suspect, he left as a matter for debate. One that continues even now.

Chapter 3

The Canterbury Tales, I: war, love, laughter

The Canterbury Tales comprises a rich array of subjects and styles. *Roman antique, fabliau,* conversion narrative, matrimonial satire, ecclesiastical critique, romance (in several forms), Breton lay, saint's life, Mariological miracle, tragedy, beast fable, and penitential treatise are all represented, but it should be emphasized that many of Chaucer's narratives resist neat classification – not least because of the broad social spectrum reflected by the tellers to which they are assigned. Rhyming couplets are the staple verse form, although in the tales told by the Man of Law, Clerk, Prioress and Second Nun, rhyme royal is deployed, to which must be added the unique *Monk's Tale* stanza (of eight five-stress lines rhyming ababbcbc), the demotic loose rhymes and rhythms of *Sir Thopas* and the accomplished didactic prose of the *Melibee* and *The Parson's Tale.*

If an all-encompassing genre is sought for *The Canterbury Tales*, then we can come up with no better than 'medieval satire'. By this I mean certain classical notions of satire as understood and interpreted in the later Middle Ages, encompassing what usually is called either *satira communis* or 'estates satire'. In Medieval Latin, the term *status* designated the various occupations, professions and vocations in accordance with which social production was organized – the term being redolent of class distinction and deference, the imperative of knowing one's place, and the existence of boundaries that could be transgressed only with difficulty (and with considerable ambition). But it would be wrong to imagine that a static and uncontentious 'medieval world picture' appertained in Chaucer's time. Quite the opposite was true. Fourteenth-century England was undergoing a period of extraordinary social upheaval and reconfiguration. This was a time of plague (with the Black Death forcing systemic change on the labour market) and of debilitating war (against the French, Scots and Irish). A time of political and religious crisis, including the longeurs and ultimate failure of King Richard II's leadership, the so-called Peasant's Revolt of 1381, the threat (real or imagined) posed by the Lollard heresy. And all this together with an identity crisis within the institution of knighthood (in part prompted by the inability of European chivalry to meet the challenge of a new crusade), the rise of what may loosely be called 'the middle class', and the emergence of a professional managerial cadre of learned laymen (Geoffrey Chaucer being one). Maybe this is why so many English writers (Gower and William Langland as much as Chaucer) turned to the discourse of estates satire. Here they found a model for the analysis of social forces that retained its usefulness (perhaps it offered some kind of reassurance?) even as it struggled to make sense of them.

The fundamental strategy of estates satire is revelation and mockery of the ways in which a representative figure or group fails to perform the requisite functions, meet the defining responsibilities and live up to the norms and aspirations of the profession and/or social role in question. A mendicant friar travesties the foundational ideals of his order by bullying people into donating gifts so that he and his confrères can enjoy a life of ease and comfort (*The Summoner's Tale*). A pardoner goes far beyond his brief of collecting alms for a London hospital by claiming priestly powers of preaching and absolution, all the better to exact money from his ill-educated victims (*The Pardoner's Prologue and Tale*). A much-married woman from Bath claims that being a wife is itself a distinct and honourable *status*, the duties of which she will readily perform. And so on.

However, the 'estates satire' element in the medieval literary theory of satire is only one aspect (albeit a vitally important one) of a tradition of major scope and scale. The three major Roman satirists, Horace, Persius and Juvenal, were studied continuously in the medieval West, and a remarkably consistent critical response emerged, which may be summarized as follows:

> Satire is that type of ethical verse, ranging in tone between bitter indignation, mocking irony, and witty humour, which in forthright, unadorned terms censures and corrects vices in society and advocates virtues, eschewing slander of individuals but sparing no guilty party, not even the poet himself.[1]

Here, then, are the principles that influenced many medieval satires. They permeate *The Canterbury Tales*. Of particular interest is satire's characteristic refusal to spare even the satirist himself. Chaucer's self-mockery in the guise of 'Chaucer the pilgrim' is one of the *Tales'* most distinctive features. Such inveterate self-irony is not, however, wholly consonant with the lofty voice of moral indignation that other aspects of satire theory promote, a form of expression that reprehends with robust moral confidence and singleness of purpose. Instead the *Tales* involve an abundance of voices, of which the Chaucer-persona's is only one. Opinions are offered and judgments made from diverse subject-positions rather than from some common vantage point of authoritative moral perception. *The Reeve's Tale* satirizes an avaricious miller,

The Friar's Tale a ruthless summoner, *The Summoner's Tale* an avaricious friar. It is true that the tone of these tales vacillates 'between bitter indignation, mocking irony, and witty humour', with vice being censured and virtue advocated 'in forthright, unadorned terms'. Yet in each case the primary motivation is marked as subjective rather than objective. Each narrator is engaged in a personal attack on a fellow pilgrim who has offended him, and the revelation of that figure's moral failings (which are based, to varying degrees, on the shortcomings of the social *status* that he or she represents) is by no means conducted in an unbiased manner. The element of personal spite interestingly complicates the satire, although without pulling its punches; indeed, in attacking others, the respective narrators lay bare their own sins. It could be said, then, that in Chaucer's *magnum opus* the univocal ethical assertiveness of *satira communis* has been personalized and privatized, dispersed over a wide range of individual voices.

Commentators on, and practitioners of, the genre of satire explained that it features a 'low' and 'light' (*levis*) style rather than an elevated one, because 'vulgar' words match quotidian, ordinary things. Those common words set its style in contrast to that of tragedy, where elevated, 'regal' words were the regular currency. Like the satyrs, those mythical woodland creatures from which the genre supposedly took its name, satire was regarded as 'naked', the point being that it deployed unadorned and unrestrained language. Here Chaucer had to hand a well-established justification for his use of lower-class speech in the *fabliaux* and elsewhere. However, in the poetics of *The Canterbury Tales*, the naked terms of satire and the elevated speech of tragedy are not in non-negotiable opposition. Chaucer included *stilus grandiloquus* (the elevated and ornate style appropriate to lofty things) as well as *stilus humilis* (the low style associated with humble persons and things) within his compilatorial experiment, with *The Knight's Tale* and *The Monk's Tale* chronicling the deeds of great men. Medieval satire theory offered strong precedent for his extensive use of 'vulgar' speech, but Chaucer's high valuation of the vernacular in *The Canterbury Tales* is altogether more rich and strange than that, the happy consequence of myriad sources and influences being mediated through a groundbreaking creative consciousness.

The Middle English noun *vulgār(e)* (cf. the Medieval Latin *vulgāre*) designated 'the native or common language of a nation';[2] in Chaucer's day English people referred to their native or mother tongue as 'the vulgar'. The word had connotations of the ordinary and usual, the commonly used and widely known; it also could mean 'common' in a derogatory way, hence the sense 'vulgar', which became the word's primary meaning in Modern English. Subsequently (in the seventeenth century) the term 'vernacular' came into use, from the Latin *vernaculus,* meaning 'domestic, native, indigenous', although also 'low-bred, proletarian'. Thus the noun *vulgāre* was displaced, and the frequent use of the word *vernacular* in a positive sense meant that the troubling ambiguity between 'the vulgar' as one's regular language and 'the vulgar' as the ordinary, plebeian, or indeed despicable, was occluded.

When Dante made his claim for the viability of an 'illustrious vernacular', he was promoting a version of Italian that was educated and upgraded far beyond its 'vulgar' or plebeian origins; a language that, through proper polishing and refinement, could rival Latin in expressive scope and social status. This belief is the basis of his polemical treatise *De vulgari eloquentia* (*On Vernacular/Vulgar Eloquence* – the challenge posed by that title should be appreciated). For his part, Chaucer seems eager to emphasize the vulgarity of 'the vulgar', the extent to which *rude* (crude), *large* (outspoken) and *brode* (unrestrained) speech features in his *Canterbury Tales.* His narrator justifies this by saying that whoever repeats someone else's tale must 'reherce' (report) all of his words, no matter how 'rudeliche and large' they may be (GP I.730–3). Obviously, figures such as the Miller and Reeve are churls, 'And harlotrie they tolden bothe two'. Yet all their tales must be re-told, 'be they bettre or werse', if the 'mateere' (subject-matter) is not to be falsified (*MilPro* I.3172–5, 82–4).

Chaucer's contemporary (and enthusiastic reader) Thomas Usk affirmed the value of 'rude' and 'boystous' (unpolished, simple) English words, which pierce the hearer's heart to its innermost point and plant *sentence* there – a direct and efficient means of communication. Let the clerics have their Latin because they are learned and know how to handle it, let the French have the 'queynt [fancy, ingenious] termes' of their own language – and let us English 'shewe our fantasyes [imaginations, conceptions] in suche wordes as we lerneden of our dames tonge [mother tongue]'.[3] Something of the same spirit pervades the penultimate section of the General Prologue and *The Miller's Prologue.* Here Chaucer highlights the *harlotrie* of certain tales to come, curiously giving them pride of place whilst reassuring his imagined audience that other performances will offer 'storial thyng [historical material]' together with 'gentillesse', 'moralitee and hoolynesse': the choice is theirs (I.3176–81).

Nowhere does Chaucer attempt to elevate *The Canterbury Tales* in its entirety, or its English in general, by drawing attention to (for instance) the grave high style of *The Knight's Tale* or the dignified rhyme royal with which he honours four tales of martyrdom and/or sacrificial female virtue. Many of the collection's most prestigious assets – or, better, assets that are prestigious in conventional terms – are, one might say, being undersold. Surely this is a careful, deliberate choice, made by a poet who has an extraordinary ear for the resources of his *dames tonge* and the varieties of expression it offers. Chaucer is willing to accommodate (even to accentuate) the rudest of the *rude*, the largest of the *large*, the broadest of the *brode*. Perhaps he supposed that when English was blatantly *boystous*, it was functioning in a manner that was distinctive, characteristic and resilient, thereby testifying to the strengths (the rude health, one might say) of the language in general.

Dante sought to value his Italian vernacular by making it the vehicle for the highest possible subject – the organization of the afterlife; the fate of the souls of humankind in the three other-worldly kingdoms, of purgatory, hell and heaven. Chaucer sought to value his English vernacular rather by encompassing a wide range of subjects, using many different linguistic registers (including dialect), mixing together high and low, religious and lay, male and female. Whereas in the *Comedy* Virgil was the authority figure Dante measured himself against and sought to surpass, in *The Canterbury Tales* Chaucer positions himself as a reporter of tales told after many men and women. In place of the Dantean egotistical sublime, we have delegated, decentralized authorship in the extreme, the ultimate tour de force of a self-ironical writer.

Moral virtue and cursed rite: the Knight's *roman antique*

The 'Luttrell Psalter', produced *c*.1320–40, includes an illumination of a finely dressed knight besting a sinister yet ridiculous figure with blue skin and distorted facial appearance, who rides a goofy horse and bears a shield decorated with a bust that exploits the stereotypical features of an 'Ethiopian', meaning a black African (figure 3). This is usually interpreted as a Christian fantasy of victory over the Saracen foe, as Richard 'the Lionheart' defeats a caricatured Saladin (Ṣalāḥ ad-Dīn Yūsuf ibn Ayyūb), with the shield image depicting some dark demonic god or the prophet Mohammed. Nothing of the sort actually happened; in real life, Saladin was the definitive victor, having recaptured Jerusalem from the Christians in 1187 and defended his gains against all counter-attacks, including those led by King Richard. In 1192 they negotiated a treaty that left Jerusalem in Muslim hands but ensured the safety of Christian pilgrims. The two rulers addressed each other in terms of mutual respect. Indeed, among Christian writers Saladin was often praised for his chivalry, and for the relative leniency he had shown following his capture of Jerusalem – in stark contrast to the bloodbath that ensued when a Christian army took the town in 1099, thus ending the First Crusade.

The conflicting impulses here at work are very much in evidence in the Knight's *roman antique*. This admiring account of pagan noblemen who live up to the highest standards of honour and chivalry could be seen as a reflex of

tam deo fusceptor meus es.

Figure 3. An illumination possibly depicting King Richard jousting with Saladin. British Library, MS Add. 42130, fol. 82r.

the narrator's personal experiences of contemporary pagans – those Muslims against whom he had fought 'for oure feith' (I.62), and whose military prowess he had witnessed at firsthand. Indeed, he also had fought alongside heathen against other heathen (I.65–6). In *The Knight's Tale* certain aspects of the pagan Other are being idealized, from a safe distance. It is tempting to read this narrative as the Knight's reaction against – maybe even as an escape from – the vicious chaos of the campaigns in which he was involved, with the ever-successful warlord Duke Theseus as the perfect military commander, an idealization that can easily be read as overreaching but is comprehensible given the lack of leadership and general ineptitude that characterized so much waging of war in the later Middle Ages, including the campaigns on which he fought (as listed at GP I.51–67). However, the extent to which the tale may be read as revelatory of the teller's character is a matter of some debate, given that (as already noted) the narrative we know as *The Knight's Tale* seems to have been written some time before Chaucer embarked on his ambitious *Canterbury Tales* project. But there is no doubting the story's admiration for pagan feats in war and love – or the deep suspicion it harbours concerning the exotic pagan gods that are worshipped so devoutly during its course. The demonization of those deities had, for Chaucer and his contemporaries, a factual basis: the fallen angels banished by God from heaven had become the objects of worship by gullible peoples who were led astray, brought to destruction, by the likes of Jove, Apollo and Mars and 'swich rascaille [rascals]' (*Troilus and Criseyde*, V.1853). The colourful imagery with which they are adorned is a far cry from the ugly (to Western eyes) idol on Saladin's shield, as depicted in the

Luttrell Psalter. But they are equally deceitful and deadly, wishing no good to humankind.

From the tale's primary source, Boccaccio's *Teseida*, Chaucer inherited the imposing figure of Duke Theseus. In his turn, Boccaccio had been inspired by Statius' *Thebaid* (written *c*.80–*c*.92 CE), particularly its final book, in which, returning from a war against the Scythians, Theseus is importuned by Argive widows whose dead relatives have been denied burial by the tyrannical Creon. Theseus leads his army to victory against the Thebans; Creon falls victim to his spear, and the widows rush to seek out and cremate their dead. At this point the narrative ends, followed by an epilogue in which Statius prays for the success of his work and modestly proclaims its inferiority to the *Aeneid*. Of the divisive and deadly love of Arcita and Palemone there is no trace; Boccaccio made that up.

Boccaccio's characterization of Theseus differs from Statius' in crucial details and in general spirit; in his turn, Chaucer diverged sharply from Boccaccio's text. The episode in which Theseus avenges the Argive widows has an even greater impact in the English narrative, not least because Chaucer has drastically abbreviated the account of the war with the Amazons that precedes it, and the account of the war against the Thebans which follows it, in the *Teseida*. *The Knight's Tale* sharply focusses on the way in which Theseus orders his men to fight in yet another foreign field, and they obey him without question – a fantasy of military discipline and logistics that must have prompted feelings of admiration and envy (if not of incredulity) in Chaucer's aristocratic readers. Theseus' superlative moral virtue, together with his supreme power, are therefore established at the outset.

They are maintained throughout the tale. Having embarked on what was, according to late-medieval standards, a Just War, Theseus pursues it in a just manner – indeed, in a manner more than just, to judge by the brutal realities of Chaucer's time. When we are told that, at Thebes, he knocked down 'bothe wall and sparre and rafter' (I.990) this may well describe the Athenians' initial breach of the town's defences, or perhaps a subsequent dismantling to render the area easier to control. At any rate, there is no account of large-scale killing, raping and looting, or the destruction of major buildings – all of which would have been justifiable behaviour, according to then-current laws of war, because Thebes was taken 'by assaut [assault]', meaning that a breach was made in the city's walls, following its refusal to surrender (I.989). In relation to the standards of crusading warfare (and of the Hundred Years War), Theseus was exceptionally squeamish. When Alexandria fell to the forces of Peter I of Cyprus in 1365 – a victory in which Chaucer's Knight supposedly participated (see GP

I.51, 72) – the town was said to have been taken *par assaut*, as for example in Guillaume de Machaut's *Prise d'Alixandre*.[4] The fall of Jerusalem during the First Crusade also fitted the same classification. On both occasions, massacres and systematic despoliation followed. In marked contrast, Theseus' restraint at Thebes seems rather reminiscent of Saladin's relatively generous treatment of the inhabitants of Jerusalem in 1187.

The Duke's final plan for the conduct of the culminating conflict over Emelye bespeaks a similar desire to control violence. Boccaccio's version of events was heavily influenced by his antiquarian knowledge of gladiatorial combat, of fights to the death in vast amphitheatres. Chaucer seems to be thinking more in terms of a medieval mock-battle or tournament, a friendly, sporting affair in which the intention was to get the better of one's opponent without inflicting extreme physical harm on him. Hence the restrictions imposed by Theseus on the types of weapon used and his insistence that the defeated should not be killed but conveyed to a place of safety. Near the end of the *Teseida* we hear of numerous funeral pyres burning; many good men have perished. In *The Knight's Tale*, there is only one pyre – Arcite's. Theseus does everything in his power to prevent his or any other warrior's death; it is only when the gods intervene that a brave man dies.

Whereas Boccaccio had the final battle take place in an existing amphitheatre, Chaucer's Theseus commands that a new structure be built – and on the very site where he had discovered the young lovers fighting over Emelye (I.1862). What was illegally hidden has been brought into a public forum of judgment; the young men's passions are contained within socially acceptable bounds. The 'oratories' of Venus, Diana and Mars, in which Palamon, Emelye and Arcite pray to their respective deities, are also new constructions, richly adorned with 'noble kervyng' and 'portreitures' (1915, cf. 1938, 1968, etc.). Theseus directs the entire operation, wields the authority needed to make it happen – and pays for everything himself (2089–92). Thus the most virtuous of Chaucer's virtuous heathen seeks to bring order out of chaos, civilization out of strife, and to replace potential destruction with actual construction.

The Duke's final speech offers an enlightened monotheistic vision of the first and unmoved mover (here identified with Jupiter) who made the fair chain of love that forms the bond of the universe (I.2987–3074). Theseus draws the moral that it is pointless to fight against the way in which the Prime Mover has organized the corruptible world (with the 'speces of thynges' surviving 'by successiouns', as individual members of each species are born and die). However, men are free to meet the inevitable with dignity and honour, thus making 'vertu of necessitee' (I.3042), creating humane value in response to impersonal forces. These principles demand, he concludes, that following a period of mourning it is now a time for joy; Emelye must take the 'gentil Palamon' for 'housbonde and for lord' (3077, 3081). Here, then, we seem to be hearing the words of a philosopher ruler of the kind commended by Boethius (who was, of course, echoing Plato's *Republic*): 'happy those states would be where philosophers were kings or their governors were philosophers' (*DCP* I, pr. 4, 18–25).

Fine words indeed. But is Theseus' philosophical disquisition not a rationalization (and a diplomatic obfuscation) of political expediency? This speech is made in the context of an Athenian parliament that is addressing the state's alliances with certain countries, and the perceived need to have 'fully of Thebans obeisaunce [obedience, submissiveness]' (I.2974). What better way to bring Thebes into full submission than to marry off Theseus' sister-in-law to a prominent member of the Theban ruling class? This is not the first time that Theseus has exploited young love for the benefit of his empire. When he spares the lives of Palamon and Arcite following their illicit duel, this is done on condition that they vow never to make war on Athens. The cousins accept Theseus as their overlord, subjecting themselves to his will (1821–8). The Duke's actions, it could be said, are driven by *Realpolitik* rather than abstract ideals of love and chivalry.

To which it may be responded that, for a medieval king, action of this kind was an act of moral virtue. A good ruler should work in defence of his people and his land, exercising the finest leadership skills to ensure 'great victories over their enemies' and to maintain peace and prosperity at home, to quote the *Livre de chevalerie* of Geoffroi de Charny, a French knight who died in 1356 at the Battle of Poitiers.[5]

But what are we to make of Theseus' claim that 'it is best, as for a worthy fame', for a man to die 'whan that he is best of name' (I.3055–6)? Of course, it was frequently stated that Fame was 'the spur that the clear spirit doth raise' to superlative feats of chivalry.[6] Geoffroi de Charny urged 'all knights and all men-at-arms' to aim 'to attain those heights of valor whereby so many good deeds are performed', thereby winning recognition during their 'lifetime . . . and for so long after their death'.[7] However, it was a commonplace of late-medieval classicism that even the best of the virtuous heathen could be too concerned with public reputation and merely earthly glory (as viewed from a supposedly superior Christian perspective). That may be what Chaucer has in mind here.

The young people whose lives Theseus governs may lag behind him in metaphysical insight, but there is no question of the intensity of their piety. Arcite earnestly performs his 'sacrifice' to Mars 'with alle the rytes of his payen wyse' (I.2368–70); Emelye and Palamon do likewise in the temples of the gods who are special to them. But it brings them little comfort during their existential crises. Palamon voices a deep suspicion of the

> ... crueel goddes that governe
> This world with byndyng of youre word eterne,
> And writen in the table of atthamaunt   *adamant (hardest of stones)*
> Youre parlement and youre eterne graunt,
> What is mankynde moore unto you holde
> Than is the sheep that rouketh in the folde?   *cowers*
> (I.1303–8)

A man may be killed like some beast cowering in a pen, or imprisoned, or suffer sickness and great misfortune, even though he is guiltless. Where's the justice in that? Even worse, Palamon continues, it seems that beasts fare better than men. A beast, while alive, may act on all its impulses and does not suffer punishment in an afterlife, whereas men are subject to firm constraints in their lives and they must 'wepe and pleyne [lament]' in their afterlives (1320). Palamon leaves this problem for the theologians to solve but is quite convinced that 'in this world greet pyne [pain] ys' (1323–4).

He locates the source of his own pain and imprisonment in the intervention of two jealous and angry gods, Saturn and Juno, who, because they bear a grudge against the royal 'blood | Of Thebes', have destroyed almost all of it (I.1328–31). Arcite agrees with him on this at least: 'Som wikke aspect or disposicioun | Of Saturne, by sum constellacioun, | Hath yeven us this' (1087–9). Contrary to the classical tradition of the 'Golden Age' when Saturn ruled and justice prevailed throughout the world, Chaucer is giving priority to the astronomical/astrological aspect of this planet-god, which was highly negative. According to the standard account, Saturn was a malevolent planet, cold, leaden and dry (and therefore portrayed as an old man in pagan fables). Alan of Lille writes that in the abode of Saturn, grief, groans, tears, discord, terror, sadness, wanness, mourning and injustice hold sway.[8] All of this squares with the description that 'pale Saturnus the colde' (2443) offers of himself: 'Min is the drenchyng [drowning] in the see so wan; | Min is the prisoun in the derke cote [dark hovel] ... ' (2454–65). It would seem, then, that any course of action proposed by this terrifying power can be expected to be deadly and unjust. 'In elde [old age] is bothe wysdom and usage', and old Saturn finds 'in his olde experience an art' (a trick) whereby 'he ful soone hath plesed every part' (2445–8) – that is, he devises a way of satisfying the warring gods Mars and Venus but without caring about the impact that his action will have on the world of men. Mars asked for victory, Palamon asked for Emelye. Saturn seizes on this, ordering Pluto to send the infernal fury that causes Arcite's horse to throw, and mortally wound, his rider (2684–93), thereby ensuring that Palamon gets the girl. The opportunism, and self-serving legalism, of his 'art' are manifest.

The crucial role Saturn plays in *The Knight's Tale* is without precedent in the *Teseida*, where the deities make up their collective mind without needing to call upon the cold god's services. Chaucer also added the episode wherein the exiled Arcite dreams of Mercury appearing to him, 'Arrayed . . . | As he was whan that Argus took his sleep' (I.1389–90). This alludes to an incident described in Ovid's *Metamorphoses* in which Jupiter sends Mercury to kill 'Argus of the hundred eyes'. Mercury first soothes Argus by playing music on his reed pipes, then lulls him to sleep with a story, whereupon the god strikes 'off the nodding head and from the rock' throws 'it all bloody, spattering the cliff with gore' (I.714–21). For Mercury to appear looking as he did on this murderous occasion, hardly bodes well for Arcite's future. He is urged to return to Athens, 'Ther is thee shapen of thy wo an ende' (I.1392). This is dangerously ambiguous: Arcite's woes will come to an end either because he will find happiness (which is how the young man seems to understand the god's words) or because he will meet his death. In a similar vein is the answer that Mars gave to Arcite, who had asked him for victory in the battle for Emelye. The hauberk on the statue of Mars begins to ring, and the word 'Victorie' issues from 'a murmurynge | Ful lowe and dym [muffled]' (2431–3). Here, once again, Chaucer parts company with the *Teseida*. Boccaccio regarded a moving statue, sweet music, and unspecified 'signs' as sufficient for a 'wondering Arcita' to infer that his prayer had been well received.[9] In Chaucer, that *basso profundo* 'Victory!' makes the fact of divine duplicity, or at least economy with the truth, even more palpable. Here are examples of 'amphibological' oracles of the kind condemned by Criseyde: 'Goddes speken in amphibologies, | And for o soth they tellen twenty lyes' (*Troilus and Criseyde*, IV.1406–7; cf. p. 41 above). Those whom the gods would destroy they first deceive.

Chaucer seems to have in mind a firm distinction between the exemplary moral virtue of his noble heathen and the contemptible shortcomings of their rascally gods, who (in Shakespearean phrase) kill men for their sport, caring no more for humankind than for the sheep that cowers in its fold. The Knight's narrative leaves no doubt that the heroic denizens of ancient Athens and Thebes were ill rewarded for faithful adherence to the 'secte' into which they were born (to return to the Squire's idiom; V.17). This exclamation from *Troilus and Criseyde* applies equally well here:

> Lo here, of payens corsed olde rites!
> Lo here, what alle hire goddes may availle!
>
> (V.1849–50)

Marvels, magic and machines: the Squire, Sir Thopas and the Franklin

In *The Squire's Tale* there is neither duplicitous pagan god nor cursed rite in sight: its (tantalizingly incomplete) narrative does not feature a heathen prayer or religious performance, let alone a resounding condemnation of such practice. This is all the more surprising given that the tale prominently features marvelous devices and events – strange phenomena that could easily have been explained with reference to the involvement of devils, those false gods mistakenly worshipped by the pagans. We hear of a bronze flying horse that can transport a person to any place in the world within a mere 24 hours; a large glass mirror in which a king can see any misfortunes that will befall his kingdom and a woman can see the future infidelity of the man she loves; a golden ring that gives its wearer the power to understand the language of birds; an armour-piercing sword that will heal any wound it inflicts.

All of these wonders are gifts from the 'kyng of Arabe and of Inde' to Cambyuskan on the occasion of the feast that celebrates his twenty years of rule. At first sight, they may seem like the stuff of poetic fiction (some observers think of Pegasus the flying horse), or sleight of hand (comparable to the supposed 'magyk' performed by conjurers at great feasts), or indeed deceitful in a more troubling sense, as when the horse crafted by Synon enabled Greek warriors to get within the walls of Troy (V.204–11). But ultimately they are presented as human inventions susceptible of rational analysis and 'scientific' explanation – here once again I use *science* in the sense of expert, specialized knowledge, a body of information judged to be reliable (cf. p. 41 above). The Squire seems in no doubt that the bronze horse is a mere machine, albeit a highly sophisticated one, 'wroghte' during a long period of time by an ingenious craftsman (128). In Chaucer's day elaborate artifacts were features of extravagant court occasions, such as the metal golden angel that bent down from its tower to present Richard II with a crown at his coronation pageant in 1377; the mechanical enactment of the capture of Jerusalem in 1099 (featuring a large model boat that seemed to travel on water) with which Charles V of France entertained his guest, the Emperor Charles IV, in 1378 or the articulated white stag that was part of the welcome afforded to Charles VI's queen, Isabeau of Bavaria, on her first visit to Paris in 1389. We would expect the great Cambyuskan's celebration to be even more memorable, and the Squire does not disappoint.

The bronze horse works through the turning of a system of pegs and manipulation of its reins (V.312–33); no evil spirit is involved. At ll.180–5 we are told that this contraption stands as if glued to the ground because a person who 'kan [knows] nat the craft' is unable to move it. However, Cambyuskan receives the requisite instruction – in private – from the knight who had piloted it (317). In general, says the Squire, 'lewed peple' think the worst about things 'that been maad moore subtilly | Than they kan in hir lewednesse comprehende' (221–3). That should not be read as a blanket condemnation of Cambyuskan's puzzled courtiers as being uneducated and ignorant people; rather the point is that, if a person does not have sufficient knowledge of how something works, he may deem it threatening, judge 'to the badder ende' (224). Moreover, if no explanation for a given phenomenon is forthcoming, this is not because one does not exist, but simply because one has not yet been discovered. It is well known that glass is made from ashes of fern (that being actual medieval practice), which may seem strange, given that glass looks nothing like ashes of fern. But that is the fact of the matter, and therefore there is neither cause for debate nor need for wonder concerning this particular artifact (253–7). In contrast, room for speculation remains concerning the origins of thunder, of the ebb and flow of the tides, of spiders' webs, and of mist (258–9) – and indeed, 'of alle thing, til that the cause is wyst [known]' (260). In that category may be included those three marvels: the mirror, sword and ring. Perhaps the mirror may be explained with reference to optical theory, one courtier opines; it may function 'naturelly', through angles and cunning reflections. Here Chaucer has been influenced by a passage in the *Roman de la Rose* that discusses vision and reflection (18123–268, cf. 17983–8030); for good measure he drops the names of Alhazen, Vitello and Aristotle, authorities on *perspectiva*, which is what the study of light and sight was called in the later Middle Ages. The sword? Achilles had a spear that could both wound and heal; perhaps a special hardening of the metal, combined with a medicinal compound, would do the trick? Canacee's ring is a tougher proposition, a 'wonder thyng' indeed – but do not Moses and King Solomon (highly respectable authorities both) have the reputation for 'konnyng [knowledge] in swich art' (247–51)?

Thus Cambyuskan's courtiers try to make 'skiles after hir fantasies' (205), seek to turn their imaginings into firm explanations, in a passage which occupies an impressive seventy-three lines. This evokes a feeling – one expressed with increasing frequency in Chaucer's day – that many a 'wonder thyng' has a natural rather than a supernatural cause; there is no need to postulate some special divine intervention or put the blame on demonic agency. Around 1370 Nicole Oresme wrote his *De causis mirabilium*

> ... to show the causes of some effects which seem to be marvels and to show that the effects occur naturally.... There is no reason to take recourse to the heavens, the last refuge of the weak, or demons, or to our glorious God as if He would produce these effects directly, more so than those effects whose causes we believe are well known to us.[10]

This is not to say that some late-medieval thinkers were denying the possibility of divine miracles; simply that they were seeking to restrict the sphere of the miraculous. Nature has its own marvels, and people may be 'well satisfied with natural causes', to cite Oresme again.[11] That poet of secular estate, Geoffrey Chaucer, can be numbered among those satisfied people. He was happy to have one of his lay creations, the Squire, affirm that certain men could make 'ful many a gyn' (ingenious contrivance, 128), thanks to their expert knowledge of natural causes. The appeal to *science* is a regular feature of Chaucer's depictions of pagan antiquity.

It is absent, however, in the first tale that Chaucer the pilgrim assigns to himself, the tail-end romance of *Sir Thopas*, a brilliant parody of a genre that could hardly be farther from the poet's usual literary preferences and intellectual tastes, although the amount of attention he pays to stylistic and metrical detail may be taken as evidence of affection rather than antipathy. The unmanliest of men, Thopas is described in terms traditionally applied to beautiful women, excels at the non-aristocratic sports of archery and wrestling, and postpones a fight with a giant, insisting that he will come back the next day, when he has put on the right armour (a process that takes up most of the second 'fit' or section). At which point the giant contemptuously fires stones at him with a slingshot – a comic inversion of David's encounter with Goliath. Thopas has entered 'the contree of Fairye' in search of 'an elf-queene' he saw in a dream, for no woman in the ordinary world is worthy to be his mate (VII.784–806). This nebulous love object lacks any distinguishing features, a far cry from the singular individual who becomes a nobleman's one true love, as per the courtly love convention. The fairy queen and 'Olifaunt' the giant (807–14) are predictable denizens of popular romance, requiring no account of their origins or explanation for their existence. They are as typical of the genre as the minstrel opening with its call to listen carefully, the long catalogues (of herbs, birds and heroes), the minutely detailed accounts of arming – and the relentless tail-rhymes that Chaucer has reduced to exquisite 'dogerel' (925).

Science is firmly in place once more in the Franklin's follow-up to the Squire's story, which he may or may not have interrupted (critical opinion is divided). Given its identification as a Breton Lay (V.709–15) one might expect a tale of fairy-world wonders and enchantments, featuring magic of a kind quite impervious to rationalization. A story, in short, of the kind parodied in *Sir Thopas*. Instead we get a narrative in which 'natural causes' (to apply Oresme's term) are sought, and usually found, for wonderful events. The Franklin tries his hand at a *roman antique*, set in heathen Brittany. However, lacking the aristocratic insouciance of the Squire and Knight, he over-anxiously attempts to distance himself from 'swiche illusiouns and swiche meschaunces [evil practices] | As hethen folk useden [practised] in thilke dayes' (1291–3).

The prime candidate for an 'illusioun and meschaunce' in this narrative is the apparent removal by a 'magicien' of the rocks from the coast of Brittany, following Dorigen's promise (if so it can be called) that she will sleep with Aurelius if that threat to her husband's returning ship is removed. Yet this mysterious event is presented primarily as a marvel with a scientific basis rather than as the outcome of a daemonic pact. It is true that Aurelius builds up an expectation of some cataclysmic event by praying for a 'miracle' (V.1056, 1065; cf. 1299) in the form of a high tide of abnormal duration, requiring interference with the moon's natural course for two whole years – a terrifying prospect, evocative of the young man's reckless desires (1066–70). Or, he continues, the Moon/Lucina/Diana/Proserpina should sink every rock down into her own dark region, the underworld (1073–5). But neither of these processes is shown as actually occurring during the Franklin's description of the Breton clerk's skilled procedure (1261–96), which is curiously unthreatening. Instead the emphasis falls on what *seems* to have happened, on how things look: 'for a wyke or tweye, | It *semed* that alle the rokkes were aweye' (1295–6; my emphasis). The Franklin's references to 'illusioun', 'apparence' and 'jogel-rye' (1264–5) tend to reduce the magician's activity to the level of sleight of hand, a mere conjuring trick, which may be devious but is certainly not devilish.

This impression is reinforced by two other passages in the tale, the first being the reminiscences of Aurelius's brother about his college days at Orléans. He recalls a book of 'magyk natureel' – presumably about natural processes rather than something more sinister, an interpretation encouraged by the brother's statement that it taught the art of 'illusioun', which he then puts on a par with the 'diverse apparences' that clever conjurers create at banquets (1139–51). Here we may detect an echo of the Squire's reference to the 'magyk' shows that conjurers put on at great feasts. Secondly, there is the Franklin's account of how the magician entertains his guests before supper with marvelous images (1186–218), which may be read as actual examples of those aforementioned dinnertime diversions. Although it may be difficult to explain these phenomena purely and simply by reference to the elaborate mechanical devices that, as already noted, were a feature of extravagant court entertainments, that is the context in which we are being invited to place and understand them.

Most telling of all is the fact that when the magician goes about his work, he uses nothing more disquieting than a set of accurate astrological tables ('tables Tolletanes..., | Ful wel corrected'; V.1273–4). These enable him to predict, not to control, the future. Furthermore, a strong emphasis is placed on the subtlety of his calculations, 'hise equacions in every thyng' (1279). It seems that the magician has the credentials of a scientist. The implication is that, thanks to his knowledge of planetary motions, he learns that a high tide is coming, which will cover all the coastal rocks. An unusual event perhaps (at least in terms of its size) but not unnatural; it may last for 'a wyke or tweye' but certainly not for the two years that Aurelius had requested in his 'ravyng' (1026). Chaucer's attribution of astronomical/astrological lore to the magician cannot be taken as prima facie evidence that his character is dubious, any more than we should blame the Physician for his use of 'magyk natureel' in diagnosing his patients (GP I.416); in Chaucer's day crucial distinctions were made between acceptable and non-acceptable forms of astrology (cf. pp. 39–40 above). For good measure the Franklin launches an attack on 'supersticious cursednesse' (1272), but that sounds like a nervous over-reaction, for the magic has been rendered rather tame.

It certainly is tame by comparison with the ghastly ritual pursued by the sorcerer and devil-worshipper portrayed by Menedon in Boccaccio's *Filocolo*, a possible source and certainly a close analogue of *The Franklin's Tale*.[12] (Boccaccio's other version of the story, as included in the *Decameron*, is a lot less close.) A blatant anachronism in a tale wherein no attempt is made to create an antique setting, Tebano lives in Thessaly where, according to Ovid, Jason brought the sorceress Medea to restore his aged father to youth, and his cursed old rite is obviously modeled on the one employed by Medea on that occasion. Roughly a quarter of Menedon's tale is given over to this bizarre ceremony, in which Hecate and Ceres are invoked, and Tebano reveals that his skills include necromancy and the means of interfering with the moon's natural course. He has the power to perform those dreadful actions that Aurelius had prayed for but whose magician lacked either the will or the means to carry out.

Arveragus may be regarded as the Franklin's attempt to invent a noble pagan of the stature of Troilus, Theseus or Cambyuskan. Invoking a merciful God of whom he has imperfect knowledge, he acts with the highest motives possible to him, affirming that 'Trouthe is the hyeste thyng that man may kepe' (V.1479), even if this means sending his wife to have sex with another man. In Boccaccio's *Filocolo* the corresponding character is said to have acted with unnecessary generosity, for his marriage contract with the lady rendered her subsequent oath invalid. There a firm distinction is made between generosity and wisdom: the husband-figure was certainly generous with his wife, but maybe he was foolish to do what he did, and risked losing honour of a kind which cannot be recovered.[13] No such distinction is offered in *The Franklin's Tale*; Arveragus may be seen as behaving in a way that was rigorous but commendable. He has not lost any honour but gained some – if we place any weight on Aurelius's praise of the 'grete gentillesse' he has shown to Dorigen (1527).

How much simpler it would have been had Arveragus simply ordered Dorigen not to go, perhaps declaring (in line with the *Filocolo*) that the promise was not legally binding. But the most noble of the 'good pagans' were absolute for sacrifice and even death, being not numbered in the roll of common men. In Arveragus's mind, a woman's gossamer-thin promise obligates two people in love to act in ways at variance with their true desires. He is driven by moral conviction of an intensity that far transcends the specifics of the contrived and barely credible love-triangle which serves as its occasion. Does this go beyond the needs of the Franklin's narrative? Or has the Franklin failed to rise to the needs of his narrative?

Masculinity and female agency: Dorigen and Canacee

In *Troilus and Criseyde*, Criseyde becomes an object of male exchange within a patriarchal society, rendered passive by the devices and desires of powerful males. Chaucer's Emelye clearly fits that same mould. She may pray to Diana that she should remain chaste all her life, but that is never going to happen. As a major prize in the marriage market, Emelye is destined to be bestowed upon the man who best supports her family's sociopolitical ambitions. Indeed, it could be said that her worship of Diana functions to emphasize her virginity not as an ideal religious state but as an asset in any future marriage negotiations. Good girls do not worship Venus.

Should Dorigen, then, be seen as yet another trafficked woman? Even as, in *The Knight's Tale*, two men compete over Emelye, at the end of *The Franklin's Tale*, three men compete to see who is the most 'fre' (liberal, generous) in a situation which was – quite inadvertently – set in motion by Dorigen and over which she has no subsequent control. Hence she may be deemed the mere pretext for rival performances of male prowess, a piece of property that the men pass from one to the other to assert their status. However, certain elements in the tale resist such a clear conclusion.

First is the fact that Chaucer puts into Dorigen's mouth a philosophical protestation concerning a seemingly unjust and incomprehensible divine order of a type that elsewhere he reserves for male characters. The most striking thing about Dorigen's exclamation that those 'unresonable' black rocks on the Breton seashore seem to be a foul confusion rather than part of a fair creation (V.868–72), is the extent to which it presents her as thinking like a man. It has obvious similarities (due to the shared Boethian influence) with Troilus' fear that 'al that comth, comth by necessitee' and Palamon's suspicion that the 'cruel goddes' regard humankind as being of no more value than some terrified sheep (see pp. 40–1, 67 above). In all these cases, pagan protest bears a positive rather than a negative valence; we are hearing virtuous heathen struggle to break through the narrow ideologies of their 'secte', seeking a better 'lay' by which to live their lives (to use yet again the Squire's words). Furthermore, the degree of enlightenment evinced by Dorigen's speech should be noted. She believes that the world was created by 'a parfit wys God and a stable' (V.871), a God who, moreover, made man 'lyk' to His 'owene merk' (V.880), phrasing that recalls the statement in Genesis 1:26 that God made man in his own image. That is not mere anachronism, for the concept of a creator-god is allowed to good pagans in some late-medieval theological discussions and in certain vernacular works that strive to depict pagan ideology with a degree of authenticity. So, then, Dorigen's beliefs are at once historically appropriate and highly impressive. Her thoughts of self-slaughter (at V.1355–66) need not cause us to think ill of her. For a heathen heroine in dire straits, suicide is a perfectly honourable course of action, as is borne out by a treatise quoted extensively here, the *Adversus Jovinianum* which Saint Jerome wrote around 393 in vigorous defence of virginity and chastity, and indeed by Chaucer's own *Legend of Good Women*. For Christians, suicide is certainly a mortal sin, but for many pagans, both male and female, it could be the crown of a life of virtue.

Secondly, Chaucer treats Dorigen's lovesickness with the same degree of medical precision and seriousness he applies when male characters suffer the same condition. Unsurprisingly, given the masculinist inclination of medieval science, the symptoms of male lovers are the focus of attention in the professional medical treatises, and this is also a dominant feature of the poetry of courtly love. But sometimes female patients do appear, as when Guillaume de Machaut (in his *Jugement dou Roy de Navarre*) recounts how a young woman becomes gravely ill on hearing that her beloved has died in a tournament (1863–2012). Her doctors try (in vain) to restore her to health by applying the 'cure by contraries' principle. Given her sorrowful state, they declare, 'One should make merry | In her presence, . . . | And also minstrels should be summoned | To entertain her and make her laugh'. Dorigen's friends apply the same therapeutic methods. They lead her 'by ryveres and by welles, | And eek in othere places delitables' (V.898–9), dance and play at chess and backgammon (900), and plan an all-day picnic (with music provided) in a beautiful garden (901–17). Fortunately, Arveragus returns, alive and well, and so Dorigen's dark forebodings end. But the accuracy of Chaucer's pathological description should be noted. The melancholic condition was supposed to cause the sufferer to dream of black things (black bulls, bears, devils – even a man dressed all in black; cf. Chapter 1). The fact that Dorigen fantasizes about black rocks helps to identify her as a victim of *melancholia*. Such is the medical condition that prompts her rash promise to Aurelius that she will sleep with him if he removes the rocks from the Breton coast – this being in sharp contrast to the supposedly impossible task set in both of Boccaccio's versions of the story, the production of a spring garden in the middle of winter. When the Franklin says she spoke those words 'in pley' (V.988), the most likely reading of that phrase is 'not seriously meant'. Playfulness of any kind is far from the mind of this woman whose friends are failing to cheer up; neither frivolity nor flirtation are likely motives. It is intriguing that the Franklin, identified as a 'sanguine' man (and hence of an optimistic disposition), should describe a temperament so different from his own in humoural composition. Chaucer seems to be paying special attention to medical categories here, one consequence of which is that Dorigen has been afforded considerable agency in the sphere of aristocratic emotion.

But, at the end of *The Franklin's Tale*, Arveragus sends Dorigen to Aurelius, who sends her back to Arveragus. Here she seems to be dependent on male direction and lacking in agency of any kind. Or is she? This passage contains two competing, precariously balanced, elements:

> . . . she answerde, half as she were mad,
> 'Unto the gardyn, as myn housbonde bad,
> My trouthe for to holde–allas! allas!'
>
> (V.1511–13)

On the one hand, she has been ordered to go to the garden; on the other, it is her own *trouthe* that is to be upheld (cf. Aurelius's assertion, 'Ye shul youre trouthe holden, by my fay!' [1474]; the term designates her promise in particular, but also fidelity as a general moral principle). In response, Aurelius refers firstly to Arveragus's *gentilesse* and second to Dorigen's *distresse*; here is an extraordinary man who would rather suffer shame than have his wife break a promise, even though it is at variance with his husbandly rights and interests (1526–32). Male agency is given top priority here, and, however much of a virtuous heathen we may judge Arveragus to be, within the perspective of this encounter, his behaviour seems to be coercive. Perhaps now he is exercising that 'soveraynetee' or 'maistrie' against the 'wyl' of Dorigen that, at the very beginning of the tale, we saw him eschew. Alternatively, Arveragus might be affirming the principle of female 'libertee' that was valued so highly within their sophisticated (but unworkable?) attempt to reconcile the differing demands of courtly love and marriage (744–59). Dorigen made a promise, and by insisting that she should keep it, he is actually respecting her freedom of choice. However, no matter how freely her promise was made, if she is forced to keep it, surely 'libertee' flies out the window, leaving only the constraints of thralldom?

Chaucer has created an intricate moral maze, which prompts a debate on ethical choice and responsibility that goes far beyond the issue of 'Who was the most generous?' Perhaps we may find a way out of it by contrasting the denouement of *The Franklin's Tale* with what happens in the analogous story in Boccaccio's *Decameron*. Dorigen's equivalent, Madonna Dianora, angrily tells her would-be lover, the knight Ansaldo, that she has come to him only because of the orders of her husband Gilberto, who has 'more concern for the pain of your uncontrolled love than his honour or mine'. Whereupon Ansaldo declares that he will not soil the honour of the 'man who had compassion' for his love. Dianora's feelings are of little consequence. Subsequently 'a very close and loyal friendship' grew up between Ansaldo and Gilberto.[14] It is impossible to imagine such a friendship growing up between Arveragus and Aurelius. In Chaucer's tale the emphasis is placed rather on the 'sovereyn blisse' (V.1552) in which Arveragus and Dorigen proceed to live their lives. The bond of love between husband and wife seems more important here than any homosocial bond between men, and consequently the reading of Dorigen as a trafficked woman loses some of its force.

In *The Squire's Tale*, the crucial bond is between females. Here a female falcon is presented as suffering from destructive lovesickness, and Cambyuskan's daughter Canacee is described as sympathizing with her plight in a way that emphasizes and celebrates the princess's superlative womanliness. The red blood runs down the tree on which the bird perches, for it has beaten itself piteously with both wings. Canacee feels great 'compassioun' (V.463), worrying that the creature will faint and fall down. A 'gentil herte kitheth gentillesse' (483), declares the falcon, appreciating the princess's concern; a gentle heart – gentle in terms of both moral excellence and good breeding – makes gentility known. In other words, 'pitee renneth soone in gentil herte' (479). Previously that line was applied to Duke Theseus (I.1761). But here a distinctly female form of *gentil* empathy is functioning. Canacee's 'compassion' comes from that 'verray wommanly benignytee' that is part of her true nature (V.486–7). Only the noblest of women can appreciate the depths of suffering experienced by this avian aristocrat of the same gender. As Canacee listens to the falcon's sad tale, she is almost slain by the other's sorrow, weeps as if she would turn to water (462, 496). Thanks to the marvelous ring on her finger, the princess can understand the bird's language, but the basis of their communication is deeper than that: females of whatever species speak the same emotional language.

Setting herself up as the falcon's physician, Canacee seeks to diagnose her ailment in a way reminiscent of the methods followed by the doctors in Machaut's *Navarre* and by Dorigen's friends, as discussed above. An excess of joy obviously being out of the question here, Canacee confidently declares that her patient is suffering from an excess of sorrow. In a 'gentil herte', this must have one of two possible causes, other 'harms' being trivial to the high-born: 'Is this for sorwe of deeth or los of love?' (V.452, 450). It turns out to be the latter. The bird explains that she fell in love with a tercelet (a young male falcon) who seemed to be a 'welle of alle gentillesse' but left her for another. Whereupon Canacee and her ladies worry about 'hou they myghte the faucon glade' (634), just as Dorigen's friends had sought ways of inducing in her that cheer which, according to the best medical opinion of the day, was a cure for melancholy. Canacee herself expertly applies bandages to the bird's wounds and makes healing ointments from precious herbs, hoping (one may infer) to achieve cures by natural causes, to enlist *science* with a good intent. Here is a virtuous version of Medea.

The princess also fashions a *mewe* for her feathered friend, placing it at her bed's head as a mark of the favour the bird enjoys. A *mewe* was a pen or cage for hunting hawks; it could also designate a coop for confining or fattening poultry, and (more generally) 'a place of security or confinement; hiding place, shelter; cage, prison'.[15] Evidently the word bears both negative and positive connotations, as do the adornments of the tercelet's new home. Beautifully decorated with velvet cloths which symbolize the 'truthe that is in women sene', on the outside this pen is painted with images of 'false fowles' (including tercelets, no doubt), in remembrance of the bird's sad history. Here is a place of security and of confinement, of safety and of concealment. It demands comparison with the 'cage' that, a little earlier in the text, was used as a metaphor in an attempt to explain male disloyalty. Put a bird in a cage made comfortable with straw, care for the creature day and night, feed it with sugar, honey, bread and milk.... All to no avail. As soon as the door is opened the bird will fly the coop, escape to the woods where it has only worms to eat – poor fare, but in accord with the creature's nature. In like manner, 'Men loven of propre kynde newefangelnesse' (V.610), as the falcon's beloved demonstrated when he left her for a 'kyte', a scavenger bird with an unsavory reputation in medieval beast-lore. 'Gentillesse of blood' (620), good breeding, does not restrain male impulses on such an occasion. 'Alle thyng, repeirynge [returning] to his kynde, | Gladeth [gladdens] hymself': and 'newefangelnesse', a love of novelty, is identified as part of the 'propre kynde' of men (608–10).

So, then, the *cage* represents the suppression of certain male desires (which are antisocial and yet express a sexual aggression that is stereotypically male), whereas the *mewe* represents the protective measures females take against those same desires. But, given the natural desire of birds to fly free in the woods, are we really meant to view the falcon's new habitation in a positive light? A cage, however gilded (and this exquisite *mewe* sports luxurious velvet rather than straw), is still a cage. It is a beautiful artifact, but beautiful by human standards; left to their own devices, birds prefer worms to honey. Conversely, keeping hawks in captivity was a regular aristocratic practice. The love of hunting that characterized the upper classes was deemed to be an expression of their noble natures. Furthermore, falcons were regarded as the noblest of birds (as *The Parliament of Fowls* illustrates), and a natural affinity between those high-ranking creatures and their high-ranking owners was assumed. Hawk-handlers put the birds into a *mewe* to molt – this being a natural process for the gradual replacement of old, tattered or damaged feathers with new growth. What better place, then, for a distressed falcon to recuperate and repair her damaged plumage? In these terms, Canacee is acting in accordance with, rather than against, the bird's nature, facilitating a natural restorative process.

What does this mean for the female of the human species? We may recall the Franklin's assertion that 'Wommen, of kynde, desiren libertee, | And nat to be constreyned as a thral' (V.768–69). Yet the Franklin's narrative may suggest that women who are allowed a long rein get into trouble; *libertee* is a highly attractive yet dangerous gift, a quality perhaps best managed by men, who provide for women the protective sociopolitical structures within which they may (according to the ideology current in Chaucer's day) fulfill their true natures. It is perfectly true that, in *The Squire's Tale*, one female provides a protective structure for another. But Canacee may be seen as acting in (inevitable) collusion with patriarchal forces that maintain a division between male agency and female passivity. Thus read, this tale expresses a (hardly surprising) social conservatism in respect of gender roles. But there is more to it than that, for the text insists on presenting that gender division as a gulf between flighty males and languishing females, an imagination so reductive that it invites ridicule.

Furthermore, the statement of disdain and defiance ('for despit', 649) that the construction of the *mewe* makes against disloyal males is actually a strategic phase within a story that will end well. The Squire, in hurried anticipation of what is left to tell (is this Chaucer providing an overview of the remainder of a tale he had decided to leave unfinished?), assures us that the falcon will regain her lover, through the mediation of a king's son, one Cambalus – who is to win Canacee's love. In the narrative as we have it, women's desires are displaced, inasmuch as they are attributed to a falcon, whose extremes of emotional behaviour (including violent self-harming) go far beyond anything found in Chaucer's other treatments of female feeling within the *roman antique* genre. By comparison, Dorigen's outbursts seem quite decorous. And it is hard to imagine the controlling and self-controlled Canacee ever acting in such a way, although her empathy with the formel manifests her own emotional resources, the deep wells of pity, love and fidelity that (one may anticipate) will flow generously when she meets her future husband. Presumably the episode of the hapless hawk and her faithless tercelet was meant to serve as a foil to the heroine's ultimate achievement of happiness – a happiness her caged bird will share, thanks to the handsome prince who secures psychological stability for them both, in line with an optimistic vision of the 'propre kynde' of men.

In the pagan worlds we have discussed in this chapter, achieving and/or maintaining marital relationships is the ultimate measure of female success – success that involves conformity to gender norms. Emelye may (at least initially) yearn to be a maiden all her life, worshipping Diana the 'goddesse of the wodes grene' (I.2297), those same woods in which she loves to hunt. But that life of outdoor liberty is not for her. Perhaps all that she, and birds of the same feather, can hope for, is the best possible *mewe*.

Beyond grotesquerie: the Shipman, Miller, Reeve, Cook and Merchant

The following discussion of Chaucer's *fabliaux* features the *Canterbury Tales* that are usually designated as such: the *Miller's Tale*, *Reeve's Tale*, *Shipman's Tale* and *Merchant's Tale*, together with the fragmentary *Cook's Tale*. We cannot assume a precise genre with neatly defined borders, however, for *fabliau* elements (if so they may be called) may also be found in prologues and tales that have been classified in other terms in this book, particularly those involving the Friar, Summoner, Pardoner, Canon's Yeoman and Wife of Bath. A distinction may be made between *fabliaux* and beast fables because the anthropomorphized animals (and obvious debt to the tradition of moralized *fabulae*) of *The Nun's Priest's Tale* and *The Manciple's Tale* make them highly distinctive, although the ways in which they ridicule human desire and vanity is often reminiscent of certain manoeuvres in the *fabliaux*. Chaucerian comedy is no respector of boundaries and cannot be reduced to a standard repertoire of tricks. But its several manifestations appear to have certain features in common, such as a strong tendency towards satire (in the sense of 'moral reprehension', as defined earlier), although the resultant laughter is no simple instrument of moral judgment. That said, Chaucerian comedy is acutely aware of the ethical consequences of actions within the tales, and of tale-telling itself as an action that must admit of ethical scrutiny.

How best to approach stories that seem to revel in fornication and flatulence, celebrate physical payback of the crudest kind, rate virility over morality, and feature words and deeds that are downright vulgar and perhaps even obscene? The key to the character and cultural significance of the *fabliaux* has been sought in their origins. One theory sees them as fundamentally bourgeois, expressive of the values of the newly emergent 'middle class'. Another holds them as addressed primarily to an audience of aristocrats, whose worldview they affirm; the upper and powerful classes are being invited to laugh at the antics of the lower orders.

Which view is correct? In a sense, both are. For *fabliaux* seem to have been popular amongst aristocrats and members of the bourgeoisie alike and by no means can be regarded as the property of one class or social group. In different tellings to different audiences, the appropriate side would, no doubt, have been taken. Those aspects of a story that would appeal to the tastes, and refract the social position, of a given interpretive community, could easily be highlighted by a skilled raconteur. The reaction of Chaucer's pilgrims to *The Miller's Tale* is highly revealing:

> Diverse folk diversely they seyde,
> But for the moore part they loughe and pleyde.
> Ne at this tale I saugh no man him greve . . .   *get angry*
>   (I.3857–9)

Well, not quite 'no' man, for 'Osewold the Reve' is offended (3860). But that is because he, a carpenter by trade, chooses to believe that the Miller's tale of a stupid carpenter was directed against him. Most of the people are laughing. The implication seems clear. *Fabliaux* were class-neutral (or, better, capable of taking on various class inflections), widely acceptable, and could easily be regarded as harmless – unless, of course, one had a personal axe to grind. The Reeve's response is deeply personal, far removed from objective righteous distaste for immorality.

Another approach to Chaucer's *fabliaux* is based on ideas developed by the Russian philosopher and cultural critic Mikhail Bakhtin (1895–1975), who found in the 'popular, festive, and spectacle forms of the Middle Ages' a sphere wherein the lower classes and lower bodily functions dominated. The images and practices thus unleashed were 'ugly, monstrous, hideous', 'contrary to the classic images of the finished, completed man' that, in the Renaissance, became normative, marginalizing the medieval 'carnivalesque'. In the medieval grotesque body, 'the emphasis is on the apertures or convexities, or on various ramifications and offshoots: the open mouth, the genital organs, the breasts, the phallus, the potbelly, the nose'. Yet all of this, according to Bakhtin, is deeply positive, indicative of increase, abundance, (pro)creation, fullness. Medieval grotesquerie, and the festive laughter which celebrated it, presented 'an element of victory' over 'all that oppresses and restricts', disclosing the 'potentiality of an entirely different world, of another order, another way of life'.[16] Here, then, is a wishful nostalgia for a time when 'the people' (to use Bakhtin's totalizing term) could find in tolerated (or semi-tolerated) social forms and practices a means of escape from the institutions that oppressed and restricted them – medieval church and state power standing in for the communist regime of Bakhtin's actual world, which in 1920s Russia offered few if any prospects for 'another way of life'.

On the face of it, this is a powerful means of valuing those many non-classical features of *The Canterbury Tales* – most obviously, its *fabliau* elements – that violate Renaissance aesthetic norms. Medieval pilgrimages frequently had a carnivalesque aspect; the church authorities tolerated (or semi-tolerated) the storytelling and music with which pilgrims entertained themselves as they traveled to and from their chosen sacred shrine. Chaucer's pilgrims set off for Canterbury to the accompaniment of the Miller's bagpipes with Harry Bailly the innkeeper established as an unlikely 'governour' or lord of misrule; he will reward the best storyteller with a free supper back at his inn in Southwark (I.796–818).Thus food, drink and festivity are placed at the centre of this enterprise. Base bodily functions and actions feature prominently. Grotesque bodies are everywhere, including those of the Miller, the Cook, the Wife of Bath and the Pardoner.

But these images resist Bakhtinian reading because there is nothing celebratory or carnivalesque about them; they fail to convey notions of increase, abundance, (pro)creation or fullness. The laughter they provoke is far from festive. It is a lot closer to the judgmental humour characteristic of medieval satire, which (as already noted) had as its objective the reprehension of folly and vice. Rather than intimating a kind of freedom from oppressive structures, then, the non-beautiful bodies and bodily activities of *The Canterbury Tales* appear to be supporting rather than subverting the norms, biases and prejudices of Chaucer's society. Ugliness, deformity and 'unnatural' appearance signal class inferiority, mental and moral deficiencies, and gross sexual appetite or aberration, rather than offering a means of escape into some alternative universe.

Furthermore, Bakhtin's bland conception of 'the people', a proletariat unified by shared experience of oppression and the capacity for continual growth and renewal,[17] fails to do justice to the complex nuances and minutiae of the social distinctions that actually appertained in late-medieval society and to which Chaucer's tales are hyper-sensitive. Far more seems to divide Chaucer's churls than unites them. The grotesquerie these figures have in common is not presented 'as something universal, representing all the people'. If applied to *The Canterbury Tales*, Bakhtin's claim that the pre-modern body has an 'all-people's character' that sets it apart from contemporary conditions and standards 'because it is not individualized' simply fails to convince.[18] For individualization is a major tendency in Chaucer's text. Admittedly, it does not progress sufficiently far to leave behind the characteristics stereotypically associated with the various *status* of society. Yet it functions as a determining and dividing principle, as the poet describes his characters and has them engage in description of *their* characters. To some extent, the grotesque is in the eye of the beholder. And Chaucer does much to make us aware of the relativism of any such viewpoint.

More recently, the exuberant linguistic play that is characteristic of so many *fabliaux* has been emphasized, as when Howard Bloch, writing about French examples, rejects the impulse to reduce them to guileless, transparent tales of social mirth, claiming rather that they offer a sustained reflection on language whose ultimate subject is the nature of poetry itself; the poet tacitly associates himself with the key trickster character of his narrative, achieving his tale as the hero achieves his material and/or sexual reward.[19] This is highly relevant to Chaucer's *fabliaux*, particularly *The Shipman's Tale*, which ends as follows:

> Thus endeth my tale, and God us sende
> Taillynge ynough unto oure lyves ende. Amen.
>
> (VII.433–4)

By *taillynge* the Shipman means not only reckoning (in the sense of estimating debt, giving credit) but also lovemaking, *tail* being a euphemism for the sexual member. Only a few lines earlier there is a clear pun on the noun 'tally' (to use the Modern English), when the merchant's wife offers to pay her husband with her body for the hundred francs she owes him. 'I am youre wyf; score it upon my taille' (416): in other words, put it on my account, mark it on my tally stick – with an obvious obscene pun. In that final line, 'taillynge' may have acquired yet another connotation – of tale-telling. So, then, the Shipman is wishing us an abundance of money, sex and stories.

'Ye han mo slakkere dettours than am I!', the merchant's wife tells her husband, 'For I wol paye yow wel and redily | Fro day to day' (VII.413–15). Here the sense of financial debt is linked to the sense of marital debt, the notion that a husband and wife were legally obliged to pay each other the debt of their body. This canonical language derives from I Cor. 7:3, 'Let the husband render the debt to his wife: and the wife also in like manner to the husband'. St Paul goes on to say that, in this respect, the wife does not have power over her body, but the husband has. In like manner, the wife has power over her husband's body; as the Wife of Bath gleefully remarks, 'in hir bookes' men set down the principle that 'man shal yelde to his wyf hire dette' (III.129–30). Indeed, this was one of the few areas of equality between husband and wife, as legally defined. In *The Shipman's Tale*, however, a wife offers to pay back her financial debt with her body – a transaction certainly not intended by the Apostle but one that the Wife of Bath would readily understand.

Having run up a large clothes bill, the merchant's wife complains to a friendly (and freeloading) monk that her husband doesn't give her enough money for this purpose. (She adds that he isn't giving her enough sex either [VII.116–17]; while he is in financial debt, evidently his libido suffers, and therefore he is unable to pay her the debt of his body.) Whereupon the wife borrows a hundred francs from the monk to pay her financial debt – and in exchange for this, she gives him sex. (It could be said that the monk is paying off the husband's sexual debt.) In fact, the monk has borrowed that very sum of money from the husband; he then proceeds to borrow his wife. En route to Paris to set his affairs in order, the merchant visits the monk – who, thinking he has come to get his money back, tells him he already gave it to his wife. The merchant's business trip having been a great success, he returns 'riche and cleerly out of dette', and proceeds to pay his marital debt to his wife with enthusiasm (VII.376–81). When he tells her what the monk said about the hundred francs, she instantly comes up with a clever answer – I thought that was a gift rather than the payment of a debt, and anyway, I'm your wife, the only way I will pay you back is in bed. The marital debt has been substituted for a financial debt. With which the merchant must be satisfied. He has, after all, recently made a thousand francs (and just made a lot of love). His only admonition to his wife is that she should 'keep bet' her 'good' (432), handle her finances better. This may include the implication that she should keep her sexual goods more to herself (and exclusively for him), although the Shipman gives no indication that the merchant suspects his wife of infidelity; the implication may rather be for the reader's benefit.

The husband has indeed paid for all, exemplifying the state of affairs described at the beginning of the tale: 'wo is hym that payen moot for al'. Dressing a woman 'richely' – for her husband's 'owene worshipe [honour]' – involves a lot of 'dispence' (expenditure), and if the husband doesn't pay up, someone else may lend her money, 'and that is perilous' (VII.4–19). But beyond that specific point, the merchant is the source of all the financial capital that has circulated among the three characters in the story. Furthermore, he has legal rights over the sexual resource in the tale, the wife's body, which circulates between the two men. Yet that power turns out to be limited, for the wife herself acts as a merchant, using her sexual capital to acquire financial capital. It might be concluded, then, that in *The Shipman's Tale*, sex has taken the place of love, and sex itself has been reduced to a commodity, something traded for personal gain. Thus the superficiality of mercantile attitudes is revealed by wraith-like creatures who 'passen as dooth a shadwe [shadow] upon the wal' (VII.9), inspiring neither identification nor sympathy. To which it might be replied that the sheer vitality of the wordplay in this tale, the way its entire plot turns on punning connections between sex and money, holds the attention and arrests the heaviest of censures. Exuberant poetic *makynge* trumps making love or making money; tale-telling emerges as the best *taillynge*. Chaucer's writing cannot be reduced to social realism of a kind easily offered up to moral condemnation.

In *The Miller's Tale*, the main mode of linguistic play is Chaucer's deployment of the 'idiom of popular poetry',[20] particularly the chain-store version of the designer discourse of *fyn lovynge*. Nicholas, the Miller's manly man, is described as *hende*, a term used, in a positive, non-ironical sense, to designate the 'approved courtly or knightly qualities', to indicate that a given person was 'noble, courtly, well-bred, refined, sportsmanlike' and/or 'polite, handsome, mild and generous'.[21] However, those occurrences are characteristic of minstrel romances (of the type parodied in *Sir Thopas*) and secular love poems like those included in the 'Harley Lyrics'.[22] The word does not appear in Chaucer's romances of antiquity; his only other use of it is in the Friar's Prologue, where the low-brow Harry Bailly addresses the Summoner (III.1286). Evidently Chaucer regarded *hende* as a word that was inappropriate as a means of complimenting aristocrats. The term could also mean 'skilled, clever, crafty' or 'near, close by', or 'handy' in the sense of 'skilled with the hands' (as in the Modern English 'handyman'),[23] a meaning Chaucer may be evoking when Alisoun tells the impassioned Nicholas to take his hands off her (I.3287).

Hende is valued more highly in the Harley Lyric 'Betwene Mersh and Averil', wherein the love-struck speaker declares that some 'hendy hap' (fair fortune) has come his way, in the shape of one 'Alisoun', on whom his love has settled.[24] That is the name Chaucer bestows upon the 'likerous', 'wylde and yong' heroine of *The Miller's Tale* (I.3225, 3245, 334), and that is what Jenkyn calls the Wife of Bath (III.803). The name seems to have been a common one – but for a certain class of woman, if we are to believe Chaucer. The Miller's Alisoun is a pretty primrose or 'pig's eye' (another flower's name, but hardly idealizing) ready for plucking, all set for any lord to bed or any stout yeoman to wed – a clear indication that no nobleman would think of marrying one of her social station (3268–70).

Given that she has married an old carpenter, her affair with Nicholas must be kept secret; fortunately, this *hende* man is expert in 'deerne love' (and, the Miller adds, in giving sexual 'solas', 3200). The ability to keep one's desire secret is a prime qualification for an adept courtly lover, well exemplified by the behaviour of Troilus, Arcite and Palamon. However, *deerne* does not feature in any description of their behaviour; indeed, Chaucer uses it exclusively of Nicholas and Alisoun. The word is, however, straightforwardly employed in the Harley Lyrics, for example when it is claimed that no fire in hell can inflict pain worse than that suffered by the man who 'loueth derne ant dar nout telle I What him ys on [what ails him]'.[25] But Nicholas loses no time in telling his 'lemman' (another down-market word) what the matter is.

> 'Ywis, but if ich have my wille,
> For deerne love of thee, lemman, I spille'.   *secret*
> And heeld hire harde by the haunchebones,   *thighs*
> And seyde, 'Lemman, love me al atones,   *Beloved*
> Or I wol dyen, also God me save!'
>
> (I.3277–81)

The verb *spillen* means to kill or to die,[26] and Chaucer uses it in that innocent sense elsewhere. But here it may also bear the sense (as in Modern English) of causing something to overflow a container, to spill out of an orifice or passage.[27] Nicholas may be over-eager to love Alisoun 'al atones'.

Thus the Miller 'quites' the Knight's narrative (I.3119), the verb *quiten* having the sense here of requiting, calling quits, meeting a challenge, perhaps even of taking revenge (intended jocularly). One tale of two men who love the same woman has been followed by another, as the lower orders answer back with the idiom of popular poetry. In *The Reeve's Tale*, told to 'quite' *The Miller's Tale*, the most striking source of linguistic humour is the northern English dialect put in the mouths of two students who get the better of a cheating miller. The Reeve himself is from Norfolk (it has recently been argued that Chaucer gave him some linguistic features characteristic of that dialectal area),[28] and the students are studying at Cambridge, but they come from the same town 'Fer in the north; I kan nat telle where' (I.4014–15). To some extent Chaucer relies on the cheap humour that is aroused by dialectal discourse taken out of context; someone who has a different accent and/or employs words that sound strange, unfamiliar or uncouth to his listeners can provoke their laughter. However, Chaucer does not give us a crude travesty of northern dialect, but rather a plausible version of the real thing, thereby achieving a large measure of accuracy while not going beyond what would be comprehensible to his usual audience of southerners. We may assume that he has concentrated on what immediately struck the London ear as recognizably northern. Dialect is seldom amusing in a tale unless the audience has some actual experience of it, and many northerners were living and working in the capital.

That humour is for the audience. Within the tale itself, the students' adversary, Symkyn the miller, does not make fun of the way they speak. Rather he ridicules their status as young Cambridge scholars – a position of social prestige (or at least one that could bring them to positions of social prestige), which perhaps jars a little with their linguistic diminution as hickish northerners. Despite 'al the sleighte [ingenuity] in hir philosophye', he plans to trick them (4048–50), confident that 'The gretteste clerkes been noght [the] wisest men' (I.4054). When the students, duly tricked, have no option but to lodge with him, Symkyn sarcastically remarks that they should have no problem with the small amount of room available in his house, because scholars, by their clever arguments, can make a mile wide from twenty feet of space (4123–24). Those jokes depend on the students being men with some (however minor) academic status; against their classroom knowledge Symkyn pits his street smarts.

This pride on the miller's part chimes with the absurd social ambitions which drove him to take a wife 'of noble kyn' (a priest's daughter!). Ridiculously jealous over an ugly woman who herself is as 'digne [haughty] as water in a dich [ditch]' (meaning that she stinks with pride), he insists that she should be addressed with the honourific title 'dame' (I.3941–2, 3956, 3964). As for their equally unattractive daughter, the grand scheme is that she will marry well, to someone of 'worthy blood of auncetrye' (3982), with her grandfather the priest providing a substantial dowry. Those are the pretensions that the students set about deflating, first by sleeping with the miller's women and then by beating up the miller. They are now standard *fabliau* students, more interested in sex than in study. Here is no battle of wits but rather physical interaction and rough revenge.

The women become means through which men pay off scores; more specifically, because they are such a source of pride to the miller, bedding them is a direct assault on what he holds most dear. Hearing of Alayn's exploits with his daughter, Symkyn exclaims,

> 'Who dorste be so boold to disparage   *sully*
> My doghter, that is come of swich lynage?'
>   (I.4271–2)

The verb *disparagen* meant not merely to defile but to degrade socially, as when a person married below his or her below rank or without proper ceremony.[29]

Here Symkyn's daughter – intended for an upwardly mobile marriage – has been degraded, not only physically but also in terms of status, by a man of lesser worth. Indeed, it could be said that both of the miller's major social assets, his wife and daughter, have brutally been devalued. The payback the students conducted on behalf of their narrator, the Reeve, was precisely targeted. Yet it is clear that personal 'quiting' can be consonant with the ethical end of satire.

The sequence of 'quiting' continues with the Cook's Prologue. The Host having accused him of selling pies unfit for human consumption, Roger the cook vows to 'quite' him with a tale about an innkeeper – but not yet. First he will tell the story of 'Perkyn Revelour' (about a dissolute reveler). Unfortunately this breaks off with the memorable remark that Perkyn's friend's wife 'swyved for hir sustenance' (screwed for a living, 4422). We can only speculate about what kind of story would have followed, but a convincing suggestion has been offered by V. J. Scattergood, who finds in Perkyn an early example of 'the would-be fashionable, dissipated urban wastrels [often called 'gallants'] who were just becoming subjects for satirical treatment and who appear frequently and recognizably in the poetry and drama of the fifteenth and early sixteenth centuries'.[30] What comes next in *The Canterbury Tales* as we have it is the Man of Law's extensive introduction and tale. The attempt at a narrative frame that began with the General Prologue and proceeded through a series of requitals (starting with the Miller's response to *The Knight's Tale*) has been abandoned, and a fresh start made. Perkyn's profligate escapades were recounted at greater length in Pier Paolo Pasolini's film *I racconti di Canterbury* (1972) in a slapstick sequence that is one of the most successful parts of this flawed masterpiece. History repeated itself as Pasolini struggled to bring under control a riotous assembly of diverse tales and tellers.

The organizational difficulties experienced by Chaucer are much in evidence in *The Merchant's Tale*. At two points its narrator refers scathingly to people of 'seculer estaat' (IV.1251, 1322), implying that the teller originally assigned to this tale was himself not of secular state (as of course any merchant would be) but rather a member of some religious order, a monk or a friar perhaps. So, then, maybe we are seeing here what happens when a typical *fabliau* plot (about a young wife cheating on her old husband) is processed through the consciousness of a clerk – a well-trained professional, in contrast with the stereotypical students sketched by the Miller and Reeve. He draws on the treatment of marriage in St Jerome's *Adversus Jovinianum* (a text owned by the Wife of Bath's clerical husband Jenkyn), refers to the origins of the sacrament in the Garden of Eden and its traditional justification (as instituted for procreation and the avoidance of lechery), alludes to the collect that follows the marriage blessing and echoes the Song of Songs, which was interpreted as an allegory of the mystical union of Christ and his church and used to valorize earthly marriage (1323–32, 1441–55, 1703–5).

Even January's ridiculous attempt to justify the foreplay he plans to enjoy with May 'er tyme come that I wil doun descende' (1830) is marked by clerical knowingness.

> 'It is no fors how longe that we pleye;
> In trewe wedlok coupled be we tweye,
> And blessed be the yok that we been inne,   *yoke*
> For in oure actes we mowe do no synne.
> A man may do no synne with his wyf,
> Ne hurte hymselven with his owene knyf,   *knife*
> For we han leve to pleye us by the lawe'.
>
> (IV.1835–41)

That argument is utterly specious. Of course a man can hurt, even kill, himself with his own knife. And he can harm, even spiritually kill, himself with his own wife. The knife analogy features in manuals of religious instruction, where it is used to make the point that a man may endanger his soul if he acts beyond the bounds of marital propriety. As *The Parson's Tale* puts it, if a couple 'assemble oonly for amorous love', and 'accomplice thilke brennynge [burning] delit' at will, this is 'deedly synne'.[31] To some extent, sex for pleasure rather than procreation was covered by the 'good of marriage' known as *fides* (mutual fidelity, companionship) and the legal obligation of paying the 'debt' of one's body, but only to some extent; thereby it was remitted to venial sin. However, if a man used his wife not as his wife but merely as a woman, then he was going beyond what was termed 'the honesty of marriage' and committing deadly sin. This, then, is what was meant by loving too ardently, and January is doing precisely that. Or at least, he is trying to do that, as he imbibes an alarmingly large number of aphrodisiacs to increase his 'corage', heighten his sexual desire (1807–12). By the end of the tale, May seems to have fallen pregnant (witness her craving to eat small green pears, I.2328–37), but no learned clerk would have accepted that as a vindication of January's practice of marital sex. He has, we should recall, 'folwed ay [always] his bodily delyt | On women, ther as was his appetyt' (1249–50). Now sixty years old (definitely aged by medieval standards), this inveterate lecher has dared to claim the church's approbation for his continued pursuit of that same 'appetyt'.

It is easy to forget that January is a knight and May, a gentlewoman (IV.1246, 2202); we seem far from the lofty behaviour and high style of *The Knight's Tale*. Squire Damyan's love-service is ridiculously brief, in contrast with the lengthy sufferings of Arcite and Palamon, and the consummation of his desire, indecorously quick. Having pulled up May's 'smok', 'in he throng' (2532–3); like 'hende Nicholas' he wants to love 'al atones' (I.3280). After she reads Damyan's love letter, May tears it up and throws it down the 'pryvee' (1954); she has gone where, admittedly, 'every wight moot neede' (1951), but none of the characters in the Knight's narrative are said to have exercised that need. Reacting to the intensified jealousy of the now-blind January, May exclaims that, were she to shame her (presumably noble) 'kin' and damage her good name, he should strip her and drown her in a sack, like some unwanted animal. Thus she tries to emphasize that she is 'a gentil womman and no wenche' (2195–202). But such *fabliau* language is appropriate to a 'wenche', and May acts like one, here and elsewhere. For his part, January behaves in ways that belie his knightly status. Much of his discourse is mercantile, reminiscent of the idioms that distinguish *The Shipman's Tale*. In the market for a 'fresshe' wife (a nice piece of 'yong flessh', 1418), he mentally reviews the candidates.

> Many fair shap and many a fair visage   *face*
> Ther passeth thurgh his herte nyght by nyght,
> As whoso tooke a mirour, polisshed bryght,
> And sette it in a commune market-place,
> Thanne sholde he se ful many a figure pace
> By his mirour . . .   (IV.1580–5)

From this fantasy beauty pageant January takes his pick. Later he spells out for May the practical advantages attendant on being a loyal wife. 'Thre thynges, certes, shal ye wynne [gain] therby': Christ's love, personal honour, and all of January's worldly goods. Make contracts just as you like! See what is in this for you! (2170–5).

Here words and deeds are close cousins (to echo the General Prologue yet again), with the deeds determining the words spoken by and about the characters. Love and marriage have been sullied – cast in the privy, one might say – by unworthy practitioners, and treating them with the 'rude' speech of a man who cannot 'glose' (equivocate) seems just retribution, and satiric fair game (cf. l. 2351). Whatever Chaucer's original intentions for the story may have been, it has convincingly grown into a merchant's tale.

Taking the morality: *The Nun's Priest's Tale* and *The Manciple's Tale*

Two types of beast-fable were identified in medieval literary theory: the 'Aesopic' type, wherein 'dumb beasts' are 'feigned to speak among themselves', and the 'libystic' type, wherein 'men are feigned to speak with beasts or beasts with men'.[32] *The Nun's Priest's Tale* falls within the former category, *The Man-ciple's Tale* within the latter. The Nun's Priest's *fabula* of the cock and the fox has close affinities with a story found in Marie de France's collection of fables and in two of the *Reynart the Fox* beast-epics. The Manciple's story of Phebus and the crow has its ultimate ancestor in Ovid's *Metamorphoses* (II.531–65, 596–632), although Chaucer may have been working from the *Ovide moralisé*, wherein the bird is criticized for its 'vile jangling tongue' and made repre-sentative of excessive chatter, idle or even vicious speech.[33] According to the medieval schoolteachers who made extensive use of beast-fables, they offered both profit and delight and sought to reach a moral end by pleasurable means. As Walter the Englishman put it in his preface to the *Romulus* (the most popular collection of its kind in Chaucer's day), 'serious matters present a more sweetly smiling countenance when adorned [variant: mixed] with pleasantries'.[34] The relationship between those two components was negotiated in various ways by the many medieval writers who found the genre attractive. For his part, Chaucer produced an Aesopic fable in which the provocation of pleasure threatens to overwhelm the assertion of moral doctrine, and a libystic fable from which any vestige of a sweetly smiling countenance has been removed, as the Manciple reduces the form to a receptacle for dour self-interest.

The Nun's Priest's *fabula* is placed in a narrative framework that pulls it in the direction of *fabliau*. The previous narrator was the manly Monk, a fair-skinned, handsome specimen who, Harry Bailly playfully claims, would have bred strong progeny had he not been celibate (VII.1929–64). What a shame that his procreative services have been lost to the world; religion has taken away all the best breeding stock, leaving behind 'borel' (coarse and uneducated) men, mere shrimps who produce only 'ympes' (weak offshoots). The Monk would have made a superb 'tredefowel', excelled in 'tredyng' – here the Host has the copulation of birds in mind. But that pilgrim's prowess does not extend to telling a vigorous tale; the Monk's repetitive recital of sad outcomes is cut short (see pp. 134–5 below), and the Nun's Priest commanded to cheer everyone up. He responds magnificently with a story that has as its avian hero the 'tredefowel' Chauntecleer, whose sexual prowess is displayed when he feathers his beloved 'Pertelote twenty tyme, | And trad hire eke as ofte, er it was pryme [before daybreak]' (VII.3177–8). The Host rewards the Nun's Priest by lauding his own great potential as a 'trede-foul', one capable of servicing 'seven tymes seventene' hens (VII.3447–54); then he changes the avian metaphor to picture this priest as a large-breasted sparrowhawk. Here, as elsewhere, Harry Bailly has virility on the brain.

Given his vow of celibacy, the Nun's Priest has limited legal outlets for his 'corage', but there is no doubt of the vigour of his story; it succeeds as much as the Monk's performance falters. The fact that he is a man working among women, tasked with hearing the confessions of nuns ('seven tymes seventene'?), further enhances the humour, adding extra piquancy to this priest's jokes about female literacy, as when he remarks that 'wommen holde in ful gret reverence' the 'book of Launcelot de Lake', and has Chauntecleer mistranslate, for Pertelote's benefit, the Latin phrase *mulier est hominis confusio* ('woman is man's downfall') with quite the opposite meaning ('woman is man's joy and all his bliss'; VII.3211–13, 3163–6). Having remarked that 'Wommennes conseils been ful ofte colde', the Nun's Priest instantly adds the cheeky excuse that he is just following his authors – and besides, 'Thise been the cokkes wordes, and nat myne' (a type of defense previously used in the *MilPro* to justify reportage of churls' speech). In fact, the cock has rejected his wife's counsel and then refused to follow his own judgment, valuing sex over sagacity.

The Nun's Priest's Tale is the merriest of Chaucer's merry tales, an effect achieved by the extraordinary extent to which the resources and procedures of rhetoric, philosophy and even theology are brought to bear on a quite trivial incident, the capture of a cock by a fox and the fowl's subsequent escape. Pertelote's medical knowledge is impressive; she seeks a natural explanation of Chauntecleer's dream and recommends a natural solution (take a laxative!). Chauntecleer tries to trump this with Valerius Maximus (if he may be identified as the great *auctour* of line 2984), two long *exempla* which show that dreams do come true, and biblical testimonies that make the same point. As a mock-disputation, this is in a class by itself – only the Wife of Bath's rapid-fire citation of *auctoritees* can compete. The mock-epic excursus is equally remarkable. 'Evere the latter ende of joye is wo', declares the Nun's Priest (echoing the Monk's tragic discourse), and Chauntecleer's 'sorweful cas' merits the attention of a skilled 'rethor' (orator), who 'in a cronycle saufly [confidently] myghte it write | As for a sovereyn notabilitee [major notable fact]' (3204–9). The Nun's Priest then shows off his rhetorical skills by delivering a lament of some forty-eight lines (3325–73), beginning with four exclamations concerning (respectively) the dangers of flattery, the inevitability of destiny, the culpable slowness of Venus to help an enthusiastic servant and the inadequacy of his own artistry – only the peerless skills of his 'deere maister', the eminent rhetorician Geoffrey of Vinsauf (fl. 1200), could rise to this occasion! Whereupon Chauntecleer's perilous situation is likened to the death of Richard the Lionheart, as bemoaned in Geoffrey's *Poetria nova* – after all, both events took place on a Friday. Then the wailing of Chauntecleer's seven wives is compared to the laments of the Trojan women when Troy fell and King Priam was killed, and to those of the Roman wives whose husbands were slaughtered by Nero, with Pertelote being singled out for special elevation through comparison with the sorrowing wife of King Hasdrubal, who died at the fall of Carthage.

There is, of course, a major difference with this narrative: Chauntecleer survives his ordeal, and the sorrow of his hens is short-lived. He outsmarts the fox and escapes; apparently he was not destined to die on this day after all. Perhaps here is an illustration of how a freely chosen course of action can prevent something from happening that otherwise would. Or, to use the Nun's Priest's theological discourse, this is a case of conditional necessity (an event will occur if certain conditions are met) as opposed to absolute necessity (an event will occur in any case; VII.3236–50). He does not attempt to sift out further the valid arguments concerning predestination and the freedom of the human will, deferring to the expertise of Augustine, Boethius and Thomas Bradwardine (*c.*1300–49). Bradwardine, who was consecrated Archbishop of Canterbury shortly before dying of the plague, had attacked those 'new pelagians' who, in his view, afforded human merit too much importance in face of the divine gift of grace; one of his opponents was the Dominican friar Robert Holcot (*c.*1290–1349), author of a popular Wisdom commentary that may be the source of Chauntecleer's two long *exempla*. It would seem that Chaucer had some knowledge of such scholastic matters. But do they really relate to a rooster? 'My tale is of a cok, as ye may heere' (VII.3252). The bathos is beautifully timed.

At last, the Nun's Priest gets to the *moralitas*. After all that exuberant amplification of a short and simple story, it comes almost as an anticlimax. The cock points out the dangers of flattery; the fox, of opening one's mouth at the wrong time, speaking when one should be silent. We are invited to 'Taketh the moralite' (VII.3440), this tale being more than a mere 'folye' about a fox, cock and hen; as St Paul says, 'All that is written is written for our doctrine' (Romans 15:4). That same biblical text is found at the beginning of the *Ovide moralisé*, where it serves as a justification for extensive Christian moralization of pagan fable: 'Tout est pour nostre enseignement'.[35] But is *everything* in the *Nun's Priest's Tale* really for our doctrine? Or have its 'pleasantries' far exceeded their didactic function? Apparently the Nun's Priest has followed the advice of Walter the Englishman: 'If the flower [appeals] more than the fruit, gather it'.[36]

Pleasantries are in short supply in the Manciple's libystic fable. It begins with an introduction to an earth-bound Phebus, and a pet crow that 'in a cage he fostred many a day' and taught to speak (IX.130–2). Those caring actions are reminiscent of the way in which the nurturing Canacee placed a cage at her bed's head as a place of refuge for the distraught female falcon which had been spurned by a faithless tercelet (cf. p. 78 above). Here, however, the betrayal concerns Phebus's wife (called Coronis in other versions of the story), and from its vantage point the bird will witness her committing adultery, on the marital bed, with a man of little social consequence (a detail absent from the *fabula* as told in Ovid's *Metamorphoses* and the *Ovide moralisé*). Also reminiscent of *The*

Squire's Tale is the Manciple's assertion that it is impossible to change one's nature, whether animal or human (IX.160–82, cf. *SqT* V.607–20). But here the discourse turns sour. A she-wolf has such a villainous (low, debased) nature that she will copulate with the 'lewedeste [most uncouth, boorish] wolf' she can find (IX.183–6). The Manciple quickly shifts into the (unconvincing) declaration that he is thinking of men here, of how husbands with lecherous appetites like to take their pleasure with women who are less worthy than their wives – so fond is their flesh of novelty ('newefangel', IX.193). Prompted by the way the disloyal tercelet had taken up with a lesser breed of bird (V.624–7), the Squire had launched a general attack on how men by nature love 'newefangelnesse' (V.610). But there is no concealing the fact that, in the Manciple's narrative, it is the female character who has demeaned herself, by coupling with 'A man of litel reputacioun' (IX.199–200).

The Manciple calls him a 'lemman' (lover), then apologizes for using this 'knavyssh speche' (IX.203–5), a term that belongs with the speech of the lower orders; we have already noted its use in *The Miller's Tale*. Apology then moves into justification:

> The wise Plato seith, as ye may rede,
> The word moot nede accorde with the dede.
> If men shal telle proprely a thyng,
> The word moot cosyn be to the werkyng.
>
> (IX.207–10)

Initially it looks as if the Manciple is reiterating Plato's doctrine as it was appropriated in the General Prologue to *The Canterbury Tales*: the word must fit the deed, therefore a 'rude' or 'large' word is appropriately related to a 'rude' or 'large' deed (GP I.731–6). It is not just that the Manciple is a 'boystous man' (IX.211); the 'knavish' word 'lemman' seems a reasonable appellation for the knavish 'man of litel reputacioun' (IX.199–200).

But a new note is being struck here. One and the same 'werkyng', it now seems, may have several 'cosyns'. If a woman is 'dishonest' of her body, she may be called either a 'lady' (as in the language of noble love) or a 'wenche' or 'lemman' (as in *fabliau* discourse). The first term is used of a person of 'heigh degree', the others of a 'povre wenche' (IX.212–20). Same deed, different words.

The Manciple provides another example of how a deed can be named in different words: a man who murders, burns and destroys can be called either an army captain or an outlaw (IX.223–34). Then he declares that he will not talk in this way any more because he is 'noght textueel' (235), not a learned man or clerk. However, through the Manciple Chaucer is echoing what medieval clerks were talking about in their linguistic theory. The conventional nature of signification was regularly asserted: connections between words and things are determined by the common consent and usage of speakers. (In Latin the word *homo* designates 'man', but in other languages, different words are deployed for that purpose, which proves that meaning is fixed through human custom or institution.) Chaucer brings to the discussion an awareness of the importance of class and power in selecting discourse, which is quite lacking in the 'textueel' Latin accounts. A high-born lady is protected from demeaning language by her social position, just as a mighty tyrant can do much harm with impunity, and be honoured with the title *capitayn*, while a petty criminal, who has only a small group of followers to support him, is called 'an outlawe or a theef' (IX.231–4). This awareness of linguistic relativism resonates throughout the remainder of *The Manciple's Tale*, where we are warned not to risk offending the powerful, even if that means staying silent when faced with wicked deeds.

The crow tells Phebus that it witnessed a man of low degree, a mere insect compared with its mighty and superlatively musical master, 'swyve' his wife (IX.256). Here (once again) 'swyve' roughly corresponds to the Modern English 'screw', and this is yet more 'knavyssh speche'– but a knavish deed has been committed (and one involving a man who is a 'knave' in social terms). True, the crow rashly rubs it in by mimicking the speech of the cuckoo, thereby 'singing' of Phebus' cuckoldry, but the bird is factually correct. Whereupon Phebus brutally kills his wife – then regrets it, and blames the messenger. The crow is designated a 'traitour' (IX.271), which is quite unfair given that the creature is Phebus' pet and familiar, and arguably acting in its master's best interests. Phebus also calls it a 'false theef' (IX.292), echoing the earlier discussion of how a perpetrator of destructive acts can be called either a thief or a captain. Alternatively, the crow could well be addressed in honourific language, termed a truth-teller and loyal servant. But, blinded by sentimental and self-centred regret, Phebus describes his adulterous wife as 'sad' (stable), 'trewe' (loyal) and 'gilteles' (IX.275–80) and proceeds to punish the crow, which is condemned as a careless chatterer.

From this sordid little narrative the Manciple draws a *moralitas* which is demoralizing in the extreme. It fails to perform the function expected of didactic beast-fable inasmuch as no edifying course of ethical behaviour is recommended; here there is no viable morality for good men to take. Furthermore, it enervates rather than exhorts, diminishing the reader's motivation to perform moral acts. A man should guard his tongue well. That, the Manciple explains, is what his mother taught him, and she used the tale of the jangling crow to do it. 'Thus lerne children whan that they been yonge' (IX.334). Such beast-fables were a staple of the nursery and served as simple fare in grammar-school education. The one recounted by the Nun's Priest had warned against saying too much, lest the speaker has cause for repentance, as when the fox regretted opening its mouth and allowing the rooster to escape its jaws. The one recounted by the Manciple's mother, and re-told by the Manciple himself, goes far beyond that and takes a perplexing turn. For it is used to assert the principle that, on every occasion, and no matter if what one has to say is true or false, little speech is better than too much speech. Indeed, talking a lot appears to be dangerous in itself; it blurs into the sin of malicious chattering. The Manciple's mother seems to be dissolving the distinction between not saying anything wicked and not saying anything at all.

> 'My sone, be war, and be noon auctour newe
> Of tidynges, wheither they been false or trewe.
> Whereso thou come, amonges hye or lowe,
> Kepe wel thy tonge and thenk upon the crowe'.
>
> (IX.359–62)

The key point has become depressingly clear. If it's not in your best interests, don't speak out, whether to someone of low status (as when the Manciple rashly denigrates the drunken Cook, IX.25–80) or to a powerful man of the type imaged by Phebus. Which is hardly is keeping with the intention of beast-fables, as understood by medieval teachers. Those texts do purvey much worldly wisdom of a self-protective kind, but that was not deemed antithetical to a higher moral vision in the way it seems to be here. Aesop sought to 'recall irrational human nature to its true self by a comparison with brute beasts', explains one commentator.[37] The Manciple's mother appears to have no interest in the lofty heights of true human nature; her sole concern is to instill self-serving wiliness in her son. Lady Philosophy, it might be said, has been reduced to a *lemman* and a wench.

The admonition to 'be noon auctour newe' warns against exposing oneself as the source of news, but insofar as *The Manciple's Tale* is revisiting the values of the General Prologue, it implicitly raises questions about the status of that 'auctour newe' Geoffrey Chaucer, the ultimate source of the Canterbury tales that are allocated to various tellers. 'Whan he sholde telle a tale', the crow could 'countrefete the speche of every man' (IX.134–5); evidently he is good at telling 'a tale after a man' in the way commended by Chaucer the pilgrim, who then proceeds to cite Plato on the importance of words being cousins to the deeds they describe (GP I.731, 741–2). The crow is stripped of its fine feathers, deprived of speech and song. But a poet cannot be silent. And a satiric poet must speak out against vice. Satire 'censures and corrects vices in society and advocates virtues' in 'forthright, unadorned terms' (cf. p. 59 above). This genre mandates open reproof, and in the reprehension of vice 'boystous' and 'knavyssh' speech is actually licensed. Yet the Manciple adopts the position that the hierarchy of linguistic valuation (whether an elevating or belittling word should be used) is directly related to, and determined by, the social hierarchy. Thus he ends up as the type of person who cringes in the face of power, rather than telling truth to it.

Following the end of *The Manciple's Tale*, the Parson vociferously rejects Harry Bailly's request for a 'fable', citing St Paul's condemnation of those who turn aside from truth to tell 'fables and swich wrecchednesse'. That is an obvious echo of II Timothy 4:4, although the Apostle's first letter to Timothy also warns against giving 'heed to fables' and denigrates 'foolish and old wives fables' (I Timothy 1:4, 4:7). The Manciple's performance of the fable of Phebus and the Crow hardly inspires confidence in the didactic efficacy of the genre, but the Parson's condemnation goes far beyond that. Therefore, some have seen in *The Manciple's Tale* the beginnings of a general rejection of fabulation that culminates in the *Retraction* (see p. 135 below). However, we may recall that no less a theologian than St Augustine defended certain fictions in which 'men have attributed even human deeds or sayings to irrational animals and things without sense', because they have a truthful end.[38]

So, then, the Parson's reductive assertion is not the only authoritative word on the matter, and the issue of whether Chaucer wanted to give him the last word (at this stage in his work and in his life) must remain a matter of debate. Suffice it to say that, in *The Manciple's Tale*, Chaucer returns to several of the issues of literary and linguistic theory that feature prominently in earlier parts of *The Canterbury Tales*, to explore further their implications. Some of those moves may seem rather jaundiced, but they also reveal an undiminished excitement in the possibilities for interaction between 'earnest' and 'game' (cf. *MilPro* I.3186), an ongoing awareness of how earnest can follow from game, how game can be made of earnest and how both can work together, or pull apart, within the capacious praxis of satire that is the foundation of this entire collection of tales.

Chapter 4

The Canterbury Tales, II: experience and authority

Wel oughte us . . . on olde bokes leve,
There as there is non other assay by preve.

(*LGW* G Pro 27–8)

Here the textual authority of old books is set in contrast with proof by other means. Citation of *auctoritees* (extracts from the revered *auctores*) was a long-established means of discovering the truth of any matter – what some divinely inspired biblical writer had to say on a given subject was proof enough. But sometimes, as in this passage from the *Legend*, deployment of *auctoritee* and assay by *preve* were separated out, as two possible ways to truth. The latter could be quite sufficient, as when Chaucer's Knight remarks that the prime mover of the universe has fixed certain durations of time to whatever is begotten, born, and dies. In this matter 'Ther nedeth noght noon auctoritee t'allegge, | For it is preeved by experience' (*KnT* I.3000–1). Here 'preve' designates the evidence of one's own eyes.

In Chaucer's day the English terms *experience* and *experiment* (following the Latin *experientia* and *experimentum*) were regularly applied in discussion of knowledge acquired through personal observation of natural events (cf. pp. 70–1 above). However, *experientia* was not necessarily regarded as functioning in opposition to what one read in some old book. What to us is textual authority may have been personal experience to a given *auctor*, and/or one's personal experience could be quite consonant with what a given *auctor* had said. Very often *auctoritee* and *experience* were treated as mutually supportive, as when, in his *Treatise on the Astrolabe* Chaucer appeals to his own experience ('had I of this conclusioun the ful experience', 'By experience I wot wel') in the course of a work compiled 'of the labour of olde astrologiens'.[1]

The same may be claimed of the *Wife of Bath's Prologue and Tale*, although here the body of knowledge is very different (and troubling questions are raised about how knowledge may be embodied). This text begins with the Wife's confident assertion that

> Experience, though noon auctoritee
> Were in this world, is right ynogh for me
> To speke of wo that is in mariage...
>
> (*WBPro* III.1–3)

Here is a clear appeal to the 'auctoryte of experyence', to borrow a phrase from the fifteenth-century writer Osbern Bokenham.[2] Yet the Wife proceeds to quote an abundance of *auctoritees* both pagan and Christian. In part this supports her own extensive experience of the 'wo that is in mariage', an experiential space in which women supposedly belong, and wherein they may be allowed authority of a kind – a kind that confines rather than empowers, inasmuch as it confirms male prejudice about the limited range of women's abilities. However, the text moves far beyond those predictable parameters to the world of 'prechyng and...scoles of clergye', the schools where clerics are trained. That is where the 'auctoritees' belong and where they should stay, the Friar insists to the Wife of Bath, far from the minds of women and the 'game' of the tale-telling competition (III.1270–7). But Chaucer will have none of this. The Wife of Bath's narrative participates in a literary experiment of extraordinary ambition, wherein textual and institutional sources of authority are related to the imagined lives of figures from a wide social spectrum, which sometimes confirm stereotypes (albeit often with rich elaboration) and sometimes go far beyond them.

Learning by experience: the Friar and the Summoner

The Friar's Tale begins with a brief account of a rigorous archdeacon who punishes people for breaches of ecclesiastical law by imposing fines. As his lackey he has an avaricious summoner, who acts as a bailiff or debt collector, filling his own purse in the process. Going on his rounds, this summoner meets a forester, who turns out to be a fiend in search of souls. Impressed by how similar their occupations are, the summoner rides forth with his newfound friend or 'brother', listening to the way in which people swear and send things to the devil. 'Why don't you take what these people are giving you?' he asks. The reply is that the devil can't take anything unless the people involved really mean what they say. There may be the suggestion here that the summoner is more of a devil than the devil himself, because the devil takes only what people freely give him, while the summoner just takes, his function being to force people into giving him what they do not want to give. Finally, the summoner meets one of his own victims, a poor old woman, and demands money from her, whereupon she sends the summoner to the devil – and really means it. Thus the fiend can carry him off to hell.

When the summoner encounters the fiend he is, in fact, meeting someone he knows very well (given his immoral life), yet he fails to recognize him. The devil having revealed his true identity, the summoner, far from being terrified, is eager to question him further. The exchange becomes more academic, issues being raised that are reminiscent of theological debates in the 'scoles of clergye' and that may be summarized in this 'question and answer' format.

Q. Do you have a determinate shape in hell?
A. No, we can take on any shape we please: sometimes a man's, sometimes an ape's, sometimes an angel's.

Q. Why do you go about in different shapes, and not in one?
A. To take our prey the more easily.

Q. What is the reason for all your labour?
A. If I told you, you wouldn't understand it all. Suffice it to say that sometimes we are God's instruments; in any case, we cannot do whatever God does not allow.

Q. Do you make your various bodies (the shapes of humans, apes, etc.) out of elements?
A. No. Sometimes we create illusions and sometimes we rise with dead bodies, in many ways, and speak as rationally and well as Samuel did with the Witch of Endor when she seemed to bring him back from the dead. (I Paralip.10:13)

'Some men seye' that Samuel was not really present then, the devil adds, but he is contemptuous of such speculation, unimpressed by 'youre dyvynytee' [theology] (III.1511–12). What humans believe they see is often erroneous, and even their most erudite knowledge does not reach very far.

Here we may recall, once more, the opening lines of the *Legend of Good Women*, where the narrator remarks that he has heard men say 'A thousand tymes . . . | That ther ys joy in hevene and peyne in helle' (F Pro 1–2). Which he is quite willing to believe, although he knows that there is no person 'dwellyng in this contree' (living on this earth) who has been to either place. In such a situation, one is reliant on textual authority, 'For by assay ther may no man hit preve' (9). Men should not just believe what they can see with their own eyes,

> For, God wot, thing is never the lasse sooth,   *nevertheless true*
> Thogh every wight ne may hit nat ysee.
> (F Pro 14–15)

However, in the very near future, the Friar's summoner will indeed be able to 'preve' the matters under discussion 'by assay', understand well through personal experience. Resident in hell, he will have more expert knowledge of its 'peyne' than Virgil or Dante (who allegedly visited the underworld while they were alive).

> Thou shalt herafterward, my brother deere,
> Com there thee nedeth nat of me to leere,   *learn*
> For thou shalt, *by thyn owene experience*,
> Konne in a chayer rede of this sentence
> Bet than Virgile, while he was on lyve,   *alive*
> Or Dant also.
>
>   (*FrT* III.1515–20; my emphasis)

That 'chayer' is the magisterial chair from which a university lecture would be delivered (the verb 'rede' means to read aloud, give a lecture; cf. the Latin verb *legere* and the related noun *lectio*). This discourse is echoed at the tale's climax, when the devil says that he will take the summoner to hell that very night, where he 'shalt knowen of our privetee [secrets] | Moore than a maister of dyvynytee' (III.1636–8).

So, then, in large measure this is a tale about 'learning by experience' – or, more precisely, about how a summoner, having failed to learn from the evidence of his own experience in this life, must make up for it with painful experience in the next.[3] The fiend he would have as his friend is no distant *auctor* but a source of crucial information who stands right before him, and yet the summoner behaves as if he is engaged in some abstract academic exercise that has no consequence for his immediate future. As an interpreter of language, he is a poor pupil, unable to recognize the heavy irony permeating the fiend's statements or to appreciate that knowledge of a speaker's intention is crucial for understanding his meaning. Rounding off his tale, the Friar warns his audience to be wary of the temptations of the devil, who wishes to enslave us. Yet it can hardly be said that, in this story, the devil has led the summoner astray. The Friar's summoner has, very effectively, done that to himself.

Enraged by this attack on his profession, Chaucer's Summoner responds by telling a tale against a friar who is ridiculously proud of his professional status, delighting to be addressed as 'maister' (*magister*). Friar John has indeed received 'in scole' (at university) this 'honour' (of a master's degree), he simperingly tells the secular lord to whom he appeals for support after his humiliation by a flatulent victim, going on to say, with false modesty, that such a title should not actually be used, following the injunction of Matthew 23:8 to 'be not . . . called Rabbi', because God alone is our master/teacher. Here, then, is a fully qualified schoolman and preacher ('in prechyng is my diligence', 1819), who shall be revealed as exploiting his position as a licensed interpreter of *auctoritees* for his personal good and that of his fellow-friars, in blatant violation of the foundational ideals of his order.

A common charge brought against the friars was that they enjoyed material comforts far in excess of the necessities of life, occupying grand buildings well stocked with food and drink – a far cry from the tiny, rundown Church of the Portiuncula, which was the Franciscan order's first home. St Francis, the son of a wealthy cloth merchant from Assisi, gave up his worldly goods to marry his 'Lady Poverty'; by Chaucer's time, the claim of his spiritual descendants to be 'wedded to poverte and continence' (III.1907) had worn thin. We do not actually *own* anything (ran the standard Franciscan justification), either individually or collectively; rather we merely *use* worldly goods, in the pursuit of our evangelical mission. The parish clergy – real-life equivalents of men like the 'curat' who has heard the sick man's confession before Friar John could get to him (III.2094–8), and the genuinely 'povre Persoun of a Toun' portrayed in the General Prologue (I.477–9) – were unimpressed by such an argument, claiming that the wandering friars were depriving them of their livelihood.

Another crucial aspect of this problematic 'rags to riches' story was that the orders of friars produced most of the finest theologians of the later Middle Ages, men of the calibre of Thomas Aquinas and Bonaventure, who held prestigious university chairs right across Europe. This development was justified with reference to the importance of having a learned clergy that could combat heresy and undertake missions to convert the heathen. Furthermore, the conviction that Holy Scripture excels all other bodies of knowledge meant that a high degree of learning was deemed necessary for preachers. But the friars were anxious to insist that they put people before books. Dominicans relished the tale of how their founder reacted to the suffering caused by the terrible famine that devastated Spain in 1191, when he was completing his theological studies. Eager to raise money to relieve distress, Dominic de Guzmán went so far as to sell off his precious manuscripts. When his companions expressed astonishment that he should do this, he asked, 'Would you have me study off these dead skins' – parchment is made from sheepskin – 'when men are dying of hunger?'[4] Friar John's emphasis is rather different. His community owes a large sum of money for building works, and if they cannot raise this,

> ... moste we oure books selle.
> And if yow lake oure predicacioun,   *lack, preaching*
> Thanne goth the world al to destruccioun.
>
> (*SumT* III.2108–10)

In this case the sale of books would fund improvements to their (already opulent) living conditions, rather than ease the sufferings of the poor – and these decadent friars value their personal comfort over their *predicacioun*. Moreover, Friar John blatantly abuses his book learning, by interpreting 'the text of hooly writ' for his own ends: 'Glosynge is a glorious thyng' indeed! (III.1788–94). In defense of this self-serving scholarship he enlists the authority of St Paul: 'The letter killeth, but the spirit giveth life' (II Cor. 3:6). This statement was sometimes used to affirm the superiority of allegorical over literal reading. But exegetical method in itself is not the issue here, rather it is the uses to which that method is put.

As the Summoner's narrative progresses, it is Friar John's pride in being called *maister* that becomes the central target of the satire. The sick householder promises him a gift on the condition that it be shared equally among all twelve of the members of his convent (which is quite fitting, given that friars had given up the right to own individual property). All he produces is a fart. The angry friar rushes to complain to a group of aristocrats who turn out to have some knowledge of the techniques of logical reasoning (evidently such academic techniques had traveled beyond the schools). They proceed to give the 'probleme' the 'churl' supposedly posed to the friar the full scholastic treatment, handling it like a topic of serious academic research. Why, declares the honourable lord in charge of this household, this 'mateere' is of such difficulty that the devil must have put it into the churl's mind! (III.2219, 2221, 2272). The point being that an uneducated man could not have gained such knowledge by any other means. (As we know from *The Friar's Tale*, all the inhabitants of the other world, devils included, have access to vast amounts of information.) How *can* a fart be divided into twelve equal parts, he asks, musing on the fact that its 'rumblynge', and indeed every sound, is but a reverberation of air (2223–5; cf. the similar discussion of sound movement in *The House of Fame*). Therefore, how is it possible to ensure that all the friars will share the experience equally, each getting his fair share of 'soun', 'savour' and 'stynk' (2226, 2273–4)?

The lord's squire manages to come up with a 'preeve which that is demonstratif', a secure conclusion based on rigorous inference. This is the language of logic, in this case a logic that proceeds by *experientia*, personal observation of natural events, and produces a conclusion with immediate consequences for the sensory experience of Friar John and his brethren. A major source of humour here is the extent to which low bodily functions are elevated to the very seat of learning. An orificial act is being afforded the same respect normally bestowed upon experiments of a more elevated kind. Set twelve friars at the end of each spoke of a wheel, set the churl in its middle 'and make hym lete a fart' (III.2253–86). Problem solved!

At this point all of the household members proceed to praise the churl's 'subtiltee I And heigh wit', which enabled him to speak as well as Euclid or Ptolemy – he was neither a fool nor a demoniac. Are these layfolk supposed to be acting with genuine or mock seriousness? In either case, the result is the same. Friar John's intellectual pretensions, and blatant abuse of the authority which learning brings, have been subjected to ridicule of an exact and appropriate kind. Quite an educational experience.

Spiritual versus material economies: the Pardoner and the Canon's Yeoman

'I trowe he were a geldyng or a mare' (GP I.691): Chaucer the pilgrim likens the Pardoner to a castrated horse or a mare. Furthermore, he asserts that this individual is unable to grow a beard – the beard being a traditional cultural marker of masculinity. Does this mean that the Pardoner is a homosexual (or, to make a more historically nuanced point, a man who is disposed to homosexual acts)? Or some kind of 'eunuch'? In Chaucer's day eunuchry could cover several possible medical conditions, ranging from the absence of testicles (as with *castrati*) to undescended or abnormal ones. A man could look feminoid for reasons other than those: he might have been born a 'womanly man' because he was generated on the left side or in the middle of his mother's womb, or (paradoxically enough) he could have become effeminate due to his inordinate desire for women.

The complexity of Chaucer's presentation of the Pardoner extends far beyond the matter of his problematic sexuality. As a depiction of a *questor* (a seeker after alms, or fundraiser), this is the most sophisticated to have survived in any medieval vernacular literature. The figure did not come to Chaucer ready-made from estates satire. Rather he took many of the standard complaints about pardoners and added to them materials relating to other types of ecclesiastical hypocrisy and malpractice (including preaching for gain and the display of false relics). The result is a composite character who is much more than the sum of his parts and resists reduction to any of them.

Chaucer's Pardoner is *not* selling relics. Rather he is selling *access* to relics and the spiritual power associated with them. More precisely, in exchange for a donation, a client is allowed to venerate his relics, use them to effect a cure for some disease of man or beast or petition for good fortune. Hence the references to a healing potion made when the bone of a 'hooly Jewes sheep' is dipped in a well, and to a glove with miraculous powers, which the Pardoner will permit a man to wear – all for a fee, of course (VI.350–76). That specially treated water will restore the health of any cow, calf, sheep or ox; moreover, if the 'good-man' (head of the household) himself drinks it or dons that glove, then his 'beestes and his stoor [stock] shal multiplie', as shall his crops. Farmers left offerings at shrines and venerated their prized relics, hoping that the relevant saints would bless them with good harvests and ensure that their animals stayed healthy and bred well. These practices are well documented historically, and, however Chaucer may have viewed them, hardly deserve our ridicule. The Pardoner is exploiting the fears of vulnerable and credulous people for his own ends. Only authentic relics can possibly bring them any benefits (according to the prevailing belief), and Chaucer goes out of his way to emphasize that the collection described here consists of worthless fakes.

This figure is almost certainly a layman. A pardoner was basically a fundraiser, working for the maintenance of a hospital, church or cathedral or for some other good cause; there was no need for such tasks to be carried out by ordained clergymen (although sometimes this did happen). Indeed, many pardoners were ordinary artisans, and some of them worked only part-time, also pursuing other professions. We need not be surprised, then, that Chaucer's character should tell the Wife of Bath that he is thinking of getting married (III.166–8), a life choice that was canonically impossible for a priest, deacon or sub-deacon.

A 'pardon' or indulgence may be understood as the remission – or, more precisely, the payment by others – of a sinner's debt of punishment for sins already forgiven through the sacrament of penance, as administered by a priest, wherein moral guilt was removed. That debt was paid out of the Church's vast spiritual treasury, as filled by the innumerable merits of Christ and the saints. To develop the treasury metaphor further, a credit from the inexhaustible resources of the heavenly bank was transferred into the sinner's overdrawn personal account, reducing the amount of debt he owed or (in the case of a plenary or 'full' indulgence) eradicating it entirely. Without such assistance, the sinner faced the prospect of a long and painful period of punishment in purgatory to render him fit to enter heaven. An indulgence's remit did not extend to hell, where the irredeemable would suffer for all eternity, or to heaven, for the blessed had no need of them.

In their discussions of indulgences, medieval theologians addressed the difficult relationship between the two economies, the material and the spiritual; between the offering of money or earthly goods made by the penitent and the spiritual benefits he received as part of this transaction – but not in direct exchange, for no amount of payment could activate a pardon unless the sinner had made a sincerely contrite and full confession. They struggled to justify a practice that was beyond their control and pushed at the limits of their powers of rationalization. Such explanations as they did come up with were often so complicated that accurate dissemination was impossible, and even some of the best educated people of the day misunderstood them. This general confusion made the system even more open to abuse at all levels – from supreme pontiffs to lowly pardoners.

The standard complaints regularly made against those lowly pardoners are well illustrated by Bishop John de Grandisson's condemnation, in 1356, of 'impious questors' who are 'neither friars nor clergy but often laymen or married men'. They absolve clients from the most grievous of sins, in a manner that far exceeds their authority; likewise they ply 'their business in the office of preaching', even though they are not authorized to preach.[5] That description fits Chaucer's Pardoner very well. The confidence with which he claims the power to absolve people from sin, 'by the auctoritee | Which that by bulle ygraunted was to me' (VI.387–8), is shocking. Later in the text he goes so far as to declare that, by his 'heigh power', he is able to absolve his clients so cleanly and purely that they shall enter heaven without hindrance (VI.913–5). You are quite honoured, he assures his listeners, to have a pardoner travelling in your company who can cater for all your needs in terms of absolution, as you ride across the country and risk all kinds of accidents. In fact, *questores* were only the 'announcers' of indulgences, tasked merely with publicizing them to the populace. The spiritual power that pardons bore came from their authorization by some pope or bishop; the lowly credentials of mere pardoners were of no consequence. Furthermore, there is confusion here – a deliberate ploy, perhaps, on the Pardoner's part – between absolution in the sense of remission of punishment thanks to an indulgence (the power deriving from the pardon itself, certainly not from any pardoner) and that which is obtained only through confession to an ordained clergyman (which Chaucer's character apparently is not). The Pardoner is implying he has authority of a kind reserved for priests alone. Moreover, the sheer amount of absolution he offers his companions is breathtaking.

In respect of preaching also, the Pardoner has usurped an office to which he has no legal right. 'I stonde *lyk* a clerk in my pulpet' (V1.391, italics mine). The point being, he is not an actual *clerk*, and hence an inappropriate occupant of that *pulpet*. By virtue of their occupation, pardoners did not possess 'the office of preaching'. They were supposed to explain the origins and objective of a given indulgence, the reasons for its issue. This activity could easily be regarded as, or mistaken for, or shade into, 'preaching'; moreover, the term 'preaching' itself could be used in loose, colloquial senses. But that is inadequate as an explanation of the way in which Chaucer's Pardoner is presented. In his prologue he claims the right and the wherewithal to preach in the full professional and technical sense of the term; indeed, this text reads as a collage of materials from medieval preaching manuals. First and foremost, the Pardoner prides himself on being a preacher. Hence there is no doubt of the extent to which he is trespassing on the territory traditionally reserved for the priest.

The use of *exempla* (morally edifying stories) in sermons to the laity was often recommended in the preaching manuals; the Pardoner sneeringly remarks that 'lewed peple loven tales olde' (VI.437). When he engages in excessive bodily movements and singles out individuals for condemnation, he is doing precisely what those texts warn against. Furthermore, Chaucer displays some awareness of issues relating to preaching that had been debated in the *scoles of clergye* (cf. III.1277) for well over a century: can an immoral man preach effectively, and can preaching for financial reward ever be justified? It was sometimes argued that fundraising may be regarded as an acceptable secondary consideration in preaching, providing that the spiritual well-being of his congregation remained paramount in the preacher's mind. The Pardoner inverts that classification by declaring that making other people turn away from greed and sorely repent is not his *principal entente*: 'I preche nothyng but for coveitise' (VI.432–3). It was also argued that a sermon from a mercenary preacher was better than no sermon at all, and preaching by an immoral man could be efficacious, especially if the congregation was unaware of his immorality. Chaucer has no truck with that evasion: the Pardoner makes his ethical shortcomings public knowledge (at least on this occasion). Therefore the brazen claim that, although he himself is a 'ful vicious man', he can tell a 'moral tale' (VI.459–60), is presented in its most challenging form.

In responding to that challenge, Chaucer's recent readers have often praised the rhetorical force of this *questor*'s tale of a quest for death, wherein three revellers end up killing each other, as they fight over a material treasury, around eight bushels in size, of 'floryns [gold coins] . . . faire and brighte' (VI.774). The mysterious old man who directs them to their doom is a tantalizingly sinister creation, all the more effective because Chaucer leaves him unexplained. Is this Death himself or one of Death's agents? Or a version of the 'Wandering Jew' or Cain-figure who wanders the earth in perpetual exile as punishment for his sin, whether the denial of Christ or fratricide or some other grave crime? (Later echoes of that type may be found in Coleridge's *Ancient Mariner* and Wagner's *Flying Dutchman*.) In the Pardoner's narrative, the perils of greed (which comprises gluttony) are vividly illustrated, this sin being identified as one of the distinctive 'sins of the mouth'; the others include drunkenness, lechery and blasphemy ('gret sweryng', VI.631). Along with gambling, these vices are seen as aspects of 'sacrifise' to the devil, cursed forms of worship within the 'develes temple' (VI.470) that is the tavern. There a cruel parody of the Eucharistic rite takes place, when blasphemers, by their swearing, break the body of Christ in a horrific replication of His sufferings on the cross ('Oure blissed Lordes body they totere [tear apart]', VI.474). Furthermore, the elaborate dishes made by cooks to satisfy the greed of delicate palates, wherein the original appearance and taste of the ingredients are totally lost, is described in terms of a turning of 'substaunce into accident' (VI.539). Perhaps here we may detect an allusion to the Eucharistic controversy of Chaucer's day, wherein John Wyclif and his followers had questioned the doctrine of transubstantiation, the belief that the sacramental bread and wine become the very body and blood of Christ, while their accidents (all that is accessible to the senses) remain unchanged.

In the Pardoner's treatment of tavern sins as devil worship may be found an explanation of his claim, made near the end of the tale, that Harry Bailly is 'moost envoluped in synne' (VI.942) and therefore should be the first to venerate his relics. If the inn is the 'develes temple', then as an innkeeper Harry is some sort of devil's priest, enveloped in sin indeed. Little wonder that he should react so robustly, saying that the Pardoner is so unscrupulous he would have him kiss his shit-stained breeches, promising this is the genuine relic of some saint (VI.946ff.). Harry then exclaims that his companion should have his *coillons* cut off, 'in stide' of relics or a reliquary – probably meaning 'in the position occupied by' rather than 'instead of', given that the next line's reference to enshrinement (albeit in a hog's turd) develops the idea of the Pardoner's parts *as* a relic. Opinion is divided as to whether the Host is angry here, or rather revelling in a joke that shifts around somewhat in the very telling; the Pardoner's anger, which renders him speechless, is obvious. At any rate, in seeking to understand the dynamic of this exchange, there is no need to implicate homophobia, to impute to Harry contempt towards a man he perceives as a homosexual and hence insults by calling his manhood in question. Assuming for the moment that the Pardoner does possess a viable version of testicles, the implication that they would make a fine relic could be taken as a compliment; this is, after all, a man who has bragged about having a girl in every town (VI.453). But if the Pardoner is, so to speak, all talk and no action in that area, then he would hardly need Harry's help in carrying an organ that one might imagine as diminutive. Either way, the joke could be fundamentally heterosexist.

However one reacts to the ending of *The Pardoner's Tale*, it would be rash to find in Chaucer's creation a Proto-Protestant attack on the issuing of indulgences in general, or going on pilgrimage to acquire them. The availability of substantial indulgences at Becket's shrine was a major reason for travelling there. Real-life Canterbury pilgrims believed that genuine pardons and relics awaited them at the cathedral, and there is no evidence whatever that the poet had any qualms about such activities.

Chaucer's satire of the Pardoner has much in common with his robust criticism of duplicitous alchemists who, in search of the 'philosophres stoon' (*CYT* VIII.862) that has the power to turn base metals into gold and silver, pretend to possess more knowledge than they actually have, and dupe people into giving them money to fund their unsuccessful experiments. As with the Pardoner, greed is the major motivating force behind such fraudulent practice; these would-be philosophers are not remotely interested in storing up 'treasures in heaven, . . . where thieves do not break through, nor steal' (in the words of Matt. 6:20). They themselves are the thieves (indeed they live among thieves), and nothing they offer is of any value. However, although the Pardoner's relics are utter fakes, his pardons may well be genuine, 'from Rome al hoot' (GP I.687), and offering abundant spiritual riches from the heavenly treasury. All that the over-heating Canon can offer is the false promise of earthly riches. His profusely sweating forehead is likened to a 'stillatorie' (VIII.576–81), a distillation vessel of the kind that will feature in the Yeoman's narrative, and a parodic parallel to the boiling cauldron in which the miraculously sweat-free Cecile was martyred (as described in the previous tale; *SNT* VIII.19–25).

The Canon is a 'passyng [outstanding] man' of 'heigh discrecioun' (VIII.613–14) and the possessor of knowledge both dangerous and dark. At least that is how he likes to be thought of, and how the Yeoman first describes him. The Canon is an ordained clergyman (whereas the Pardoner is not). His identification as a regular (or Augustinian or 'Black') canon has generally been accepted; he seems to have the same status as that held by the protagonist of the second part of the tale, a canon possessed of even 'moore subtiltee' (VIII.1091) and whose social position is made perfectly clear. On that assumption, the Canon is a member of a community bound by the vows of chastity, poverty and obedience.

So, then, what is Chaucer's character doing lurking in haunts and blind alleys in some unsafe suburb, and why is he of 'sluttish' (slovenly) appearance, wearing a dirty and torn cassock (VIII.633–9)? Apparently he has deserted his calling and is living in blatant violation of his vows. We need not leap to the conclusion that the Canon is in hiding as the persecuted follower of a prohibited craft. When church and authorities issued legislation to restrict the practice of alchemy, they were seeking primarily to counter the threat of counterfeiting, the use of fake chemical compounds in the production of unauthorized coins; the art itself was not necessarily being condemned. No less a figure than Thomas Aquinas opined that if 'real gold were to be produced by alchemy, it would not be unlawful to sell it for the genuine article, for nothing prevents art from employing certain natural causes for the production of natural and true effects'.[6] On this reasoning, alchemy is not against nature but works with nature. As John Gower put it, 'This craft is wroght be weie of kinde, | So that ther is no fallas [falseness] inne' (*Confessio Amantis*, IV.2508–9). Furthermore, in an age when almost all the highly educated men were inevitably clerics, his interest in 'elvysshe [mysterious] craft' (VIII.751) would not necessarily render the Canon suspect. Perhaps the answer is that he has been brought low by that addictive quest for the Philosopher's Stone his servant describes so vividly.

Later the Yeoman will remark, on being asked why alchemists dress so shabbily, that they claim this is a protective measure, a means of hiding knowledge so great that they might be killed for it. But what is really being concealed is their miserable lack of success (VIII.892–7). So, then, it seems that the Canon is really indigent. That would explain his desperate desire to join the Canterbury pilgrims; a parasite like the Pardoner, he has hopes of leeching off the unwary. For here are no altruistic researchers but men on the make. He and the Yeoman create 'illusioun' (672) and 'sleightes' (773) to deceive their victims – and alchemists also deceive themselves, when they think they may be observing gold and silver being produced. No amount of staring can make that happen.

> If that youre eyen kan nat seen aright,
> Looke that youre mynde lakke noght his sight.
> For though ye looken never so brode and stare,   *with wide-open eyes*
> Ye shul nothyng wynne on that chaffare...   *business*
>
> (VIII.1418–21)

Firsthand experience, the testimony of one's own eyes, has its limits. We should rely rather on the mind's eye and its powers of reason – which the duped priest of the final part of *The Canon Yeoman's Tale* fails to do, believing the canon's assurance that he will 'seen heer, by experience', quicksilver becoming a precious metal 'right in [his] sighte anon, withouten lye' (VIII.1125–30).

The extent of Chaucer's knowledge of the 'slidynge [slippery/unreliable] science' of alchemy (VIII.732) is a matter of debate, as is the issue of whether he had any genuine belief in it. At the very least he was familiar with many of the relevant 'clergial' and 'queynte' terms (VIII.752), as when Arnold of Villa Nova (d.1311) is quoted as following the belief of the putative founder of the art, Hermes Trismegistus, that the dragon never dies unless his brother is also slain. Decoding the secret speech of alchemical *pryvetee*, this means that mercury cannot be 'mortified' or solidified except in association with sulphur, as a crucial stage in the transmutation of metals. The dragon image (a staple of alchemical tradition) is vividly illustrated in an alchemical scroll (dated *c*.1570) that contains an English translation of material from one of Arnold's treatises,

Figure 4. An alchemical dragon. Yale University, Beinecke Library, MS Mellon MS 41, unfol.

together with verses ascribed to the fifteenth-century alchemist George Ripley, a real-life Augustinian canon (see figure 4).[7] It probably represents mercury, as in Chaucer's tale, while the toad may be an image of the First Matter which has to be worked on to obtain the Philosopher's Stone (hence the reference to the taming of venom, meaning the elimination of impurities).

With such a device 'philosophres' could perform the secular equivalent of miracles of the kind the Pardoner claims for his relics (although, as already noted, alchemists claimed to be working with nature rather than effecting miracles which transcended nature). The Pardoner promises increase and augmentation of animal and plant life (VI.352–76), whereas the Yeoman speaks of 'multiplication' – a key term in alchemical discourse – in the sense of making two pounds of gold from one, or even producing enough precious metal to pave with gold and silver the road from here to Canterbury (VIII.623–6). But this obsessive search for occult doctrine teaches a lesson that is quite easy to learn: alchemists do the opposite of what they promise, by turning gain into lack, making a man's happiness into sorrow, and emptying rather than filling large purses. Here is a strange form of return for one's investment, a material economy which generates loss rather than reward.

A man may lightly lerne, if he have aught,	*anything*
To multiplie, and brynge his good to naught!	
Lo! swich a lucre is in this lusty game,	*profit, vigorous/tempting*
A mannes myrthe it wol turne unto grame,	*sorrow*
And empten also grete and hevye purses . . .	

(VIII.1400–4)

Rather than bringing 'avantage' to himself, this slippery 'science' has rendered the Yeoman 'bare', deprived him of his worldly goods, while constant exposure to fumes has damaged his health, 'consumed and wasted' his 'reednesse' or complexion (VIII.731–3, 1100): a far cry from alchemy's promise of an elixir of life, which confers youth and longevity. Instead of enjoying increase and augmentation, he (in common with other would-be masters of the occult art) has suffered diminution and deterioration.

At the present time, then, this 'lore' is fruitless, no 'conclusioun' having been achieved; here is a 'science' so far ahead of our knowledge that it is impossible to 'overtake', catch up with (VIII.672, 680–2). But what of future time (875), will it continue to slide away? The Yeoman ends his tale with an anecdote about how Plato refused to name the secret stone; indeed, all the philosophers swore an oath of silence. Even more decisively, Jesus Christ himself holds the art so dear that he wills it should not be explained, until such a time as it will please His deity to enlighten, and to protect, certain men, in respect of such knowledge (VIII.1428–71). There is no categorical prohibition of alchemical inquiry here, but rather the possibility that, one day, Christ might reveal its secrets to the right people. (The converse is that anyone who makes God his opponent will be unable to get anywhere in the pursuit of this knowledge.) We are not dealing with impossibilities of nature, pseudo-knowledge that can never be true, but rather with a body of genuine knowledge so significant that it is 'lief [beloved] and deere' to Christ himself (a specific claim unparalleled in any known source of the Yeoman's tale). Assuming, of course, that we are hearing the voice of Chaucer here, rather than that of a narrator who is habouring false hopes, despite all the disappointments and deprivations he has endured on account of this 'elvysshe nyce [foolish] loore'(VIII.842). If we can indeed make that assumption, and regard alchemy as 'a site where modernizing values could take root', then the Canon's Yeoman may be seen as offering intimations of 'Chaucerian modernity'.[8]

However, all intellectual roads do not lead directly and inexorably to the present, as is abundantly demonstrated by recent interest in alchemy as a proto-science that contributed to the development of modern chemistry and medicine, rather than being brushed aside in their inevitable progress. That founding father of modern science, Isaac Newton (1642–1726), studied alchemy extensively and wrote treatises on the subject; indeed, it has been argued that this research 'constituted one of the pillars supporting his mature scientific edifice'.[9] So, then, the new did not demolish the old but was under-pinned by it. We should not think in simplistic terms 'of light overcoming darkness, but of an animated muddle of belief, disillusion, and reinterpreta-tion that is all part of negotiating what there is to talk about in the structure of nature, and how best to learn more about it'. *The Canon Yeoman's Prologue and Tale* has its place within that muddle. 'Those skilled in alchemical procedures' may be seen as 'contributing to the creation of natural knowledge by sometimes getting their hands dirty and manipulating different substances in order to produce new effects'.[10] Such a remark might occasion a little sympathy for the real-life equivalents of Chaucer's grimy Canon and his dirty-handed servant, whose 'labour and travaille' was all 'lost' (VIII.780–1).

Authorizing women: Alisoun, Prudence, Cecile and Eglentyne

Chaucer's basic model for Alisoun of Bath was the literary type of the old woman who, as an authority on love, teaches the young how to become skilled in this art. Her ultimate prototype is Ovid's Dipsas (*Amores*, I.viii), the forerunner of 'La Vielle' in Jean de Meun's part of the *Roman de la Rose*, which is the direct source for many passages in *The Wife of Bath's Prologue*, including its opening lines, wherein the authority of experience is affirmed. I never went to a school where they taught the theory of love, La Vielle had declared. Rather, 'I know everything by practice (*practique*)'; 'Experiments (*experimenz*), which I have followed my whole life, have made me wise in love' (*Rose*, 12774–6).

However, Chaucer grants Alisoun a much wider area of expertise, putting into her mouth many *auctoritees* that transcend those boundaries. But how could a woman, and a laywoman at that, have acquired such information? Because her fifth husband, Jankyn, had been at 'scole' in Oxford (III.527–8), where he had been trained in reading, writing and disputation. Jankyn reads aloud from his 'book of wikked wyves' (685) to his wife, and she proves an apt pupil, albeit one who is able to turn the material to her own purposes (the comparisons with the self-promoting textual manipulations of the Friar and the Pardoner are obvious). Her primary target is a treatise included in that same collection, Saint Jerome's 'book agayn Jovinian' (675), wherein marriage is treated as a kind of damage-limitation exercise. Jerome had denigrated women who behaved rather like the Wife of Bath in rushing from one marriage into another. Alisoun counter-attacks with enthusiasm, being particularly skilled at undoing Jerome's readings of St Paul. The Apostle had said 'if thou take a wife, thou hast not sinned' (I Cor. 7:28, cf. 36), and that it is better to marry than to burn (I Cor. 7:8–9). Here, Jerome heavily emphasizes, Paul was not advocating such behaviour but thinking merely in terms of a concession to the human frailty he saw all around him (cf. I Cor. 7:6). Turning this argument on its head, Alisoun gleefully reads St Paul's rather grudging concession as unambiguous approval for multiple marriage: she is free to wed as often as she wants (III.49–52) and, should her husband die, no one can reprove another man for marrying her (84–6). This 'arch-wife' (cf. *ClT* IV.1195) presents virginity and continence as alternative life choices to marriage and, while acknowledging their higher status, roundly declares that they are not for her. In the face of all the theological disputations and 'glossing' of clerics, she understands well the truth of the 'gentil text', 'Be fruitful and multiply' (Genesis 1:28). Hence she has devoted her life to 'the actes and in fruyt of mariage' (III.105–114).

Alisoun is engaging not only with male authorities (and male authority in general) but also with male methods of argument, the techniques of disputation that were the staple method of intellectual inquiry in the schools, from which women were barred. If women had written the history books (which 'clerkes' traditionally have produced in their 'oratories'), 'They wolde han writen of men moore wikkednesse | Than al the mark of Adam [the entire male sex] may redresse' (III.695–6). Who painted the lion, tell me who? Here the Wife alludes to a proverb that holds that the lion is painted by the hunter; just so, the written record is in the hands of history's winners, with women being depicted disparagingly by male authors. A few years after Chaucer's death, similar sentiments were being expressed by Christine de Pizan. Reacting against Jean de Meun's satire on marriage, Christine remarks, 'because I am a woman I can speak better in this matter than one who has not had the experience (*experience*)'.[11] Given that (obviously) Chaucer lacks such female *experience*, it is difficult to know what to make of remarks in *The Wife of Bath's Prologue* that blatantly take the lion's side of the debate, particularly because elsewhere in the Prologue, Alisoun's Ovidian ancestry is made obvious, as she becomes the stereotypical nagging wife who marries for money and hastens her aged husbands' progress to the grave, only to make two imprudent marriages to younger men who, in turn, are after her money. On the other hand, she does manage to achieve a reconciliation with Jenkyn, after he burns his antifeminist anthology, an act that symbolizes how the Wife has gained mastery (in the sense of dominance and sovereignty) both within her marriage and over the 'masters', the authoritative teachers represented in that same book. Indeed, sometimes Alisoun sounds like a genuine *magister* rather than a conventionally outrageous teacher of the art of love, a debater who could give the glibly glossing Friar a run for his money. But only sometimes.

This textual conflict plays out through Alisoun's tale as well, which inverts the values of the usual 'loathly damsel' story. As told by other medieval writers, the manly virtue of the best knight available provided the tale's moral centre and the narrative pivot. He rescues the damsel in distress; true, she must get him to marry her, but his moral virtue is necessary to make the magic work and ensure her transformation to her true, young and beautiful self. Uniquely, Chaucer's version presents a wise and wonderful old woman asserting her natural moral superiority over a repugnant young knight who violently raped a maiden. This character makes himself even more despicable by complaining, it's a great pity that 'any of my nacioun' – a person of his distinguished family – should be 'disparaged' in so 'foule' a manner (1068–9), by being forced into an inappropriate marriage. It is not simply that his bride-to-be is old and ugly – that being quite enough for the other versions of the story – but she is of low birth as well. That protest is what Alisoun's wise old woman reacts against most vigorously, devoting 67 lines out of 106 (III.1109–214, the extent of her moral disquisition proper) to the argument that gentle is as gentle does. The problem of her 'poverte' receives 29, and her 'filthe and elde', a mere 9. The aspect of her status that is of greatest importance in the traditional narrative – her ugly appearance – is here judged to be the least important. Furthermore, *gentillesse* is the first topic to be discussed within this sequence, the clear implication being that, by acting in a morally churlish manner ('vileyns sinful dedes make a cherl'), the knight with no name has obscured his noble ancestry; how are the mighty fallen! At this point there is no mention of the knight's specific crime of rape. Probably there is no need for that, for he stands in sharp contrast to the woman of low birth who is one of nature's nobles; her *gentilesse* comes from personal actions, undertaken freely and with the aid of divine grace, rather than from social privilege. In sum, its source is God (1162–4).

However, at the end of the tale, this authoritative figure performs a sort of striptease, throwing off her moral garb to transform into a young woman who is, admittedly, both fair and good (thereby refuting the antifeminist implication that a woman cannot be both), but the final emphasis seems to be placed on the fact that she is good in bed, well able to 'fulfille' the keen sexual 'appetit' (cf. III.1218) of her partner, as previously expressed in that initial act of violent rape. (In Chaucer's day, marriage was often seen as a means of containing male desire, keeping it within acceptable bounds.) Evidently the Wife wishes to associate herself with this sexual plenitude, for she goes on to make a general prayer for husbands just like him: may 'Jhesu Crist us sende | Housbondes meeke [compliant], yonge, and fressh abedde' (1258–9). Here we are reminded that she, too, is in the market for (yet another) husband. Ovidian sexuality and satire against women's wiles are back in position; the strident tones of Jean de Meun's Vielle are heard once more. A richly overdetermined character has reverted to a disempowering stereotype. But the ending of the Wife's tale cannot be taken as Chaucer's last word on the matter, for there is no 'last word' offered at any stage of her performance, rather an elaboration of discourses that resist easy reconciliation.

At one point the rapist knight shows some signs of grace.

> 'My lady and my love, and wyf so deere,
> I put me in youre wise governance;
> Cheseth youreself which may be most pleasance   *Choose*
> And moost honour to yow and me also'.
>
> (III.1230–3)

Following this extraordinary declaration of respect and deference, the lady herself asks, then have I got *maistrie* over you? and he replies, Yes, certainly, wife; I hold it best. Here, it may be argued, is real mastery: sovereignty of soul, a spiritual dominance so manifest that it can be accepted without reservation. Although still 'loothly' and 'oold' at this point, she is, the knight seems to believe, wise enough to make the crucial decision for both of them – and eminently capable of acting in a way which will redound to their mutual 'honour'. That phrase recalls Jankyn's pacific words to Alisoun –

> 'Myn owene trewe wyf,
> Do as thee lust the terme of al thy lyf;
> Keep thyn honour, and keep eek myn estaat'
>
> (III.819–21)

– although the rapprochement of that much odder couple, the loathy damsel and the rapist-knight, has been achieved with greater speed and relative ease. This yarn is, after all, a fairytale, set in the days of King Arthur, when all this land was filled with fairies, and the hag makes her appearance on a green, following a dance of a kind associated with the elf-queen (III.989–99, cf. 857–61). But there is much more to it than that. The knight's words recall the discourse of mutual respect and deference found in Chaucer's *Tale of Melibee*, wherein the rich and powerful Melibeus gradually comes to accept the superior wisdom of his wife Prudence.

> '. . . wyf, by cause of thy sweete wordes, and eek for I have assayed and preved thy grete sapience and thy grete trouthe, I wol governe me by thy conseil in alle thyng'.
>
> 'Dame', quod Melibee, 'dooth youre wil and youre likynge; for I putte me hoolly in youre disposicioun and ordinaunce'.[12]

Read in light of these statements, it is hard to read the nameless knight's acceptance of his wife's 'wise governance' as spoken through the gritted teeth of a man who has been browbeaten into submission.

Chaucer sets up *The Tale of Melibee* with considerable gravity. Briskly distancing himself from the 'drasty' rhymes of *Sir Thopas*, and the Host's description of him as doll-like and 'elvyssh' (here meaning abstracted/other-worldly), he claims a literary kinship with the Four Evangelists who spoke of 'the peyne of Jhesu Crist' (VII.701–4, 943–12). While staying true to, and preserving the truth of, the overall 'sentence'[profound meaning], each of those writers conducted his 'tellyng' in his own way. Just so, Chaucer will give his own version of another story that has been 'told somtyme in sondry wyse | Of sondry folk', the 'moral tale vertuous' of Melibee (940–2). Several versions of this story do indeed survive from the later Middle Ages. Originally written in Latin by Albertinus of Brescia, sometime after 1336 Renaud de Louens made a French translation. Chaucer follows Renaud closely. There is little difference, then, between the French and English treatises, not only in *sentence* but also in textual detail. Obviously, the languages are different, but Chaucer does not mention that matter here, in marked contrast with the prologue to *The Second Nun's Tale*, where the fact that important doctrine is being explained 'in Englissh' is given considerable emphasis (VIII.2, 87, 106). Perhaps that particular difference is being occluded even as the point about narrative differences is being exaggerated to bring Chaucer somewhat closer to the *auctores* of Holy Writ, so that some of their prestige may rub off on him: authority by association.

The *Tale of Melibee* itself is a discourse on the operation of prudence – 'right reason applied to action' (to quote Aquinas),[13] a virtue that resides in the practical reason, first taking counsel, then judging what is best to be done, and finally commanding that this should be implemented in action. Hence prudence is a crucial virtue for the 'active life' as followed by men of secular estate – men like Melibee, who must decide on whether vengeance and punishment or 'grace and mercy' is the best way to respond to the assault on his daughter Sophie (representative of wisdom). Eventually Melibee listens to Prudence, and forgives his enemies. But initially he treats her as a lippy wife rather than the authoritative voice of right reason – an entertaining disjunction between vehicle and tenor. If I followed your advice and ceded you 'power', he tells Prudence, 'Every wight wolde holde me thane a fool', not least because 'alle women been wikke [wicked]'.[14] Even in the neverland of personification allegory, it seems, normative gender roles must be affirmed, and the pedagogic authority of women held suspect. The threat posed by female *maistrie* is as acute here as it is in the *Wife of Bath's Prologue and Tale*, although Prudence's rapid-fire allegation of *auctoritees* is far less problematic than Alisoun's.

Melibee resists giving Prudence the 'maistrie' over him on the grounds that 'if the wyf have maistrie, she is contrarious to hir housbonde'.[15] Likewise, in *The Parson's Tale* may be found the assertion that, where the woman has the mastery, there is too much confusion. Christ did not make Eve out of the head of Adam, 'for she sholde nat clayme to greet lordshipe. For ther as the womman hath the maistrie, she maketh to muche desray [disorder]'.[16] But Prudence is scrupulously careful not to claim 'greet lordshipe' over Melibee. If a man were advised only by those who have 'lordshipe and maistrie of his persone', then he would receive little counsel, she declares. The point is that as a woman and a wife, she does not possess such power. Rather than asserting the authority she possesses as the personification of prudence, Chaucer's text has her defer to Melibee's husbandly authority. It is important to notice that Prudence's teaching (Melibee certainly regards his wife's counsel as such) takes place in the private space of the family home, and when she shows her husband's adversaries the error of their ways, this is done likewise in 'a pryvee place', well out of the public eye. In persuading Melibee to listen to her, Prudence cites as precedents four biblical women (Rebekah, Judith, Abigail and Esther) who, according to the orthodox theological treatment, did not presume to preach or teach publicly but advised their relatives and leaders in a discreet manner. Melibee's blushes are spared, his manly *maistrie* left intact.

A family home was deemed 'private' space, as indeed was a nunnery, whereas a church pulpit and a university classroom were regarded as 'public' spaces, and hence prohibited to women, on the grounds that 'it is a shame for a woman to speak in the church'; if women 'would learn anything, let them ask their husbands at home' (I Cor. 14:34–35). Thus St Paul. Elsewhere he declares, 'I suffer not a woman to teach, nor to use authority over the man' (I Tim. 2:12). Those statements are reiterated again and again in late-medieval denials of priestly authority to women. But some of Wyclif's opponents felt that he had challenged this status quo, as when Thomas Netter, Carmelite theologian and confessor to King Henry V, accused him of being a shameless worker for women, having dared to claim that a woman might be suitable as a priest or bishop, even as a pope. Netter goes on to raise the spectre of heretical female preachers celebrating masses and other sacraments. In fact, Wyclif's few comments on the subject are much less exciting than Netter's comments would have us think, and Lollard women priests seem to have existed mainly in the fantasies of fearful churchmen. But in 1393 a Welsh Lollard, Walter Brut, was tried for a number of heresies, including the belief that women have the power to preach and, in certain situations, administer the sacraments. Here, then, is a useful context within which to read Chaucer's 'lyf of Seinte Cecile' (VIII.554).

The Second Nun does allow Cecile a preaching role, but of a carefully limited kind and within the historical context of the persecution of the early church in pagan Rome. On their wedding night, in bed with Valerian, the man she has been forced to marry, Cecile instructs him 'pryvely' concerning her vocation, revealing that a guardian angel will strike him dead if he should seek anything other than 'clene love' with her, a spiritual marriage involving sexual abstinence (VIII.141–61). Having converted Valerian, Cecile moves on to her brother-in-law Tiburce, telling him about the Holy Trinity and preaching to him, on a one-to-one basis, about Christ's coming and death (VIII.338–47). Subsequently, thanks to her 'wise loore' the officers who are sent to force her to sacrifice to Jupiter also become Christians (VIII.414–16). However, Cecile's most substantial proselytizing – an act of public instruction – does not come until the time of her martyrdom. Half-dead, with her head partially severed from her body, she manages to teach and preach for three whole days:

> ... nevere cessed hem the feith to teche
> That she hadde fostred; hem she gan to preche ...
>
> (VIII.538–9)

Thus Cecile's specially privileged position is dramatically, indeed shockingly, established. Orthodox churchmen accepted that women had the right to preach publicly in special situations, and situations do not get more special than this.

The extent to which Cecile defers to the ubiquitous Pope Urban, a saint in hiding but available when needed, is quite remarkable. She may have converted Valerian and Tiburce, but Urban baptizes them – as he has every right to do, as an ordained clergyman with the authority to administer the sacraments. Furthermore, following the conversion by Valerian and Tiburce of the head-prefect Maximus and several torturers, she promptly brings a team of priests to this gathering, so that all may be christened (VIII.372–80). Given the exceptional situation in which this beleaguered group of Christians is struggling to survive, lay baptism would have been perfectly acceptable (as per the standard teaching on this most fundamental of all the sacraments), but Chaucer does not do anything to complicate the doctrine that the sacrament of baptism should be handled by the proper officials. He seems keen to keep the saint well away from the subversive possibilities that Wyclif and his followers had explored. Institutional church authority is being respected to a remarkably high degree.

In any case, this manner of presenting Saint Cecelia is quite appropriate for a nun, who lacked access to the public space of the university classroom, or any direct experience of disputation technique of the kind the Wife of Bath had managed to acquire by dint of her association with an Oxford student. Here Chaucer seems to be reusing a text he had prepared earlier (the 'Lyf of Seynt Cecile' is included in a list of the poet's works in *LGW* F Pro 426), and it is tempting to see *The Second Nun's Prologue* as the statement of an ambitious male translator, who is commending to his readers – the nun's listening audience of Canterbury pilgrims not getting a look in here – a virtuoso rendering of a Latin saint's life in rhyme royal stanzas, his achievement being topped off with the prayer to the Virgin Mary that Dante had put in St Bernard of Clairvaux's mouth in *Paradiso*, XXXIII. On the other hand, we would expect a nun to be familiar with Marian hymnology, and few, if any, among Chaucer's initial audience could have identified the Dantean material.

The 'konnyng' of the first nun on Chaucer's fictional pilgrimage, the Prioress, is also determined by what she would have learned through 'the service dyvyne' (GP I.122), the liturgy. Her initial text is Psalm 8:2–3, 'O Lord, our Lord, how admirable is thy name in the whole earth! For thy magnificence is elevated above the heavens. Out of the mouth of infants and of sucklings thou hast perfected praise' (cf. *PrPro* VII.453–9). These verses form the Introit that begins the Mass of the Innocents in Sarum Use. Eglentyne uses them to emphasize that divine praise is performed not only by 'men of dignitee' but also 'by the mouth of children', for 'on the brest soukynge | Somtime shewen they thyn heriynge [worship]'. Psalm 8:2 is echoed later, when the Prioress speaks of how 'grete God' has 'parfournest' (perfected) his 'laude | By mouth of innocentz, lo, heere thy myght!' (VII.607–8). This comes just before the 'litel clergeon [schoolboy]', his throat cut, resumes his performance of the *Alma redemptoris mater*, the liturgical song at the very centre of the Prioress's own 'song' (487) – and in itself further evidence of this nun's religious training, for it is one of the four antiphons of the Blessed Virgin sung at the end of the office of Compline.

The Prioress allies herself with young innocents, infants and sucklings to a quite remarkable extent, rather than (as one might expect) adopting a maternal role in relation to them, in emulation of the motherhood of Mary that she celebrates so effusively in her prologue and illustrates so spectacularly in her tale. Several prominent medieval theologians, including Augustine, Anselm and Bernard of Clairvaux, had likened the divine love for humanity to that which a mother lavishes on her child, both in her womb and during its early experience in the world; the comparison was developed substantially by the English holy woman Julian of Norwich (d. *c.*1416). In particular, the process of nourishment whereby a Christian is fed by the divine word was sometimes compared to breastfeeding. Hildegard of Bingen (1098–1179) cast herself in the role of nurturing mother when she predicted how 'these daughters of mine' (the nuns whom she, as an abbess, had in her charge) 'will lament when their mother dies, for they will no longer suckle her breasts'.[17]

In light of these testimonies, the extent and nature of Madame Eglentyne's self-effacement is remarkable. Rather than offering herself as a source of spiritual nurture, she herself, it seems, is in need of nurture. Every bit as much as the murdered *clergeon*, the Prioress requires divine grace to guide her song, this being (as she presents the issue) the ultimate, and the only, basis of its authority. Indeed, in relation to the Virgin Mary's supreme 'magnificence' (VII.474), Eglentyne is comparable to an even younger child.

> But as a child of twelf month oold, or lesse,
> That kan unnethes any word expresse,   *hardly*
> Right so fare I, and therfore I yow preye,
> Gydeth my song that I shal of yow seye.
>
> (VII.484–7)

The *clergeon*'s own youthfulness is emphasized, along with the parenting skills of his earthly mother, a widow woman who taught him to worship Christ's mother, thereby prompting his (fatal) interest in the *Alma redemptoris*, with its praise of the 'kind mother of the Redeemer'. This 'newe Rachel' (VII.627) follows the model of the Old Testament figure who wept for her children (Jer. 31:15), a passage read in Matt. 2:18 as a prophecy of Herod's Massacre of the Innocents (and which was part of the gospel for the Mass of the Holy Innocents). Moreover, Rachel was often seen as a prefiguration of the Virgin Mary, who wept for her son at the Crucifixion. A long line of lamenting mother figures is thereby established. The self-infantalizing Prioress is not part of it.

How should we regard this self-infantalization? Being childlike is a good thing, according to Christ Himself. At Matt. 18:2–3 we read of how Jesus called 'unto him a little child, set him in the midst of them. And said . . . unless you be converted and become as little children, you shall not enter into the kingdom of heaven'. Which is consonant with Christ's earlier statement that the 'Lord of heaven and earth' has hid many things 'from the wise and prudent and hast revealed them to little ones' (Matt. 11:25). But the suspicion remains that the Prioress is like a child in a negative sense – childish, trivial, immature. A harsh reading of her piety would find here an image of ignorance posing as innocence. A nun whose 'wayk' and superficial 'konnyng' has been learnt by rote, even as the little *clergeon* learned the *Alma redemptoris*. And whose misplaced love of little creatures (her small dogs, the mouse caught in a trap, GP I.144–9) finds expression in her sentimental portrait of the suffering 'litel' (an adjective repeated again and again), 'smale' and 'tendre' body of the murdered child. On the other hand, this could be read as good tear-jerking technique, the child's vulnerability being heightened to enlist an intensely affective response. At the tale's end the abbot and monks of the convent weep profusely, and the Canterbury pilgrims are rendered wonderfully 'sobre' (VII.692). Eglentyne's emotionalism seems to be valued highly. An alternative interpretation is that at least certain aspects of her narrative – particularly its crass anti-Semitism – are reprehensibly naïve, the target of a satirist who wishes to distance himself from some of those views. But is such an interpretive move an act of wish fulfilment by modern readers who wish to rescue Geoffrey Chaucer from the charge of anti-Semitism? That too would be reprehensibly naïve.

Yet views better than Eglentyne's were available. Medieval popes condemned that most grotesque version of the depiction of Jews as infanticides, the so-called Blood Libel, according to which Jews murdered Christian children to obtain their blood for religious rituals. Writing in 1271–6, Gregory X offered Jews 'the shield of our protection through the clemency of Christian piety', in respect of accusations made 'of secretly carrying off and killing . . . Christian children and of making sacrifices of the heart and blood of these very children'. Sometimes Christians have simply invented such accusations to extort money, Gregory continues, and orders that 'Jews seized under such a silly pretext be freed from imprisonment'.[18] Fine words, but in the real world the papal shield of projection did not extend very far.

So, then, where do we locate cosmopolitan Chaucer, who during his European travels may have become aware of the pogroms perpetrated against Jewish communities, which suffered horrifically when crusading fervour ran high? Maybe he was aware of papal ridicule of the Blood Libel and accordingly had little if any sympathy with a character whose views can be seen as simplistic, narrow-minded and provincial. Or maybe not. Provincialism works in many ways; local piety enforces its own loyalties. In the last stanza of her tale (VII.684–90) the Prioress alludes to the death of 'yonge Hugh of Lyncoln', allegedly murdered by Jews in 1255. The cult of this boy martyr flourished in Chaucer's day, and several prominent aristocrats, including John of Gaunt, had strong ties with Lincoln Cathedral, which was a popular pilgrimage destination, thanks to Hugh's shrine. Besides, a former king of England, Henry III, had played a prominent role in the punishment of the Jews accused of Hugh's murder. Church and state had colluded in this crucial historical event, which set the stage for the general expulsion of the Jews from England in 1290. Even though few Jews were living in the country at the time when Chaucer wrote *The Prioress's Tale*, populist anti-Semitism kept the memory of such events alive; little wonder that Madame Eglentyne can remark that young Hugh was slain only 'a litel while ago' (VII.686).

Therefore it is hard to argue that Chaucer's (unique) location of the story of the martyred boy singer 'in Asye' is designed to distance its events from England and from English history. In her concluding verse, the Prioress brings it all back home. Furthermore, this remote location allows her to describe and exploit the distress of Christians who are unprotected by a Christian ruler like King Henry III. Englishmen can share a sense of victimhood with the beleaguered Asian Christians of the tale, even as their confidence in the ultimate success of their cause is vindicated. Thus *The Prioress's Tale* offers a bittersweet affect of considerable force, a powerful fantasy that has considerable religious significance and consequence for Chaucer's England. On this approach, it is hard to read the tale as satirizing a childish narrator.

And yet Chaucer has gone to considerable lengths to present this story as Eglentyne's property. The reiterated 'quod she' (VII.454, 581) reminds us of who is talking, even as the euphemistic reference to the 'wardrobe' in which the Jews purged 'hire entraille' (VII.572–3) recalls the prissy Prioress of the General Prologue, who can easily be imagined as reluctant to speak indecorously (and let a word like 'pryvee'[19] pass her lips), although she wants her audience to be revolted by the thought of Jewish defecation. In many other Canterbury Tales, discordant voices compete for authorial possession of the material. In contrast, *The Prioress's Tale* is entirely the Prioress's. No other voice intervenes to claim a piece of the action. Either Chaucer is invested in that single voice, or for some reason – whether social, intellectual, or ethical – he wants it to be heard, loud and clear, but not as his own. There we must leave the matter. Interpretation can go no further.

Power and patience: Custance, Grisilde and Virginia

> Wommen are born to thraldom and penance,
> And to been under mannes governance.
>
> (*MLT* II.286–7)

Custance's words neatly sum up the subject-position occupied by the women in the next three tales to be discussed, wherein heroines are presented as making great sacrifices for their beliefs – or, more accurately, for beliefs that they are obliged, by dominant males, to try and test. Hence they appear as more sacrificed than sacrificing. A Roman emperor sends away his daughter (who also is identified as the 'doghter of hooly chirche', II.675) to enable the Christian conversion of Muslim Syria, a role she subsequently will play in (largely) heathen Britain as well. A Lombard lord subjects his low-born wife to the most extreme of tests to discover how high womanly virtue can reach. And a pagan knight sacrifices his daughter, quite literally, rather than allowing her virtue to be sullied by a corrupt judge. All three narratives highlight the relationship between patriarchal power and 'patience', by which is meant the calm endurance of misfortune and suffering, a willingness to bear wrongs with self-restraint.[20] This virtue underpins the moral authority of Custance, Grisilde, and Virginia.

The convoluted tale of Custance is told by the 'Sargeant of the Law' as described in the General Prologue; a wealthy and well-dressed lawyer, at the top of his profession, and a prudent buyer of land. In estates satire, lawyers are frequently attacked for being avaricious and charging excessive fees. Nothing of the kind is found here – at least not obviously. On the contrary, the Man of Law's own prologue warns against the perils of poverty and commends rich merchants who enjoy secure social positions. As masters of their own destiny, they travel across 'lond and see' (II.127) as they please, going about their business freely – in obvious contrast with the lot of the passive emperor's daughter who is forced to sail to unknown lands and on two occasions is set adrift in a rudderless ship. 'All the days of povre men been wikke' (118), remarks the opinionated Sargeant, without allowing any moral or spiritual advantages to the state. His initial disquisition on poverty is based on a passage in Pope Innocent III's *De miseria condictionis humane*.[21] However, Innocent had gone on to condemn the notion that 'a person is valued according to his wealth'. The Man of Law's subsequent remarks seem rather to affirm it.

Because of their travels to many regions of the world, merchants are well informed about politics ('th'estaat | Of regnes'). Furthermore – a fascinating touch, this – they are said to be the 'fadres' of tidings and tales about both peace and strife (II.128–30). So then, Chaucer – who was to be celebrated as the father of English poetry – attributes paternity of an abundance of stories to merchants. And has his Man of Law declare that he himself would have been 'desolaat' of tales (quite lacking in stories) had he not been 'taughte' one by a merchant, the one he proceeds to tell.

It begins with an account of merchants' tales – specifically, the 'tidynges' a group of wealthy Syrian merchants bring home with them following a visit to Rome. There, according to 'the commune voys of every man' (II.155), the emperor's daughter Custance is reckoned (cf. 'rekene', 158) to surpass all other women in 'goodnesse' as well as 'beautee' (158). The 'chapmen riche' pass on this valuation of Custance to their lord the Sultan of Syria, who delights in hearing travelers' stories and learning about 'wondres' (176–82). So wondrous is Custance that the Sultan falls in love with her, this being seen as a diktat of destiny. The contrasts with Chaucer's source, a 'universal history' Nicholas Trevet wrote in Anglo-Norman, are remarkable. Having no other child, the emperor Tiberius had his daughter taught the Christian faith 'and instructed by learned masters (*mestres*) in the seven sciences', together with various languages (which will be useful during her many wanderings). In Custance's thirteenth year, a group of pagan merchants visits her father's court, 'carrying much rich and diverse merchandise', whereupon she preaches (*precha*) the Christian faith to them and has them baptized. It is these christened merchants who return to their Sultan, praising Custance for her 'very high and noble mind and wisdom' together with her 'great and wondrous beauty, and gentility and noble lineage'.[22] Chaucer's heroine simply has all the virtues appropriate to a marriageable woman of noble lineage. 'A person is valued according to his wealth' (to return to Innocent's dictum). The Man of Law's merchants judge Custance according to her value in the international marriage market, her conventional and non-threatening virtues (including her piety) being major parts of the package. This woman's heart may be a 'verray chambre of hoolynesse' (II.167), but this is manifested through decorous almsgiving rather than precocious preaching.

Here, as throughout the tale, Custance has value impressed upon her rather than being a locus of authority, a source from which value emanates. Mercantile reckoning gives way to papal recognition of the major benefits that will accrue to the Christian faith through her marriage. Therefore Custance must go to a 'strange' and 'Barbre nacioun' (II.268–9, 281), 'be bounden under subjeccioun' (270) to a man she does not know. Yet she will obey her parent's 'wille', and seek to 'fulfille' the 'heestes' (commands) of Christ. 'No fors [matter] though I spille!', she adds ruefully (282–5).

In fact, Custance survives, but the Sultan and the other Syrian converts, along with her Roman entourage, are massacred. After a long period of exile, Custance's ship makes land in pagan Northumbria, where she encounters a kindly steward and his wife, Hermengyld, who is much taken with her, and becomes a Christian. Custance's role in this process consists of prayer and penance, which Christ rewards by converting Hermengyld 'thurgh his grace' (536–9). In Trevet's chronicle we hear of how Hermengyld 'listened humbly and devoutly', and evidently at some length, 'to the teaching of the faith from the mouth of Custance', after which 'instruction' she 'devoutly begged to be baptized according to the form of Holy Church'.[23] Chaucer also downplays the part Trevet assigned to Custance in curing the blindness of one of the few surviving native Christians, even occluding the fact that this was a miracle (561–7). A comparable change is evident when Chaucer recounts how the 'theef' who attempted to rape Custance on board ship falls overboard, as she struggles 'wel and myghtily' (921); thus God gave 'this wayke womman' the strength to defend herself (932–3). Trevet's more robust and self-directed heroine came 'secretly behind his back and pushed him into the sea'.[24]

'Allas, what myghte she seye?' the narrator asks of Custance, when she has been accused of Hermengyld's murder. Indeed, she has little to say, not just here but throughout the text. On first meeting the Constable, she addresses him in 'a maner Latyn corrupt', although he manages to understand her. Trevet's character is able to speak Saxon, Olda's tongue, with considerable competence; as mentioned previously in the Anglo-Norman chronicle, she is 'skilled in various languages'.[25] But Chaucer's Custance is no Cecelia – a woman who preaches with gusto, albeit in carefully delimited circumstances. Rather Custance serves as an instrument of God's will in the first instance by furthering conversion through marriage with powerful pagans and subsequently through her role as the mother of Maurice, the future Roman emperor. Thus she must set her holiness aside a little at night to ensure that she falls pregnant with, and gives birth to, a male heir (II.708–15). This mildly salacious passage, unprecedented in Trevet, has a larger point to make. Custance's relationship with the once-pagan King Alla of Northumbria is no spiritual marriage of the kind that Cecelia achieved with Valerian. Marriage was sometimes seen as a hindrance to holiness, as in *The Second Nun's Tale*. But in this Sargeant's tale, marriage and motherhood, which entail continuous obedience and acquiescence on Custance's part, are deemed the best expressions of her holiness. We are told that Jesus 'made Alla wedden' this 'hooly mayden' – 'thus hath Crist ymaad Custance a queene' (690–3). There is no doubt where the power lies.

The devil also has his female instruments: 'Thyn instrument so . . . | Makestow of wommen, whan thou wolt bigile' (II.370–1). They appear as the tale's two mother-in-laws, the Sultaness and Donegild, who are castigated as 'mannysh' (782) and serpents in womanly guise (358–64); here are the narrative's 'feendly' creatures (cf. 751), rather than the monstrous birth of which Donegild falsely accuses Custance. Against such iniquity her conventional female virtues shine forth; this calumniated queen's acceptance of the 'governance' of God and men is required by the triumphalist narrative. Custance's roles as daughter (of the emperor and of the Holy Church) and mother ensure the smooth lineal descent and unbroken hegemony of both the Christian faith and the ruling Roman dynasty. Those interests manifestly converge when Maurice is 'Emperour | Maad by the Pope' (1121–2). Thus Chaucer makes political as well as moral virtue of passivity.

The 'pacience' of Chaucer's Grisilde involves a willingness to bear with fortitude all the adversities life (or, more specifically, her husband) throws at her. Here is no drama played out on a worldwide stage, although political and dynastic issues are involved, inasmuch as it centres on the behaviour of Walter, Marquess of Saluzzo, who, 'to speke of lynage', was the 'gentilleste yborn of Lumbardye' (IV.71–2). However, this is essentially a small-scale domestic production that has wider moral (and even theological) significance thrust upon it – a process rendered quite explicit in the text, with alternative reader-responses being on prominent display.

Gentillesse is no respector of place, whether geographic or social, according to the Wife of Bath's loathly and low-born damsel. Take fire and bear it to the darkest house between here and the Caucasus mountains, and it will burn as brightly as if twenty thousand men were beholding it (IV.1139–43). In the case of the Clerk's tale, this gift of grace has been sent to the 'west syde of Ytallie', down at the foot of Mount Vesuvius (57–8), to a woman, named Grisilde, who is the 'povrest of hem alle' (204). Walter has been encouraged by his subjects (who are eager to see him beget an heir) to marry someone 'born of the gentilleste and of the meeste | Of al this land' (131–2). Instead he marries Grisilde, on the principle that 'under low degree | Was ofte vertu hid' (425–6) and spends the rest of the tale testing this belief to the utmost, with an experimental zeal as intense as that which (to judge by the Canon's Yeoman) alchemists brought to their search for the Philosopher's Stone.

'To tempte his wyf was set al his entente' (IV.735). Here the verb bears the sense of testing someone's character, endurance, and strength. It is used frequently in *The Clerk's Tale*, as is its synonym 'assay'. Following her marriage, Grisilde proves herself worthy in every respect, performing not only traditionally female feats of household management but also serving the 'commune profit', resolving discord and, in her husband's absence, settling disputes among the nobility. Thus she successfully undergoes a rigorous process of 'assay by preve', to return to that line from the *Legend of Good Women*, G Pro. 28. But for Walter this is not enough. As Francis Petrarch (1304–74) puts it in his *Historia Griseldis* (the authoritative version of the story to which the Clerk ostentatiously defers at the beginning and the end of his own narrative), Walter was seized by a desire 'more amazing than worthy' to try further (*experiendi altius*) 'the faithfulness of his dear wife', which already had been sufficiently proved (*satis expertam*), and to repeat the test again and again (*iterum retemptandi*).[26] Chaucer renders those sentiments as follows.

He hadde assayed hire ynogh bifore,	*enough*
And foond hire evere good; what neded it	
Hire for to tempte, and alwey moore and moore,	*test*
Though som men preise it for a subtil wit?	
But as for me, I seye that yvele it sit	*evil*
To assaye a wyf whan that it is no nede,	
And putten hire in angwyssh and in drede.	*anguish*

(IV.456–62)

When the testing is finally over, Walter tries to justify himself to Grisilde by claiming that he acted not out of 'malice' or 'crueltee'| But for t'assaye in thee thy wommanheede' (1074–5). Here Petrarch has him explain that he is curious and given to experiments (*curiosum atque experientem esse*), but 'not impious: I have proved my wife rather than condemned her'.[27] Perhaps here is why the

Clerk raises the possibility that someone might praise Walter's assaying as the practice of a 'subtil wit': we would expect 'subtiltee and heigh wit' (to borrow the Summoner's idiom) from a keen researcher. But the Clerk rejects Walter's behavior as 'yvele'. When Grisilde is said to lack 'subtiltee' (at 687–95) this is seen as a good thing, indicative of the total absence of 'malice' or cruelty in her character. The 'sad' (steadfast) face (694) she presents during the traumatizing removal of her children (694) is due to virtue rather than hardheartedness. Her maternal love is plain and simple, in contrast with the zeal for intricate experimentation that drives her husband.

Walter's attempt to discover the ultimate reaches of wifely passivity has reached obsessive proportions (perhaps even fetishistic proportions: this Marquis of Saluzzo anticipates the Marquis de Sade). 'These proofs (*experimenta*) of conjugal good will and faithfulness might have been enough for the most demanding husband; but some people, having begun a course of action, will not desist. No, they press on further, clinging to their plan'.[28] Thus Petrarch. Chaucer reiterates this (IV.701–3), presenting Walter as continuing 'To tempte [test] his wyf as he was first disposed' (707). He has something of the mad scientist about him; here is a governor who treats his subjects like so many lab rats. For his exercise of raw power extends beyond the domestic sphere to the way he rules the state of Saluzzo. When put under pressure to marry, the Marquis insists on handling the situation his way, with full compliance from his advisors. He simply assumes that because Grisilde's father, Janicula, is his 'feithful lige man' he will do anything he asks (309–20). A loyal servant pretends to be an infanticide, not once but twice, on Walter's orders; he is able to get papal bulls specially forged and sent from Rome – all in order to pursue 'the experiment he had conceived'. 'Assay by preve' has its dark side; the desire to see everything with one's own eyes can lead to hell, as the Friar's over-inquisitive summoner painfully discovered.

The Clerk appeals to Petrarch not only as the teacher (IV.27, 40) and *auctour* (1141) of the tale but also as its commentator. Petrarch had reworked Boccaccio's relatively straightforward story of a selfish husband showing his wife who's boss and read it as a means of understanding the hierarchical relationship between God and man. St James is quoted as saying that on many occasions, God 'tests (*appreuve*) us and makes us suffer grievous punishment'. (Here I follow an anonymous French translation of Petrarch's *Historia Griseldis* that Chaucer seems to have used.) Therefore this tale applies to steadfast men also, although Petrarch expresses doubt 'if there are any who for our creator and redeemer Jesus Christ could suffer and patiently endure what, for her mortal husband, this poor little wife endured'.[29] Chaucer incorporated all of that. God, who 'preeveth folk al day' (1155), is identified as an appropriate and utterly justified tester, authorized by a rationale that does not apply to Walter; it is reasonable that the Almighty should try and temper his own creation ('preeve that he wroughte', 1152). Thus both the Italian laureate and the English poet seek to transcend the sufferings of a 'poor little wife' by implicating an objective large and grand enough to suit the extensive experimentation which drives the plot.

But Chaucer does not give Petrarch the last word. Instead his Clerk adds 'o word' more, remarking cynically that, these days, it would be hard to find in a large town two or three Grisildes who could endure the 'assayes' to which the original paragon was subjected. Her gold has now been alloyed with baser metal (1163–9): alchemy in reverse. Then, by way of (mock) praise of the Wife of Bath and all her 'secte' of dominating wives, he offers a 'song' asserting that Grisilde and her patience are things of the past, both dead and buried in Italy. Finally, Harry Bailly has his say; he wishes that his wife could hear this 'legende'(1212a–g). Apparently she is a member of that abovementioned 'secte' and would benefit from some Grisildan patience.

Several of the story's redactors regarded Grisilda, in all seriousness, as a 'mirror for married women'. That is Philippe de Mézières' phrase, from his own version of the story; elsewhere he wished King Richard II a wife like Grisilda.[30] The compiler of *Le Ménagier de Paris* (*c.*1392–94) adopts a similar stance: women should love their husbands in silence and submission, and likewise humankind should 'suffer patiently the tribulations that God . . . sends them'. But he also says that he does not expect such obedience from his own wife: he is no marquis, she no shepherdess. There is, he believes, excessive cruelty in the tale. And he assures his young spouse that its oppressive testing is not relevant to her own life. 'I am not so foolish, presumptuous, or immature as to fail to recognize the inappropriateness of my abusing or testing you in such ways. God keep me from trying you (*vous en essayer*) in this or any other manner, under any false pretenses!' Her worth has already been proved to him, by her good reputation and that of her forebears, together with 'what I sense and see with my own eyes and know from real experience (*de vraye experience*)'.[31] No other *assay* is necessary for the Ménagier.

It would seem, then, that certain medieval readers reacted strongly, and in different ways, to Grisilda's patience. Chaucer participated in this rich reception by seeing her, by turns, as a wife put in a state of anguish and fear, a pauper oppressed by a prince, an object of excessive experimentation, a means of justifying the ways of God to man, and a memorial of extinct female virtue. Ever and always, she is an exemplar of wifely obedience and submission in extreme circumstances. Virginia, the heroine of the Physician's rather arid little tale, exemplifies daughterly obedience and submission in similarly (or even more) extreme circumstances; in both tales Chaucer engages with the conventional didacticism of 'conduct literature' – a genre tasked with finding good reasons for deference to patriarchal authority.

The Physician's patriarchal authority figure is Virginius. Faced with a travesty of justice that brings his daughter Virginia into the power of a corrupt judge, Apius, who lusts after her, he decides she must die rather than suffer sexual defilement. The heroine's 'mooder deere' is obviously alive (VI.119) but scarcely visible in this grisly narrative, and unnamed. Virginius and Virginia are well named. A loving father asks his 'deere doghter' (208) to take her death 'in pacience' (223), because preservation of her virginity is the moral imperative, and she bows to his will with Grisilde-like passivity.

> 'Blissed be God that I shal dye a mayde!
> Yif me my deeth, er that I have a shame;
> Dooth with youre child youre wil, a Goddes name!'
>
> (VI.248–50)

Virginius then strikes off her head, and carries it by the hair to where Apius is holding court. This shocking spectacle incites the populace to rise up against a magistrate whom they distrusted in any case (and his lechery was well known); thrown into prison, he commits suicide. Others who were party to this 'cursedness' (the case involving Virginia, or Apius's corruption in general?) are hanged (275–6), but the sentence against Claudius, the servant who had been forced to bring a false charge against Virginia, is commuted to exile, thanks to Virginius' plea. His 'pitee' for that man saves his life (270–4): a telling contrast with the 'pitous hand' with which he killed his own daughter (226). Yet again, man seems to be the measure of all things, and one man has chosen to respond to the desires of another by killing its unwitting object – all in the name of absolute justice, which exists above and beyond the decadent version embodied in Apius.

For Virginius is one of Chaucer's virtuous heathen (albeit the least appealing of the pack). This nobleman's treatment of his daughter is reminiscent of the familial sacrifices made by famous pagan politicians and philosophers, as commended, for example, by Saint Augustine in *De civitate Dei*.[32] The saint's prime example is Brutus, who had his own sons put to death because they had plotted a restoration of the Tarquinian monarchy and hence conspired against Roman freedom. 'Love of country drove him, and the immense love of praise', but this deed rendered Brutus a deeply unhappy man, no matter how it 'may be celebrated in days to come' (cf. *Aeneid*, VI.820–3). Although performed within the domestic rather than the political sphere, Virginius' action is of that kind. Augustine's examples of spectacular infanticide illustrate the superiority of Christianity, which does not oblige present-day believers to suppress their paternal feelings in such an extreme manner. As described by Livy, the Physician's professed *auctor* (although the *Roman de la Rose* was Chaucer's immediate source), the highest values of Virginius' time do seem to have required such a feat.

Although the Physician's 'studie was but litel on the Bible' (GP I.438) – doctors of medicine were frequently criticized for their worldliness – he does manage to cite the Old Testament story (yet another 'rash promise' tale) of Jephthah's Daughter (see Judges 11). Having promised God that, were he granted victory in battle, he would sacrifice the first thing he saw on returning home, Jephthah is obliged to offer up his own daughter, who rushes out to greet him. However, he grants the girl a stay of execution, when she requests two months' grace, 'that I may go about the mountains . . . and may bewail my virginity' (Judges 11:37). Virginia cites that *auctoritee*, in asking her father to give her time 'My deeth for to compleyne a litel space' (VI.238–9). But the 'space' allowed is 'litel' indeed, far shorter than two months in duration. Therefore some have detected petulance in Virginia's request, a girlish rebuke of the haste with which her father acts – and a crack in her façade of passivity. Alternatively, Chaucer is upping the emotional ante, enhancing the pathos of Virginia's situation by alluding to a sadness of even longer duration. To the same end, he describes the girl putting both arms around her father's neck, as is her childish habit, when she begs for mercy (232–3). Finally she asks that he should strike 'softe' with his sword (252). Here that adverb, which has 'gently' as its usual sense, probably means something like 'not roughly' or 'unobtrusively':[33] Virginia would die with as little pain as possible and/or does not want to see the blow coming. (Indeed, she seems to be in a swoon when it does.) The Man of Law's Custance reminds her father of how she was 'fostred up so softe' as a child (II.275); Virginia's use of the word intimates an awful parody, perhaps even a perversion, of such parental tenderness.

The discourse of good child-rearing also appears in the Clerk's account of how Janicula, Grisilde's 'olde povre fader', 'fostred' her 'in greet reverence and charitee' (IV.221–2). In *The Physician's Tale* it is used more extensively; indeed, it dominates much of the narrative. Virginius says he had 'fostred up' his daughter with 'swich plesaunce' that she was 'nevere out' of his 'remembraunce' (VI.219–20). A surprisingly long passage on the duties of governesses and parents appears earlier in the tale (72–104; thus Chaucer fills out the brief narrative he found in the *Rose*). Old 'maistresses' who have the daughters of lords in their care should ensure that they themselves are virtuous, to enable them to teach virtue better. If their 'honestee' was ever compromised (sexual incontinence here being implied), they should have repudiated such misconduct long ago. When innocence is betrayed, that is the worst treason of all. Then 'Ye fadres and ye moodres eek also' are addressed: no matter how few children you may have, ensure that you keep them under careful 'surveiaunce'; show them good models of behavior in their own lives, and do not neglect your duty of 'chastisynge'. Spare the rod, and spoil the child.

The relevance of any of this to the narrative is questionable. Neither 'maistresse' nor mother is shown as involved in Virginia's education. Furthermore, not sparing the rod is one thing; substituting a sword for it is something else. Careless fosterage may indeed cause a child to 'perisse' (VI.99), but so will a violent paternal act; inflicting death seems a strange means of protecting one's offspring. In any case, the tale that follows is about the unkindness of strangers rather than familial negligence. To cap it all, the Physician proceeds to say that Virginia needed no instructor, 'no maistresse' at all (106), her virtue being innate, a product of nature – and her life was as a book to other young women, who could read there every good word and deed that is appropriate to maidenly conduct. So, then, this fourteen-year-old was, so to speak, self-taught, and functioned as a teacher of sorts. The moral message the Physician is struggling to assign to his tale seems to reach out to readers with instructional needs and moral dilemmas very different from those that concern its protagonists.

A similar point may be made about the tale's concluding passage (VI.277–86). Death comes unexpectedly; no one knows when and where God will 'smyte'. Moreover, even though their wickedness may be hidden from others, sinners suffer from their secret knowledge thereof; the worm of conscience gnaws within them. Who has the Physician in mind here? Apius, or even Claudius? The tale offers no account of any conscience-induced fears on their part; their sins quickly become the subject of public punishment. If the worm of conscience promoted Apius to commit suicide, we hear nothing of that. And the smiting at the centre of the story involves the death of an innocent rather than of a sinner. The Physician has told a self-deconstructing tale of nature and nurture, wherein the patient heroine's death seems due to a rigorous excess of fosterage rather than a deficit.

Endings: the Monk and the Parson

'This world nys but a thurghfare ful of wo,   *thoroughfare*
And we been pilgrymes, passynge to and fro'.
(*KnT* I.2847–8)

That is the *sentence* of Egeus, the aged father of Theseus. As a man who knows this world's mutability, and has seen it change 'bothe up and doun, | Joye after wo, and wo after gladnesse' (2839–41), he seeks to counsel his son. Theseus' response is necessarily selective: he has a vast empire to rule and a dynastic marriage to arrange. So the duke chooses to accentuate the upside, the 'joye' that follows 'wo'. 'After wo I rede us to me merye', he tells the assembled populace; indeed, they can make two sorrows into one perfect joy, by ensuring that Palamon and Emily marry (3067–72). Which, of course, they do, and *The Knight's Tale* ends with them living in happiness, prosperity and good health. What was a tragedy for Arcite, 'now in his colde grave' (2778), is a 'comedy' for them, to use the term in its medieval literary-theoretical sense of a narrative with a happy ending.

Such is the balance which the Knight intimates in his vigorous reaction against the Monk's collection of stories that inevitably end in 'wo' rather than 'joye'. This worldly prelate, who regards the Rule of St Benedict as too old and too strict for the present day (GP I.165–207), has chosen to present a relentlessly tragic vision of human life.

> Tragedie is to seyn a certeyn storie,
> As olde bookes maken us memorie,
> Of hym that stood in greet prosperitee,
> And is yfallen out of heigh degree
> Into myserie, and endeth wrecchedly.
> (VII.1973–7)

The 'contrarie' of this, the Knight retorts, is 'joye and greet solas', as when a man who has been in a lowly situation 'clymbeth up and wexeth [becomes] fortunat' – and stays that way, rather than falling back into misery (2771–9). Such a thing would be pleasing to hear. But Daun Piers (so named at 2792) is not interested in telling such a tale. Even the Host's invitation to say something about hunting (his greatest pleasure in life; cf. GP I.166) does not draw him out. He will talk of tragedy, and nothing else.

The Monk's theory of tragedy is essentially Boethian, derived from ideas in *De consolatione philosophiae*. At Book II, pr. 2, 38–40, Dame Philosophy poses the rhetorical question, 'What else is the cry of tragedy but a lament (*clamor*) that happy states are overthrown by the indiscriminate blows of fortune?' This underlies the Monk's statement, made at the beginning of his tale, that he 'wol biwaille [lament] in manere of tragedie | The harm of hem that stoode in heigh degree'. When good fortune decides to leave a man, that is the end of the matter; no one should trust in 'blynd prosperitee' (VII.1991–7). The implication is that those actions are indiscriminate. Certainly there is no suggestion that they are punitive. However, that alternative view of tragedy appears at the end of the tale, just before the Knight's intervention.

> Tragediës noon oother maner thyng
> Ne kan in syngyng crie ne biwaille   *bewail*
> But that Fortune alwey wole assaille
> With unwar strook the regnes that been proude...   *unexpected stroke,*
>   (VII.2761–4)   *kings*

Here Fortune is defined as functioning retributively, reacting against and punishing sin.

During his tale Daun Piers veers from one viewpoint to the other. Lucifer fell 'for his synne' (VII.2002), Adam for his 'mysgovernaunce' (2012). Sampson stupidly shared the secret of his power with Dalida (2047–94); Croesus, Nabugodonosor, Balthasar, Nero, Holofernes and Anthiochus are castigated for their pride. The case of Balthasar is particularly clear, because here the forsaking of Fortune (2241) is associated with an act of direct divine intervention. Because he was proud and did not fear God, the almighty inflicted great 'wreche' (vengeance) upon that ruler, and 'hym birafte the regne that he hadde' (2212–14). Others are ostensibly praised for their valour and might, including Hercules, Peter of Spain, Peter of Cyprus, Alexander and Julius Ceasar. No punishable fault is imputed to those once-powerful figures – an effect achieved by the omission of details that would enable a more nuanced judgment. The Ugolino narrative takes editorial obfuscation even further. Piers refers us to Dante for the full story (2459–63), without mentioning that 'the grete poete of Ytaille' had condemned the count of Donoratico to hell on account of his political treachery: any disruption of the horror, and hence the pathos, of this attenuated tale is thus avoided. In other cases the compression is so severe that the narrative line is hard to follow, and its moral significance even harder to gauge. However, the only woman in the collection, Cenobia, is allowed a modicum of complexity (2247–374). She fled 'office of wommen' (a bad thing to do according to *The Man of Law's Tale*)[34] but became a great warrior-queen (a good thing, inasmuch as it aligns her with King Alexander and his kind).

The standard medieval *auctoritees* concerning the nature of tragedy have not been reconciled. Indeed, they are fundamentally irreconcilable. So this vacillation on the Monk's part is hardly surprising. Piers struggles to stay on message by dealing in generalities, seeking to shock his audience again and again with the speed and unexpectedness of all the unfortunate falls which he recounts. There are plenty more where they came from – he has a hundred in his cell (1972). But the Knight has heard enough. A little 'hevynesse' is quite enough for many folk, he declares (2767–70). Harry Bailly agrees. The Monk's tale is annoying all the company, and if a man has no 'audience' there is no point in him telling his 'sentence' (2788–91). The Nun's Priest is asked to tell a 'myrie' tale, which he does with enthusiasm. For a moment the pilgrimage of this life seems rather more than a thoroughfare of woe.

But only for a moment. *Hevynesse* has merely been deferred. It returns at the end of the tales, when the Parson refuses to tell a mere 'fable' or fiction, quoting St Paul on the vanity of such 'wrecchednesse' (X.29–36; cf. p. 97 above). What people can expect from him is 'moralitee and virtuous mateere' (38). He will 'knytte up . . . this feeste and make an ende' accordingly, in the hope that his words, uttered at the end of their pilgrimage to Canterbury, will help direct them on the most glorious journey of all, to the Heavenly Jerusalem (48–51). He has found an audience. The pilgrims earnestly agree that it is best to 'To enden in som virtuous sentence' (63).

'A myrie tale in prose' is promised, as the Parson eschews both alliterative measure and rhyme. What we get is a treatise on penance, drawn from Latin into English, a priest's handbook made available in the vernacular to a wider audience, including layfolk. Basically, Chaucer seems to have drawn on Raymond of Peñafort's *Summa de poenitentia* and Peraldus's *Summa vitiorum*. But these works do not account for all of his materials. Other sources apparently were involved, particularly the anonymous *Summa virtutum de remediis anime*, which seems to underlie his account of the remedial virtues (which are directly opposed to the Seven Deadly Sins). Either Chaucer brought together extracts from several treatises on the virtues and vices (no simple task) or he used a compilation or compilations that have not yet been identified – or the truth lies somewhere in between.

Whatever the exact sources of the *Parson's Tale* may be, it seems obvious that the merriness it offers is rather different from that stirred by the *Nun's Priest's Tale*. Perhaps a broad definition of the term should be applied here. After all, Chaucer pronounced the staunchly moral *Melibee* a 'murye tale' (VII.964), and the holy woman Margery Kempe once claimed that 'it is full merry in heaven'.[35] A more robust response would be to question whether *The Parson's Tale* is either 'myrie' or a 'meditacioun' (X.55, cf. 69) or even a tale. It is appropriately called a 'litel tretys' in the *Retraction* (the use of 'litel' perhaps being a gesture of modesty), which proceeds to ask God to give the writer 'grace of verray penitence, confessioun and satisfaccioun to doon in this present lyf', so that he 'may been oon of hem at the day of doom that shulle be saved' – apt sentiments to follow a penitential 'tretys'. So, then, the *Retraction* seems firmly connected to *The Parson's Tale*, even as *The Parson's Prologue* is obviously designed to follow *The Manciple's Tale*. But the thematic and generic connections between *The Parson's Prologue* and *The Parson's Tale* on the one hand, and between the *Retraction* and the entire *Canterbury Tales* on the other, are matters of debate.

The Canterbury Tales is very much a work in progress. We can find statements in a given tale that do not fit the character, or the social class, or the gender of its assigned teller; the poet recycled texts he had written earlier, and sometimes the fit is hardly exact. Even though the two most important of the early copies, the so-called Ellesmere and Hengwrt manuscripts, were written by the same scribe, there are major differences in the positioning of some tales and groups of tales, and the Hengwrt lacks the *Canon Yeoman's Prologue and Tale*. This suggests that Chaucer had not settled on a definitive arrangement for his work or had failed to impose one (the Hengwrt offering testimony to an alternative arrangement and/or an earlier stage in the compilation process). The large number of spurious additions to *The Canterbury Tales* may indicate a recognition by Chaucer's early readers that the text was incomplete and hence open to amplification.

Given this context of creative contingency, the text now known as *The Parson's Tale* could be judged not as a 'tale' in any meaningful sense of that term but as rather an abandonment of the tale-telling competition (we are never told who won that free supper) and/or a disruption of the framework of the fictional pilgrimage, as Chaucer – who now knows he will never finish *The Canterbury Tales* as originally conceived – breaks away from his ambitious *fable*-making to offer a penitential treatise and to pray that God may give him a good end. (He might have undertaken the translation as a penitential act in itself – and not necessarily at the very end of his career, the decision to close the *Tales* with it being made later.) On this argument, the search for a distinctive narratorial voice in the 'tretys' is inappropriate.

Not everyone would agree with that. Some readers have heard in *The Parson's Tale* the distinctive voice of the poor small-town parson portrayed so idealistically in the General Prologue. Here, they say, may be found the standards against which the words and deeds of all the other pilgrims should be judged; thus the Parson serves as a sort of moral policeman for his fellow travellers. That same rigour has also been read as deriving from Lollard ideology. *Au contraire*, there has been some resistance to the idea that the Parson is exempt from Chaucer's all-pervasive irony; he has been seen as a pedant who delivers routine dogma in a boring way. Another reading has out-parsoned the Parson by finding fault with his supposedly negative tone, which (so the argument runs) hinders the treatise's penitential objectives. Setting aside the issue of the fit between teller and tale, Lee Patterson has praised the work as highly successful in its own terms, inasmuch as it offers a 'complete and even absolute view of experience as a whole. Its narrowness of focus does not exclude or reduce reality but on the contrary fits all of reality within a single and peculiarly intense and authoritative perspective'.[36] Praise for a penitential treatise hardly gets better than that.

The *Retraction* begins with a clear reference back to *The Parson's Tale*. That is the text Chaucer has in mind when he makes an appeal for correction by his audience, following this up with the request that they should ascribe anything which displeases them to his imperfect knowledge rather than to his will. All that is written is written for our doctrine, as St Paul says (Romans 15:4), and Chaucer has done precisely that – written for the instruction of those who will hear or read his treatise. In what follows, he does not address *The Canterbury Tales* in its totality, as a discrete work. The only 'tales of Caunterbury' here specified are those that lead into sin, and they are bracketed with other works that Chaucer now revokes, including the major dream-visions, *The Legend of Good Women* and *Troilus and Criseyde*. Chaucer then proceeds to a second grouping of texts, bringing together the *Boece* and 'othere books of legendes of seintes, and omelies, and moralitee, and devocioun'. The fact that some of them are Canterbury tales (or became Canterbury tales) is not mentioned. Chaucer's 'feeste' of tale-telling has not so much been 'knytte up' (drawn together) as ripped apart (cf. *ParP* X.46–7). The idioms of the Parson's Prologue seem far distant; they were able to collude with the fictional pilgrimage in a way that the *Retraction* is not.

Does the *Retraction* represent a level of discourse far beyond fiction, or are we, once again, faced with a carapace of literary conventions, whether of the *apologia* or of the *retractio* – conventions that can accommodate open expressions of regret alongside a listing of one's achievements, which the act of revocation has rendered permissible? For an expression of regret, this text includes a rather full list of the works it is supposed to be revoking, so could Chaucer be more interested in canon-formation than in an act of confession at once public and private? That question does not, I think, get us very far; we need not find (indeed, we have no means of finding) anything insincere in the writing. Use of conventional forms need not imply lack of commitment; even a great poet needs them to repent with and through.

The stance adopted throughout *The Canterbury Tales*, in its constant engagements with religious *auctores* and ecclesiastical institutions, is insistently lay, a version of Christian belief quite different in tenor from the values of monasticism (with its imperatives of celibacy and contemplation), which had dominated European Christianity for centuries, and remained a force to be reckoned with, despite the impact of the Aristotelian thought systems that inform the poet's understanding of *science*. The pressures troubling that version come to the fore in the *Retraction*. Again and again, Chaucer had negotiated between the competing demands of authority and experience, what we see with our own eyes and what the old books tell us to believe, what requires *preve* and what is a matter of faith. Now the limits of secularism are acknowledged. The maker of this book takes his leave, having humbled himself before his Maker. As an ending, that lacks neither power nor poignancy.

Afterword

A squire removes the hood from his falcon's head and releases it from his gloved hand. It climbs into the sky and circles, seeking its prey. Then, in an instant, feathers become metal, the silent soaring of the bird gives way to the roar of a powerful piston engine. A medieval killing machine has morphed into a modern one, a Spitfire fighter plane. When we return to the squire, he has doffed his medieval costume and now is dressed as a soldier, complete with steel helmet and fixed bayonet.

Here I have described part of the opening sequence from the 1944 film *A Canterbury Tale*, directed by Emeric Pressburger and Michael Powell. An idyllic depiction of Chaucer's pilgrims traveling towards Canterbury prefaces a tale that owes nothing to any of Chaucer's own narratives, being a whimsical account of how three strangers – a British army sergeant, an American GI and a 'Land Girl'– are accidentally thrown together in a small Kent town and confront a minor local mystery. A delicate depiction of rural England threatened by wartime change emerges. Chaucer's characters, and images of the town of Canterbury itself, have been deployed in the moving evocation of a type of Englishness that may never be the same again.

The wartime imprint on this realization of *The Canterbury Tales* is just one among many examples of how, during six hundred years of reading, interpretation and translation, Chaucer has taken on the mark of different historical moments. The poet's fifteenth-century successors, while praising 'master Chaucer' for his philosophical and ethical pronouncements, emphasized his role as a skilled rhetorician who had embellished the English language. Early comment on Chaucer's characters is rare, and what we do have tends to normalize their subversive implications, as when Thomas Hoccleve reduces the Wife of Bath to a stereotypical shrew who reacts vigorously against male attempts at moral admonition. However, Sir/St Thomas More, writing on the eve of the English Reformation[1] (to which he fell victim), delighted in Chaucer's depiction of the Pardoner, seeing here a forceful satire on abuses within the church, which the church was well equipped to counter, and certainly rise above. Following the passage in 1536 of an act of parliament 'extinguishing the authority of the bishop of Rome', such aspects of Chaucer's writing earned him a place alongside John Wyclif as a morning star of the Reformation, an early voice of protest against popish superstition.

During the sixteenth century, however, Chaucer was respected rather than imitated, his 'pleasant, easy and plain' words (as John Skelton had called them in the early 1500s) having become hard to understand and associated with a 'misty time' denigrated as barbarous and uncouth.[2] Chaucer failed to conform to the stylistic standards of humanist classicism, although (in 1597) Sir Francis Beaumont attempted to compare his comic tales to a tradition reaching back to the likes of Philemon and Menander, and his *Troilus and Criseyde* to Homer, Virgil and Horace. Edmund Spenser drank deeply from the 'well of English undefyled', as he termed Chaucer (*Faerie Queene*, IV.ii.32). However, his adventures in Chaucerian English are self-consciously anachronistic, a means of conjuring up fictional worlds ostensibly remote from the political realities of Elizabethan England – realities that, in fact, are clearly visible through the thin veils of pastoral or epic discourse. Furthermore, the fact that Spenser apparently fails to detect the parodic nature of Chaucer's *Tale of Sir Thopas* raises questions concerning the extent of his linguistic comprehension. In an account published in 1694, Joseph Addison succinctly expressed the prevailing opinion. 'Age has rusted' what that 'merry bard' wrote,

> Worn out his language, and obscur'd his wit.
> In vain he jests in his unpolish'd strain
> And tries to make his readers laugh in vain.

John Dryden (d. 1700) was more generous, moving beyond issues of verbal dust and rust by finding in *The Canterbury Tales* 'God's plenty', and enthusing about the way 'Chaucer followed Nature everywhere, but was never so bold to go beyond her'. Those statements feature in the preface to Dryden's *Fables, Ancient and Modern*, which includes modernizations of several of Chaucer's works (offered as a reverent replacement of obsolete expression). *The Wife of Bath's Tale* is included, but not her *Prologue*, Dryden 'not daring' to venture there, 'because 'tis too licentious'. 'I have confined my choice', he reassures his readers, 'to such tales of Chaucer as savour nothing of immodesty'. The young Alexander Pope did dare to produce a version of *The Wife of Bath's Prologue*, together with *The Merchant's Tale* and *The House of Fame*, duly bowdlerizing immodest passages in accordance with eighteenth-century tastes.

Dryden remarked that Chaucer took into his compass 'the various manners and humours . . . of the whole English nation'. More than a century later (in 1809), William Blake aimed even higher by proclaiming Chaucer's pilgrims 'the characters which compose all ages and nations'; 'some of the names or titles are altered by time, but the characters themselves for ever remain unaltered, and consequently they are the physiognomies or lineaments of universal human life, beyond which Nature never steps. Names alter, things never alter'. Chaucer has become at once an astute observer of common human experience and the ideal Englishman – cheerful, generous and plain-spoken, staunchly sensible yet sensitive to beauty, truth and love. He was being praised in such terms as late as 1956, as these eloquent words of Nevill Coghill, Chaucer's greatest translator into Modern English, attest: 'His vision of earth ranges from one of amused delight to one of grave compassion; these are his dawn and his dusk. His daylight is a lively April of fresh good will and kindly common sense, and if, here and there, there is a delicate frost of irony, warmth is his great characteristic'.[3] A few generations earlier, Matthew Arnold (d.1888) had credited Chaucer with a 'large, free, simple, clear yet kindly view of human life', characterizing him as a writer who had 'gained the power to survey the world from a central, a truly human point of view'. This remark should be read in light of the 'Victorian medievalism' that influenced so many poets and artists of Arnold's day, who harked back to a past supposedly marked by chivalry, honour, duty and manly piety, as they sought moral certainties and clear social responsibilities in a rapidly changing industrial age.

However, Arnold struck one of the most discordant notes ever heard in Chaucer criticism by declaring that the poet lacked 'high seriousness', a quality Arnold managed to find in Homer, Dante and Shakespeare. Chaucer's honour was vigorously defended by a succession of critics who emphasized his 'high comedy' (Coghill's phrase) and argued that 'it was humor rather than poker-faced solemnity that created the most complex vision of the world'.[4] This stance owes much to G. L. Kittredge, who in 1896 became only the second person to hold a Harvard chair dedicated to the study of English Literature.

The twentieth century saw an unprecedented burgeoning of Chaucer criticism, enabled by the growth, particularly in Britain and the United States, of university Departments of English; the Higher Education system as a whole enjoyed an era of unprecedented expansion, with students from a wider range of socioeconomic backgrounds being admitted, particularly after the Second World War. A 'bourgeois' style was identified in some of Chaucer's poems and read either as subversive of or in uneasy if ultimate alliance with the high style that conveyed aristocratic views of love and war. Even more fundamentally, whereas the previous century had emphasized Chaucer's 'realism' (often praised as a departure from the constrictions of rhetoric or French courtly style), this came to be seen as a style in itself, a way of writing constituted by distinctive conventions. Whereas in 1818, William Hazlitt had commended the poet for exhibiting 'for the most part the naked object, with little drapery thrown over it', his successors commended the many clothes that made the men they covered. No 'naked object' is in sight, certainly not Chaucer the man himself, who is obscured by a series of impermeable fictions, such as 'the narrator', the 'I-persona', 'the dreamer' and 'Chaucer the pilgrim', all of whom now speak in place of convivial Chaucer. The terms of reference cited here are those of 'New Criticism', a movement that generated much intellectual excitement in the post-war period, as its proponents professed their aim of rescuing medieval texts from the philologists and source-scholars. Chaucer was at once the greatest prize and the easiest Middle English writer to win over, given the openness of so many of his texts to 'close reading'.

However, such critics experienced strong competition – particularly in North America – from the 'exegetical' school associated with D. W. Robertson, Jr. 'Robertsonianism' may be regarded as a historicizing methodology inasmuch as it offers readings that proudly display their (supposedly) authentic period credentials. Medieval thinkers (usually theologians) are called upon to provide the keys that open up the meaning of medieval poems; otherwise modern readers may well be misled by present-day values. Here, then, is a world we have lost – and what a fascinatingly different, and more ideologically cohesive, place it is too (although its fundamental Christian values may still guide us in today's world). And yet – in exegetical criticism of Chaucer, history implodes as the worldview of the Church Fathers (particularly St Augustine) is deemed of direct relevance to fourteenth-century England and to a writer who, however learned, was a layman. Distinctions between monasticism and scholasticism, Latinity and vernacularity, the contemplative and the active lives, the clerical and the lay, are dissolved, as 'God's plenty' risks being reduced to allegories of the conflict between *caritas* (Christian love) and cupidity.

'Exegetical' criticism may be seen as a historicism of ideas, with little interest in social and political history. During the 1970s that interest found expression in Marxist and New Historicist analysis, this being part of a general 'theoretical moment' that also encompassed feminism, psychoanalysis, the carnivalesque, structuralism, deconstruction and postmodernism. New Historicism is marked by a rejection of distinctions between 'literary' works and historical documents, all of which are read as texts constructed through rhetorical devices and narrative strategies and all of which constitute the 'Cultural Poetics' of an age. Hence medieval chronicles, legal documents, public accounts and the like became the objects of bravura close reading as they were ushered into the company of poems from which they had once been segregated.

By far the most successful of those theoretical 'schools' was feminism. Indeed, so great has been its success that it can hardly be called a school anymore; rather it is now part of the mainstream, a crucial feature of any classroom discussion of (for instance) Criseyde, the Wife of Bath or Grisilde. Some elements of feminist critique helped create the wider base of gender criticism, one outcome of which has been the investigation of 'Chaucerian masculinities'. Within Medieval Studies 'queer theory' ranges from the analysis of records (or at least implications) of same-sex liaisons to an ongoing 'queering' or critique of any attempt to render certain practices and attitudes (sexual or otherwise) as normative for human behaviour. (Here literary criticism is functioning in the service of identity politics.) Much of the discussion of 'Queer Chaucer' has concentrated on the Pardoner, in response to the provocative remark about him looking like a gelding or a mare.

During the first decades of the new millennium, postcolonialist theory has been particularly fruitful in Chaucer Studies, not least because it has focussed attention on issues that have long been in need of investigation. 'Postcolonial critique emphasizes the heterogeneity of cultures, their commingling of differences in history, language, creed, custom, desire'.[5] Thus understood, it encompasses (for example) Chaucer's evident fascination with pagan antiquity, the journeys he has Custance make from Rome to Syria to Northern England and back to Rome again, and his location of the martyrdom of a 'litel clergeon' in an Asian city where heterogeneous cultures violently clash. The many meanings of 'nature' in Chaucer's time are the central concern of eco-critical readings, which have raised questions about the poet's understanding of the wild, the remote and the uncivilized. Dorigen's outcry against the grisly black rocks on the Breton coast has proved an excellent point of departure, as has the Man in Black's self-alienation in an inhospitable wood. 'Animal studies', which has much in common with eco-criticism, is taking on a life of its own, moving from the symbolic work that animals perform in Chaucer's poetry to his treatment of the divide between animals and humans, as an essential constituent of what it means to be human. High stakes indeed.

But Chaucer is not the exclusive property of professional critics, as is manifest by Jonathan Myerson's award-winning animated version of selected *Canterbury Tales* (1998) and the modernized versions of the tales directed for the BBC by John McKay and Andy de Emmony (2003), a highlight of which was Julie Walters' BAFTA award–winning performance as soap-opera star Beth (an alter ego of the Wife of Bath), who marries a handsome actor many years her junior (a version of Jenkyn, although here called Jerome – a joke at the expense of the misogynistic saint). This is creative transformation rather than adaptation. The African-American writer Gloria Naylor pays a comparable *omage* in her novel *Bailey's Café* (1992), where Harry Bailly is re-imagined as the sympathetic but insufficient host to a motley crew of customers who seek the road to self-redemption.

Chaucer's bawdy reputation is often referenced in popular culture. When, in the American TV show *The Big Bang Theory*, geeky Amy wants to tell the dirtiest story she knows, she comes up with *The Miller's Tale*. A literally naked 'Chaucer' (who has little to do with Chaucer) features in the 2001 movie *A Knight's Tale* (which has nothing to do with Chaucer's tale). Indeed, Hollywood has never taken on *The Canterbury Tales*. Perhaps that reluctance is due to bad memories surrounding Pier Paolo Pasolini's *I racconti di Canterbury* (1972), which became an organizational nightmare for its director, as he struggled to devise the best sequence for the tales (thereby reliving some of Chaucer's own creative difficulties) and which met with a mixed critical reception, in part due to its explicit sexual content. It deserves better – for, at its best, it offers a powerful 'queering' of the Middle Ages, as Pasolini reveals how the human body, whether male or female, can be exploited and debased for capitalist purposes, with sex being reduced to a commodity. That is the truly shocking thing about Pasolini's film.

Chaucer's place in the classroom remains assured, although the erosion of 'period requirements' and an emphasis on modern literature (at both university and high school levels) has not been good for him, or indeed for any pre-1800 author with the possible exception of Shakespeare. As Chaucer himself might have put it, a person cannot offer his *sentence* if he is not allowed an *audience*. Yet, institutionally, Chaucer stands alongside Shakespeare as an author whose canonical weight must inevitably be felt. Furthermore, he has found new audiences far beyond the Anglophone regions and Western Europe. The 'Global Chaucer' project has tracked down nearly fifty country/language combinations, including Arabic, Brazilian Portuguese, Bulgarian, Mandarin Chinese, Farsi, Hebrew, Japanese, Serbo-Croatian, Tamil – and Mongolian.[6] Translation offers Chaucer many possible futures (a fact recognized long ago by Dryden). There is a certain poetic justice here, given his historical position in fourteenth-century England when, in the words of poet and performance artist Caroline Bergvall, 'the spelling and fixing of Middle English was very much up for grabs. . . . He made his choices from within the language's active maelstrom of influences and confluences. Everything about Middle English was a mashup on the rise'.[7] Chaucer is deeply embedded in the mashup, the meddle, the muddle, the mingle, of world language.

Notes

Introduction: Life and historical contexts

1 Throughout this chapter, I have drawn on Martin M. Crow and Clair C. Olson, eds., *Chaucer Life-Records* (Oxford: Clarendon Press, 1966).
2 *The Testament of Love*, ed. R. Allen Shoaf (Kalamazoo, Mich.: TEAMS, 1998), p. 266.
3 *Riverside Chaucer*, p. 662.
4 *Selections from English Wycliffite Writings*, ed. Anne Hudson (Cambridge: Cambridge University Press, 1978), pp. 24–9, 150–5; Thomas Walsingham, *Chronica maiora (1376–1422)*, tr. David Preest (Woodbridge: Boydell Press, 2005), p. 293.
5 Nigel Saul, 'Chaucer and Gentility', in Barbara A. Hanawalt, ed., *Chaucer's England: Literature in Historical Context* (Minneapolis: University of Minnesota Press, 1992), pp. 41–55 (p. 48).

1 Love and lore: the shorter poems

1 V. J. Scattergood in Alastair Minnis with V. J. Scattergood and J. J. Smith, *Chaucer: The Shorter Poems* (Oxford: Clarendon Press, 1995), p. 465.
2 *Riverside Chaucer*, p. 1076.
3 References are to *Le jugement du Roy de Behaigne and Remede de fortune*, ed. James I. Wimsatt and William W. Kibler (Athens: University of Georgia Press, 1988).
4 Windeatt, tr., *Chaucer's Dream Poetry*, p. 41.
5 Mary Frances Wack, *Lovesickness in the Middle Ages: The Viaticum and Its Commentaries* (Philadelphia: University of Pennsylvania Press, 1990), pp. 188–9.
6 *Le Livre des Eschez amoureux moralisés*, ed. Françoise Guichard-Tesson and Bruno Roy (Montréal: Bibliothèque du Moyen Français, 1993), p. 191.
7 *Ovide moralisé*, vol. iv, ed. C. de Boer (Amsterdam: Koninklijke Akademie, 1936), pp. 198–219.
8 *Etymologiae*, I.iii.12.
9 *Policraticus*, tr. Cary C. Nederman (Cambridge: Cambridge University Press, 1990), pp. 3–4.
10 Guido, *Historia destructionis Troiae*, tr. M. E. Meek (Bloomington, Ind., 1974), p. 1.
11 Ibid., p. 265. (With one alteration.)
12 *Etymologiae*, I.xl.1, and V. xxvii.26.

13 Martin Irvine, 'Medieval Grammatical Theory and Chaucer's *House of Fame*', *Speculum*, 60 (1985), 850–76 (p. 855).

14 Assuming that *The House of Fame* predates *Troilus and Criseyde*, where the Muses are also invoked, at II.8–9 and III.45–6, respectively. Cf. also *Anelida and Arcite*, 15–19.

15 *Legend of Good Women*, F 420–1; apparently an early version of *The Knight's Tale*. Helen Cooper has argued persuasively for this later dating: 'The Four Last Things in Dante and Chaucer: Ugolino in the House of Rumour', *New Medieval Literatures*, 3 (1999), 39–66 (pp. 58–60).

16 H. A. Kelly, *Chaucer and the Cult of Saint Valentine* (Leiden: Brill, 1986), esp. pp. 45–63, 77–98.

17 Alan of Lille, *The Plaint of Nature*, tr. James J. Sheridan (Toronto: Pontifical Institute, 1980), pp. 73–105.

18 Ibid., pp. 131–2.

19 Ibid., pp. 118–19.

20 Ibid., p. 119.

21 *Commentary on the Dream of Scipio by Macrobius*, tr. W. H. Stahl (New York: Columbia University Press, 1952), p. 71.

22 *The Governance of Kings and Princes: John Trevisa's Middle English Translation of the De regimine principum of Aegidius Romanus*, ed. David C. Fowler et al. (New York: Garland, 1997), pp. 182–4, 187. Cf. *Nicomachean Ethics*, VIII.12 (1162a).

23 Oresme, *Le Livre de Yconomque d'Aristote*, ed. A. D. Menut (Philadelphia: American Philosophical Society, 1957), p. 813.

2   Fictions of antiquity: *Troilus and Criseyde* and *The Legend of Good Women*

1 There is some debate concerning this identification. An alternative candidate is Genghis's grandson Batu Khan (1207–55), founder of the Kipchak Khanate.

2 Walter Hilton, *The Scale of Perfection*, II.3, ed. Thomas H. Bestul (Kalamazoo, Mich.: TEAMS, 2000), p. 139.

3 *De civitate Dei*, VIII. 9 and 10; tr. R. W. Dyson (Cambridge: Cambridge University Press, 1998), pp. 324–5, 326–7.

4 *Riverside Chaucer*, p. 671.

5 By contrast, 'general' predictions of such great terrestrial events as plagues, famines, floods, great wars, the falls of empires and the like were at once possible and permissible (although some warned of the difficulty of obtaining precise results). Another – quite unproblematic – branch of the science sought to know beforehand what the weather had in store, in respect of winds, storms, and the like.

6 Havely, tr., *Chaucer's Boccaccio*, p. 71.

7 *Speculum doctrinale*, iii.92, in *Speculum quadruplex, sive Speculum maius* (Douai: B. Bellerie, 1624, rpt. Graz: Akademische Druck- u. Verlaganstalt, 1964–5), ii, fol. 51r.

8 Oresme, *Livre de divinacions* (1361–5), ed. G. W. Coopland, *Nicole Oresme and the Astrologers* (Cambridge, Mass.: Harvard University Press, 1952), pp. 94–7.

9 I draw on Maggie Humm's discussion of Rubin in her anthology *Modern Feminisms: Political, Literary, Cultural* (New York: Columbia University Press, 1992), p. 256.

10 *MED*, s.v. *corage*.

11 *Chaucer, Langland and the Creative Imagination* (London and Boston: Routledge & Kegan Paul, 1980), pp. 120, 122.

12 *The Allegory of Love: A Study in Medieval Tradition* (Oxford: The Clarendon Press, 1936), pp. 185–6, 189–90.

13 The following discussion is based on Alastair Minnis and Eric Johnson, 'Criseyde's Feminine Fear', in Jocelyn Wogan-Browne et al., eds., *Medieval Women: Texts and Contexts in Late-Medieval Britain: Essays for Felicity Riddy* (Turnhout: Brepols, 2000), pp. 199–216.

14 Havely, tr., *Chaucer's Boccaccio*, pp. 167, 175, 178–80.

15 Guido, *Historia destructionis Troiae*, tr. Meek, p. 157.

16 Havely, tr., *Chaucer's Boccaccio*, pp. 101 and 38.

17 Ibid., p. 73.

18 *Poems of Cupid, God of Love*, ed. T. S. Fenster and M. C. Erler (Leiden: Brill, 1990), p. 67.

19 *Riverside Chaucer*, p. 328.

20 The F prologue is usually dated *c*.1386. Some of the narratives may have been written before that; we have no way of knowing.

21 Christine de Pizan, *The Book of the City of Ladies*, tr. Rosalind Brown-Grant (Harmondsworth: Penguin, 1999), pp. 63, 82–5, 173–5.

22 *The Judgment of the King of Navarre*, ed. R. Barton Palmer (New York: Garland, 1988). All *Navarre* references are to this edition.

23 Augustine, *De civitate Dei*, I.19; tr. Dyson, pp. 29–31.

24 Ibid., p. 31.

25 *The Middle Scots Poets*, ed. A. M. Kinghorn (London: Edward Arnold, 1970), pp. 162–3.

3 *The Canterbury Tales*, I: war, love, laughter

1 Paul Miller, 'John Gower, Satiric Poet', in Alastair Minnis, ed., *Gower's Confessio Amantis: Responses and Reassessments* (Cambridge: D. S. Brewer, 1983), pp. 79–105 (p. 82).

2 *MED*, s.v. *vulgār(e)*.

3 *Testament of Love*, ed. Shoaf, p. 49.

4 *La prise d'Alixandre*, 2600, 2697, 2794, 2805, 3137, 3177. References are to the edition by R. Barton Palmer (New York: Routledge, 2002).

5 Geoffroi de Charnay, *The Book of Chivalry*, tr. R. W. Kaeuper and Elspeth Kennedy (Philadelphia: University of Pennsylvania Press, 1996), pp. 142–5.

6 To borrow a phrase from Milton's *Lycidas*, 70–1.

7 *Book of Chivalry*, p. 163.

8 *Anticlaudianus*, IV.482–3, ed. R. Bossuat (Paris: Vrin, 1955), p. 121.

9 Havely, tr., *Chaucer's Boccaccio*, p. 128.

10 *Nicole Oresme and The Marvels of Nature*, ed. Bert Hansen (Toronto: Pontifical Institute of Mediaeval Studies, 1985), p. 137.

11 *Marvels of Nature*, ed. Hansen, p. 361.

12 *S&A*, i.222–9.

13 Ibid., i.232–9.

14 Ibid., i.238–45.

15 *MED*, s.v. *meue* (n. 1).

16 Mikhail Bakhtin, *Rabelais and His World*, tr. Hélène Iswolsky (Bloomington, Ind.: Indiana University Press, 1984), pp. 25–7, 48, 92.

17 Ibid., p. 19.

18 Ibid.

19 R. Howard Bloch, *The Scandal of the Fabliaux* (Chicago: University of Chicago Press, 1986), esp. pp. 19, 69–70.

20 As Talbot Donaldson nicely called it in his *Speaking of Chaucer* (London: Athlone Press, 1970), pp. 13–29.

21 *MED*, s.v. *hende* (adj.), 1 and 2.

22 Preserved in British Library, MS Harley 2253; ed. G. L. Brook; *The Harley Lyrics*, 4th edn (Manchester: Manchester University Press, 1968).

23 *MED*, s.v. *hende* (adj.), 3 and 4.

24 *Harley Lyrics*, ed. Brook, p. 33.

25 Ibid., pp. 40–1.

26 *MED*, s.v. *spillen* 4(a).

27 Ibid. 7 (a).

28 Simon Horobin, 'Chaucer's Norfolk Reeve', *Neophilologus*, 86 (2002), 609–12.

29 *MED*, s.v. *disparagen*.

30 V. J. Scattergood, 'Perkyn Revelour and the *Cook's Tale*', *ChR*, 19 (1984), 14–23 (p. 16).

31 *Riverside Chaucer*, p. 322.

32 Isidore of Seville, *Etymologiae*, 1.xl.1–4.

33 *S&A*, ii.754–5.

34 See *The Poems of Robert Henryson*, ed. Denton Fox (Oxford: Clarendon Press, 1981), p. 190.

35 *Ovide moralisé*, vol. 1, ed. de Boer, p. 61.

36 *The Fables of 'Walter of England'*, ed. Aaron E. Wright (Toronto: Pontifical Institute, 1997), p. 19.

37 Alastair Minnis and A. B. Scott with David Wallace, eds., *Medieval Literary Theory and Criticism c.1100–c.1375: The Commentary Tradition*, rev. edn (Oxford: Clarendon Press, 1991), p. 38.

38 Ibid., p. 209.

4   *The Canterbury Tales*, II: experience and authority

1 *Riverside Chaucer*, pp. 669, 670, 662.

2 *MED*, s.v. *experience*, 2(a).

3 Cf. W. G. East, 'By Preeve Which That Is Demonstratif', *ChR*, 12 (1977), 78–82.

4 Michael C. Thomsett, *The Inquisition: A History* (Jefferson, N.C.: McFarland & Co., 2010), p. 54.

5 See Alastair Minnis, *Fallible Authors: Chaucer's Pardoner and Wife of Bath* (Philadelphia: University of Pennsylvania Press, 2007), p. 118.

6 *Summa theologiae*, 2a 2ae, qu.77, art.2, reply to obj. 1.

7 Beinecke Library, MS Mellon 41. Ripley is the author of *The Compound of Alchymie* (1471), an English poem of more than 2,500 lines of verse, in rhyme royal stanzas.

8 Lee Patterson, *Temporal Circumstances: Form and History in the Canterbury Tales* (New York: Palgrave Macmillan, 2006), pp. 171, 176.

9 Betty Jo Teeter Dobbs, *The Janus Faces of Genius: The Role of Alchemy in Newton's Thought* (Cambridge: Cambridge University Press, 1991), pp. 1, 3.

10 Bruce T. Moran, *Distilling Knowledge: Alchemy, Chemistry, and the Scientific Revolution* (Cambridge, Mass.: Harvard University Press, 2005), pp. 7, 4–5.

11 *La Querelle de la Rose: Letters and Documents*, tr. Joseph L. Baird and John R. Kane (Chapel Hill: University of North Carolina Press, 1978), pp. 52–3.

12 *Riverside Chaucer*, pp. 221–2, 236.

13 *Summa theologiae*, 2a 2ae, qu. 47, art. 8, resp.

14 *Riverside Chaucer*, p. 220.

15 Ibid.

16 Ibid., p. 321.

17 *The Personal Correspondence of Hildegard of Bingen*, tr. Joseph L. Baird (Oxford: Oxford University Press, 2006), p. 37.

18 Brian Tierney, *The Middle Ages*, 2nd edn (New York: Knopf, 1977), i.231.

19 Cf. *The Merchant's Tale*, IV.1954.

20 *MED*, s.v. *pacience*, 1 & 2.

21 *S&A*, ii.14, pp. 294–5. Chaucer made a translation of this treatise (according to *LGW* F Pro 414), which has been lost.

22 Ibid., ii.298–9.

23 Ibid., ii.304–5.

24 Ibid., ii.316–17.

25 Ibid., ii.302–3.

26 Ibid., i.118–19.

27 Ibid., i.128–9.

28 Ibid., i.122–3.

29 Ibid., i.166–7.

30 *The Good Wife's Guide, Le Ménagier de Paris*, tr. Gina L. Greco and Christine M. Rose (Ithaca, N.Y.: Cornell University Press, 2009), p. 31.

31 Ibid., pp. 118–19. Critical opinion is divided on whether Chaucer knew *Le Ménagier*.

32 Augustine, *De civitate Dei*, V.18; tr. Dyson, pp. 218–23.

33 Cf. *MED*, s.v. *softe*, 3(a).

34 Cf. *MlT* II.362–4, 370–1.

35 *The Book of Margery Kempe*, I.3, ed. Barry Windeatt (Cambridge: D. S. Brewer, 2004), p. 61.

36 'The *Parson's Tale* and the quitting of the *Canterbury Tales*', *Traditio*, 34 (1978), 331–80 (pp. 346–7).

Afterword

1 In his *Dialogue Concerning Heresies* (1529).
2 All of the quotations used in this chapter that are not specifically referenced may conveniently be found in Derek Brewer's two-volume collection, *Chaucer: The Critical Heritage* (London and Boston: Routledge & Paul, 1978).
3 *The Collected Papers of Nevill Coghill*, ed. Douglas Gray (Brighton: Harvester Press, 1988), p. 49.
4 As Ethan Knapp nicely puts it; 'Chaucer Criticism and Its Legacies', in Steve Ellis, ed., *Chaucer: An Oxford Guide* (Oxford: Oxford University Press, 2005), pp. 324–56 (p. 340).
5 Jeffrey J. Cohen, 'Postcolonialism', in Ellis, ed., *Chaucer: An Oxford Guide*, pp. 448–62 (p. 448).
6 See http://globalchaucers.wordpress.com, an initiative of Candace Barrington and Jonathan Hsy.
7 *Meddle English* (Callicoon, N.Y.: Nightboat Books, 2011), p. 13. In the following sentence, I have adopted some of Bergvall's creative phrasings.

Further reading

Editions

The basic text for both scholarship and teaching is *The Riverside Chaucer*, general ed. Larry D. Benson, 3rd edn (Oxford: Oxford University Press, 2008). Given their appended critical essays and historical materials, the Norton Critical Editions (published by W. W. Norton and Company, New York) are excellent for classroom use: *The Canterbury Tales: Fifteen Tales and the General Prologue*, 2nd edn, ed. V. A. Kolve and Glending Olson (2005), *Troilus and Criseyde*, ed. Stephen Barney (2006), and *Dream Visions and Other Poems*, ed. Kathyrn L. Lynch (2006). Among the many editions of specific texts in the original Middle English, particularly recommended are *Troilus and Criseyde*, ed. Barry A. Windeatt (London and New York: Longman, 1984); *Chaucer's Dream Poetry*, ed. Helen Phillips and N. R. Havely (London and New York: Longman, 1997); and *The Canterbury Tales*, ed. Jill Mann (Harmondsworth: Penguin Books, 2005).

Guides and introductory materials

Excellent brief accounts of Chaucer are provided in David Wallace, ed., *The Cambridge History of Medieval English Literature* (Cambridge: Cambridge University Press, 1999), pp. 566–88 (by Glending Olson); Roger Ellis, ed., *The Oxford History of Literary Translation in English*, vol. 2 (Oxford: Oxford University Press, 2008), pp. 137–48 (by Barry Windeatt); and Larry Scanlon, ed., *The Cambridge Companion to Medieval English Literature, 1100–1500* (Cambridge: Cambridge University Press, 2009), pp. 165–78 (by Larry Scanlon). An abundance of introductory books is available, including Peter Brown, ed., *A Companion to Chaucer* (Oxford: Blackwell, 2000); Steve Ellis, ed., *Chaucer: An Oxford Guide* (Oxford: Oxford University Press, 2005); Seth Lerer, ed., *The Yale Companion to Chaucer* (New Haven, Conn.: Yale University Press, 2006); Corinne Saunders, ed., *A Concise Companion to Chaucer* (Oxford: Blackwell,

2006); and Susanna Fein and David Raybin, eds., *Chaucer: Contemporary Approaches* (University Park, Pa.: Pennsylvania State University Press, 2010). Oxford University Press has published three volumes comprising the Oxford Guides to Chaucer series: Barry Windeatt, *Troilus and Criseyde* (1992); Alastair Minnis with V. J. Scattergood and J. J. Smith, *The Shorter Poems* (1995); and Helen Cooper, *The Canterbury Tales*, 2nd edn (1996). Winthrop Wetherbee, *The Canterbury Tales* (Cambridge: Cambridge University Press, 1990), is an impressive short introduction to the *Tales*; for a fuller treatment see Derek Pearsall, *The Canterbury Tales* (London and New York: Routledge, 1993). For *Troilus*, a good place to start is Jenni Nuttall, *Troilus and Criseyde: A Reader's Guide* (Cambridge: Cambridge University Press, 2013). Among the collections of original essays, particularly recommended is Piero Boitani and Jill Mann, eds., *The Cambridge Companion to Chaucer*, 2nd edn (Cambridge: Cambridge University Press, 2003).

Manuscript studies; history of the book

A major milestone was the discovery by A. I. Doyle and M. B. Parkes that the Ellesmere and Hengwrt manuscripts of the *Tales* were written by the same scribe; 'The Production of Copies of the *Canterbury Tales* and the *Confessio Amantis* in the Early Fifteenth Century', in M. B. Parkes and Andrew G. Watson, eds., *Medieval Scribes, Manuscripts and Libraries: Essays Presented to N. R. Ker* (London: Scolar Press, 1978), pp. 163–210. For the argument that this was Adam Pinkhurst, Scrivener and Clerk of the Guildhall, see Linne R. Mooney, 'Chaucer's Scribe', *Speculum*, 81 (2006), 97–138, and Linne R. Mooney and Estelle Stubbs, *Scribes and the City: London Guildhall Clerks and the Dissemination of Middle English Literature, 1375–1425* (York: York Medieval Press with Boydell & Brewer, 2013). However, this remains controversial; see Jane Roberts, 'On Giving Scribe B a Name and a Clutch of London Manuscripts from *c*.1400', *Medium Ævum*, 80 (2011), 247–70; and Ralph Hanna, *Introducing English Medieval Book History: Manuscripts, Their Producers and Their Readers* (Liverpool: Liverpool University Press, 2013), pp. 132–65. Important recent work involving the structure and sequence of the *Tales* includes Ralph Hanna, *Pursuing History: Middle English Manuscripts and Their Texts* (Stanford, Calif.: Stanford University Press, 1996), pp. 97–194, 247–57; and Simon Horobin, 'Compiling the *Canterbury Tales* in Fifteenth-Century Manuscripts', *ChR*, 47 (2013), 372–89. There is much relevant material in Alexandra Gillespie and Daniel Wakelin, eds., *The Production of Books in England, 1350–1500* (Cambridge: Cambridge University Press, 2011); and Kathryn Kerby-Fulton, Maidie

Hilmo and Linda Olson, *Opening Up Middle English Manuscripts: Literary and Visual Approaches* (Ithaca, N.Y.: Cornell University Press, 2013).

Language and versification

A fine introduction has been provided by Simon Horobin, *Chaucer's Language*, 2nd edn (New York: Palgrave Macmillan, 2012). For historiographical and sociolinguistic discussion see Christopher Cannon, *The Making of Chaucer's English: A Study of Words* (Cambridge: Cambridge University Press, 1998); Tim William Machan, *English in the Middle Ages* (Oxford: Oxford University Press, 2003); and Simon Horobin, *The Language of the Chaucer Tradition* (Cambridge: D. S. Brewer, 2003). On Chaucer's versification, the definitive short account is by Norman Davis in *The Riverside Chaucer*, pp. xlii–xlv. (The first paragraph describes the early tetrameters, and the rest is devoted to the pentameter.) Nicholas Barber and Charles Barber, 'The Versification of the *Canterbury Tales*: A Computer-Based Statistical Survey', *Leeds Studies in English*, 21 (1990), 81–103 and 22 (1991), 57–84, use computer-generated scansions to show that Chaucer's lines were regularly (hen)decasyllabic (i.e. pentametric), and that historical final -e was nearly always counted in the metre except before vowels or h-. Martin Duffell has argued that although Chaucer selected elements from French and Italian metrics, he created a quintessentially English metre by emphasizing stress accent as much as syllable count; '"The Craft So Long to Lerne": Chaucer's Invention of the Iambic Pentameter', *ChR*, 34 (2000), 269–88.

Life, times and history

For a superb brief overview see Douglas Gray, 'Chaucer, Geoffrey (*c.*1340–1400)', *Oxford Dictionary of National Biography* (Oxford University Press, 2004); online edn, May 2012, at www.oxforddnb.com/view/article/5191. The best general biography remains Derek Pearsall, *The Life of Geoffrey Chaucer: A Critical Biography* (Oxford: Blackwell, 1992). Historicizing and historicist discussions of Chaucer include Richard Firth Green, *Poets and Princepleasers: Literature and the English Court in the Late Middle Ages* (Toronto: University of Toronto Press, 1980); David Aers, *Chaucer, Langland, and the Creative Imagination* (London and Boston: Routledge & Kegan Paul, 1980), pp. 80–195; Paul Strohm, *Social Chaucer* (Cambridge, Mass.: Harvard University Press, 1989);

Lee Patterson, *Chaucer and the Subject of History* (Madison: University of Wisconsin Press, 1991); Richard Firth Green, *A Crisis of Truth: Literature and Law in Ricardian England* (Philadelphia: University of Pennsylvania Press, 1999); Lynn Staley, *Languages of Power in the Age of Richard II* (University Park: Pennsylvania State University Press, 2005); Jenni Nuttall, *The Creation of Lancastrian Kingship: Literature, Language and Politics in Late Medieval England* (Cambridge: Cambridge University Press, 2007); and Peter Brown, *Geoffrey Chaucer* (Oxford: Oxford University Press, 2011). For Chaucer as a London poet see Ardis Butterfield, ed., *Chaucer and the City* (Woodbridge: Boydell & Brewer, 2006); and Marion Turner, *Chaucerian Conflict: Languages of Antagonism in Late Fourteenth-Century London* (Oxford: Clarendon Press, 2007). On Chaucer and 'nation' see the essays by Peggy Knapp and Kathleen Davis in Kathy Lavezzo, ed., *Imagining a Medieval English Nation* (Minneapolis: University of Minnesota Press, 2004), pp. 131–87.

Sources, analogues and continental intersections

For sources and analogues see Barry A. Windeatt, tr., *Chaucer's Dream Poetry: Sources and Analogues* (Cambridge: D. S. Brewer, 1982); N. R. Havely, tr., *Chaucer's Boccaccio: Sources of Troilus and the Knight's and Franklin's Tales* (Woodbridge: Boydell & Brewer, 1980); Robert M. Correale and Mary Hamel, eds., *Sources and Analogues of the Canterbury Tales*, 2 vols. (Cambridge: D. S. Brewer, 2002–5). For intersections with France see especially James I. Wimsatt, *Chaucer and his French Contemporaries: Natural Music in the Fourteenth Century* (Toronto: University of Toronto Press, 1991); and Ardis Butterfield, *The Familiar Enemy: Chaucer, Language, and Nation in the Hundred Years War* (Oxford: Oxford University Press, 2009). For Chaucer's deployment of first-person narrators (which often follows French precedent) see David Lawton, *Chaucer's Narrators* (Cambridge: D. S. Brewer, 1985), and two superb monographs by A. C. Spearing, *Textual Subjectivity: The Encoding of Subjectivity in Medieval Narratives and Lyrics* (Oxford: Oxford University Press, 2005), esp. pp. 68–136, and *Medieval Autographies: The 'I' of the Text* (Notre Dame, Ind.: University of Notre Dame Press, 2013), esp. pp. 65–98. For more on the *fabliaux* see John Hines, *The Fabliau in English* (London: Longman, 1993). For the French of England (as spoken by Chaucer's Prioress), the best starting point is Jocelyn Wogan-Browne et al., eds., *Language and Culture in Medieval Britain: The French of England c.1100–c.1500* (York: York Medieval Press with Boydell & Brewer, 2009). The literature on Chaucer and Italy is more extensive. Specially recommended are Piero Boitani, *Chaucer and the Imaginary World of Fame* (Cambridge: D. S. Brewer, 1984); and Boitani, ed., *Chaucer and the Italian Trecento* (Cambridge: Cambridge University Press, 1983); David Wallace, *Chaucer and the Early Writings of Boccaccio* (Cambridge: D. S. Brewer, 1985) and *Chaucerian Polity: Absolutist Lineages and Associational Forms in England and Italy* (Stanford, Calif.: Stanford University Press, 1997); Warren Ginsberg, *Chaucer's Italian Tradition* (Ann Arbor: University of Michigan Press, 2002); Robert R. Edwards, *Chaucer and Boccaccio: Antiquity and Modernity* (New York: Palgrave, 2002); and K. P. Clarke, *Chaucer and Italian Textuality* (Oxford: Oxford University Press, 2011). More broadly, see Piero Boitani, ed., *The European Tragedy of Troilus* (Oxford: Oxford University Press, 1989); and David Wallace, *Premodern Places: Calais to Surinam, Chaucer to Aphra Behn* (Oxford: Blackwell, 2004).

Latin legacies

On Chaucer and the Latin poets see John M. Fyler, *Chaucer and Ovid* (New Haven: Yale University Press, 1979); John P. McCall, *Chaucer among the Gods: The Poetics of Classical Myth* (University Park: Pennsylvania State University Press, 1979); Winthrop Wetherbee, *Chaucer and the Poets* (Ithaca, N.Y.: Cornell University Press, 1984); Christopher Baswell, *Virgil in Medieval England: Figuring the Aeneid from the Twelfth Century to Chaucer* (Cambridge: Cambridge University Press, 1995), pp. 220–69; and Jamie C. Fumo, *The Legacy of Apollo: Antiquity, Authority, and Chaucerian Poetics* (Toronto: University of Toronto Press, 2010). On Chaucer's debt to Latin grammatical and rhetorical traditions see Rita Copeland, *Rhetoric, Hermeneutics, and Translation in the Middle Ages: Academic Traditions and Vernacular Texts* (Cambridge: Cambridge University Press, 1991). For the 'set texts' studied in medieval grammar schools and their significance for Chaucer, see Edward Wheatley, *Mastering Aesop: Medieval Education, Chaucer, and his Followers* (Gainesville, Fla.: University Press of Florida, 2000); and Jill Mann, '"He Knew Nat Catoun": Medieval School-Texts and Middle English Literature', in Jill Mann and Maura Nolan, eds., *The Text in the Community: Essays on Medieval Works, Manuscripts, Authors, and Readers* (Notre Dame, Ind.: University of Notre Dame Press, 2006), pp. 41–74. See further Peter W. Travis, *Disseminal Chaucer: Rereading The Nun's Priest's Tale* (Notre Dame, Ind.: University of Notre Dame Press, 2010). The pre-eminent study of Chaucer and the medieval theory and praxis of satire (which has its roots in Roman satire) is Jill Mann, *Chaucer and Medieval Estates Satire* (Cambridge: Cambridge University Press, 1973). On Chaucer and medieval knowledge (and ignorance) of classical ideas of tragedy, see H. A. Kelly, *Ideas and Forms of Tragedy from Aristotle to the Middle Ages* (Cambridge: Cambridge University Press, 1993); and *Chaucerian Tragedy* (Cambridge: D. S. Brewer, 1997). For the ways in which vernacular writers deployed Latin literary theory to claim authority for their own writings and those of distinguished contemporaries, see Alastair Minnis, *Medieval Theory of Authorship: Scholastic Literary Attitudes in the Later Middle Ages*, 2nd edn with a new preface (Philadelphia: University of Pennsylvania Press, 2010), pp. 160–210; and Alastair Minnis and Ian Johnson, eds., *The Cambridge History of Literary Criticism, Vol. 2: The Middle Ages* (Cambridge: Cambridge University Press, 2005), pp. 363–421. On Chaucer and the vernacular *roman antique* genre (which developed from classical models) see Barbara Nolan, *Chaucer and the Tradition of the Roman Antique* (Cambridge: Cambridge University Press, 1992). For the argument that Chaucer's imaginary of pagan antiquity allows some measure of sympathy, indeed admiration, for his heathen heroes and heroines, see Alastair Minnis, *Chaucer and Pagan Antiquity* (Cambridge: D. S. Brewer, 1982), and the pertinent discussion in Frank Grady, *Representing Righteous Heathens in Late Medieval England* (New York: Palgrave Macmillan, 2005). A very different line is taken by John V. Fleming, *Classical Imitation and Interpretation in Chaucer's Troilus* (Lincoln: University of Nebraska Press, 1990), who holds that Chaucer is deeply critical of the pagan values he presents. This is an exercise in moralizing 'exegetical' criticism of the kind established by D. W. Robertson's monumental *A Preface to Chaucer: Studies in Medieval Perspectives* (Princeton: Princeton University Press, 1962).

Love and marriage

On the origins and cultural significance of aristocratic love, see Francis X. Newman, *The Meaning of Courtly Love* (Albany: State University of New York Press, 1968); R. Howard Bloch, *Medieval Misogyny and the Invention of Western Romantic Love* (Chicago: University of Chicago Press, 1991); and James A. Schultz, *Courtly Love, the Love of Courtliness, and the History of Sexuality* (Chicago: University of Chicago Press, 2006). The medical doctrines that underpin so many aspects of noble love are well brought out by Mary Frances Wack, *Lovesickness in the Middle Ages* (Philadelphia: University of Pennsylvania Press, 1990). Freudian psychoanalytic theory is deployed by L. O. Aranye Fradenburg, *Sacrifice Your Love: Psychoanalysis, Historicism, Chaucer* (Minneapolis: University of Minnesota Press, 2002). On love and marriage see H. A. Kelly, *Love and Marriage in the Age of Chaucer* (Ithaca, N.Y.: Cornell University

Press, 1975); and Cathy Hume, *Chaucer and the Cultures of Love and Marriage* (Cambridge: D. S. Brewer, 2012). More specific studies include Michael A. Calabrese, *Chaucer's Ovidian Arts of Love* (Gainesville: University Press of Florida, 1994); N. S. Thompson, *Chaucer, Boccaccio, and the Debate of Love: A Comparative Study of The Decameron and The Canterbury Tales* (Oxford: Clarendon Press, 1996); and Marilynn Desmond, *Ovid's Art and the Wife of Bath: The Ethics of Erotic Violence* (Ithaca, N.Y.: Cornell University Press, 2006).

Gender and sexualities

Carolyn Dinshaw's two groundbreaking monographs are essential reading: *Chaucer's Sexual Poetics* (Madison: University of Wisconsin Press, 1989) and *Getting Medieval: Sexualities and Communities, Pre- and Postmodern* (Durham, N.C.: Duke University Press, 1999), along with the essays in Ruth Evans and Lesley Johnson, eds., *Feminist Readings in Middle English Literature: The Wife of Bath and All Her Sect* (London and New York: Routledge, 1994), particularly those by Mary Carruthers, 'The Wife of Bath and the Painting of Lions' (pp. 22–53), and Felicity Riddy, 'Engendering Pity in the *Franklin's Tale*' (pp. 54–71). Also important are Elaine Tuttle Hansen, *Chaucer and the Fictions of Gender* (Berkeley: University of California Press, 1992); Susan Crane, *Gender and Romance in Chaucer's Canterbury Tales* (Princeton, N.J.: Princeton University Press, 1994); Marilynn Desmond, *Reading Dido: Gender, Textuality, and the Medieval Aeneid* (Minneapolis: University of Minnesota Press, 1994), pp. 128–51; Corinne Saunders, *Rape and Ravishment in the Literature of Medieval England* (Cambridge: D. S. Brewer, 2001); Jill Mann, *Feminizing Chaucer*, 2nd edn (Cambridge: D. S. Brewer, 2002); Alcuin Blamires, *Chaucer, Ethics, and Gender* (Oxford: Oxford University Press, 2006); and Jane Gilbert, *Living Death in Medieval French and English Literature* (Cambridge: Cambridge University Press, 2011), pp. 191–214. On Chaucerian masculinities see Peter G. Beidler, ed., *Masculinities in Chaucer: Approaches to Maleness in The Canterbury Tales and Troilus and Criseyde* (Cambridge: D. S. Brewer, 1998); Bruce W. Holsinger, *Music, Body, and Desire in Medieval Culture: Hildegard of Bingen to Chaucer* (Stanford, Calif.: Stanford University Press, 2001), esp. pp. 137–87, 259–92, and 261–3; Holly A. Crocker, *Chaucer's Visions of Manhood* (New York: Palgrave Macmillan, 2007); Isabel Davis, *Writing Masculinity in the Later Middle Ages* (Cambridge: Cambridge University Press, 2007), pp. 108–37; and Tison Pugh and Marcia Smith Marzec, eds., *Men and Masculinities in Chaucer's Troilus and Criseyde* (Cambridge: D. S. Brewer, 2008). On Chaucer and queer theory see Monica McAlpine, 'The Pardoner's Homosexuality and How It Matters',

PMLA, 95 (1980), 8–22; Steven Kruger, 'Claiming the Pardoner: Toward a Gay Reading of Chaucer's *Pardoner's Tale*', *Exemplaria*, 6 (1994), 115–39; Glenn Burger, 'Kissing the Pardoner', *PMLA*, 107 (1992), 1143–73, and *Chaucer's Queer Nation* (Minneapolis: University of Minnesota Press, 2003); Robert S. Sturges, *Chaucer's Pardoner and Gender Theory: Bodies of Discourse* (New York: Palgrave Macmillan, 2000); John Bowers, 'Queering the Summoner: Same-Sex Union in Chaucer's *Canterbury Tales*', in Robert F. Yeager and Charlotte C. Morse, eds., *Speaking Images: Essays in Honor of V. A. Kolve* (Asheville, N.C.: Pegasus Press, 2001), pp. 301–24; and Alastair Minnis, 'Chaucer and the Queering Eunuch', *New Medieval Literatures*, 6 (2003), 107–28.

Religion

See Lawrence Besserman, *Chaucer's Biblical Poetics* (Norman: University of Oklahoma Press, 1998); David Benson and Elizabeth Robertson, eds., *Chaucer's Religious Tales* (Cambridge: D. S. Brewer, 1990); David Aers and Lynn Staley, *The Powers of the Holy: Religion, Politics, and Gender in Late Medieval English Culture* (University Park: Pennsylvania State University Press, 1996), esp. pp. 179–59; Alan J. Fletcher, *Preaching, Politics and Poetry in Late-Medieval England* (Dublin: Four Courts, 1998), pp. 249–303; Helen Phillips, ed., *Chaucer and Religion* (Cambridge: D. S. Brewer, 2010); David Raybin and Linda Tarte Holley, eds., *Closure in the Canterbury Tales: The Role of The Parson's Tale* (Kalamazoo, Mich.: Medieval Institute Publications, 2000); James F. Rhodes, *Poetry Does Theology: Chaucer, Grosseteste, and the Pearl-Poet* (Notre Dame, Ind.: University of Notre Dame Press, 2001); and Alastair Minnis, *Translations of Authority in Medieval English Literature: Valuing the Vernacular* (Cambridge: Cambridge University Press, 2009), pp. 38–67. For two succinct (and fascinatingly different) attempts to determine Chaucer's religious position, see Alcuin Blamires, 'Chaucer the Reactionary: Ideology and the General Prologue to *The Canterbury Tales*', *The Review of English Studies*, n.s. 51, no. 204 (2000), 523–39, and Nicholas Watson, 'Chaucer's Public Christianity', *Religion & Literature*, 37 (2005), 99–114. Much of the recent discussion has involved the issue of whether Chaucer had any sympathy for Lollardy. See Alan J. Fletcher, 'Chaucer the Heretic', *SAC*, 25 (2003), 53–121; Alastair Minnis, *Fallible Authors: Chaucer's Pardoner and Wife of Bath* (Philadelphia: University of Pennsylvania Press, 2007); and Andrew Cole, *Literature and Heresy in the Age of Chaucer* (Cambridge: Cambridge University Press, 2008). On the fraught subject of Chaucer and the Jews, see Sheila Delany, ed., *Chaucer and the Jews: Sources, Contexts, Meanings* (London and New York: Routledge, 2002); Roger Dahood,

'The Punishment of the Jews, Hugh of Lincoln, and the Question of Satire in Chaucer's *Prioress's Tale'*, *Viator*, 36 (2005), 465–91; Lee Patterson,'"The Living Witnesses of our Redemption": Martyrdom and Imitation in Chaucer's *Prioress's Tale'*, in Patterson, *Temporal Circumstances: Form and History in the Canterbury Tales* (New York: Palgrave Macmillan, 2006), pp. 129–57; and Anthony Bale, *The Jew in the Medieval Book: English Antisemitisms, 1350–1500* (Cambridge: Cambridge University Press, 2006), pp. 55–103.

Secularity, philosophy and science

On the idea of secularity see Alastair Minnis, '*I speke of folk in seculer estaat*: Vernacularity and Secularity in the Age of Chaucer', *SAC*, 27 (2005), 25–58. See further Stephen H. Rigby, *Wisdom and Chivalry: Chaucer's Knight's Tale and Medieval Political Theory* (Leiden: Brill, 2009), which reads *The Knight's Tale* in terms of Aristotelian political philosophy. Chaucer's main philosophical source was the *De consolatione philosophiae* of Boethius, on which see Alastair Minnis, ed., *Chaucer's Boece and the Medieval Tradition of Boethius* (Cambridge: D. S. Brewer, 1993), and Tim William Machan, ed., *Sources of the Boece* (Athens: University of Georgia Press, 2005). The connections between sexuality and philosophical analysis of agency are explored by Mark Miller, *Philosophical Chaucer* (Cambridge: Cambridge University Press, 2004). See also Jessica Rosenfeld, *Ethics and Enjoyment in Late Medieval Poetry: Love after Aristotle* (Cambridge: Cambridge University Press, 2010). A cogent introduction to astronomy/astrology has been provided by Hilary Carey, *Courting Disaster: Astrology at the English Court and University in the Later Middle Ages* (Houndmills, Basingstoke: Macmillan, 1992). See further John North, *Chaucer's Universe* (Oxford: Clarendon Press, 1988), which is brilliant on the science although some of his textual datings on the basis of astronomical events are controversial, together with his *God's Clockmaker: Richard of Wallingford and the Invention of Time* (London and New York: Hambledon and Palgrave Macmillan, 2005). For Chaucer's interest in the astrolabe (a scientific instrument used to make astronomical measurements) see Marijane Osborn, *Time and the Astrolabe in The Canterbury Tales* (Norman: University of Oklahoma Press, 2002). On alchemy, much needs to be done, but see Robert Schuler, 'The Renaissance Chaucer as Alchemist', *Viator*, 15 (1984), 305–33; Stanton J. Linden, *Darke hierogliphicks: Alchemy in English Literature from Chaucer to the Restoration* (Lexington: University Press of Kentucky, 1996); Michela Pereira, 'Alchemy and the Use of Vernacular Languages in the Late Middle Ages', *Speculum*, 74 (1999), 336–56; Mark J. Bruhn, 'Art, Anxiety, and Alchemy in the

Canon's Yeoman's Tale, ChR, 33 (1999), 288–313; and Lee Patterson, 'Perpetual Motion: Alchemy and the Technology of the Self', in Patterson, *Temporal Circumstances* (full reference under 'Religion'), pp. 159–76. Medieval medicine offered secular explanations for a wide range of human conditions and phenomena, including personality, lovesickness, sex difference, and dreams. See Wack, *Lovesickness in the Middle Ages* (full reference under 'Love and marriage'); Steven Kruger, *Dreaming in the Middle Ages* (Cambridge: Cambridge University Press, 1992); Joan Cadden, *Meanings of Sex Difference in the Middle Ages: Medicine, Science, and Culture* (Cambridge: Cambridge University Press, 1993); Carol Falvo Heffernan, *The Melancholy Muse: Chaucer, Shakespeare, and Early Medicine* (Pittsburgh, Pa.: Duquesne University Press, 1995); and Kathryn L. Lynch, *Chaucer's Philosophical Visions* (Cambridge: D. S. Brewer, 2000).

Iconography, aesthetics, ecocriticism and animal studies

On the influence of iconography (both religious and secular) on Chaucer's poetics see especially V. A. Kolve's two monographs, *Chaucer and the Imagery of Narrative: The First Five Canterbury Tales* (Stanford, Calif.: Stanford University Press, 1984), and *Telling Images: Chaucer and the Imagery of Narrative, II* (Stanford, Calif.: Stanford University Press, 2009), which may be supplemented with Michael Camille, *The Gothic Idol: Ideology and Image-making in Medieval Art* (Cambridge: Cambridge University Press, 1989, rpt. 1991). On Chaucer and aesthetic inquiry see especially Peggy A. Knapp, *Chaucerian Aesthetics* (New York: Palgrave Macmillan, 2008). For ecocritical interpretations see Lisa J. Kiser, 'Chaucer and the Politics of Nature', in Karla Armbruster and Kathleen R. Wallace, eds., *Beyond Nature Writing: Expanding the Boundaries of Ecocriticism* (Charlottesville, VA: University Press of Virginia, 2001), pp. 41–56; Sarah Stanbury, 'EcoChaucer: Green Ethics and Medieval Nature', *ChR*, 39 (2004), 1–16; Gillian Rudd, *Greenery: Ecocritical Readings of Late Medieval English Literature* (Manchester: Manchester University Press, 2007), esp. pp. 50–67, 67–74 and 138–48; and Barbara A. Hanawalt and Lisa J. Kiser, eds., *Engaging with Nature: Essays on the Natural World in Medieval and Early Modern Europe* (Notre-Dame, Ind.: University of Notre Dame Press, 2008). 'Animal studies' interpretations range from historically oriented discussions of the medieval animal world (and of the animal/human divide) to politically committed cultural criticism. See Susan Crane, 'For the Birds', *SAC*, 29 (2007), 23–41, and her monograph, *Animal Encounters: Contacts and Concepts in Medieval Britain* (Philadelphia: University of Pennsylvania Press, 2013);

Bruce Holsinger, 'Of Pigs and Parchment: Medieval Studies and the Coming of the Animal', *PMLA*, 124 (2009) 616–22; Jill Mann, *From Aesop to Reynard: Beast Literature in Medieval Britain* (Oxford: Oxford University Press, 2009), esp. pp.192–219 and 250–61; also the relevant material in Jeffrey Jerome Cohen's monographs, *Of Giants: Sex, Monsters, and the Middle Ages* (Minneapolis: University of Minnesota Press, 1999), *Medieval Identity Machines* (Minneapolis: University of Minnesota Press, 2003), and *Hybridity, Identity, and Monstrosity in Medieval Britain: On Difficult Middles* (New York: Palgrave Macmillan, 2006), together with his edited collection, *Animal, Vegetable, Mineral: Ethics and Objects* (Washington, D.C.: Oliphaunt Books, 2012).

Afterlives

On changing responses over the centuries to Chaucer's writing see Alice S. Miskimin, *The Renaissance Chaucer* (New Haven, Conn.: Yale University Press, 1975); Derek Brewer, ed., *Chaucer: The Critical Heritage*, 2 vols. (London and Boston: Routledge & Keegan Paul, 1978); Ruth Morse and Barry Windeatt, eds, *Chaucer Traditions: Studies in Honour of Derek Brewer* (Cambridge: Cambridge University Press, 1990); Seth Lerer, *Chaucer and His Readers: Imagining the Author in Late-Medieval England* (Princeton, N.J.: Princeton University Press, 1993); Stephanie Trigg, *Congenial Souls: Reading Chaucer from Medieval to Postmodern* (Minneapolis: University of Minnesota Press, 2001); Velma Bourgeois Richmond, *Chaucer as Children's Literature: Retellings from the Victorian and Edwardian Eras* (Jefferson, N.C.: McFarland, 2004); Alexandra Gillespie, *Print Culture and the Medieval Author: Chaucer, Lydgate, and Their Books, 1473–1557* (Oxford: Oxford University Press, 2006); and Robert J. Meyer-Lee, *Poets and Power from Chaucer to Wyatt* (Cambridge: Cambridge University Press, 2007). For Chaucer in relation to medievalism, an approach that addresses the various uses and valuations made of 'the medieval' in later cultures, including contemporary popular culture, see Steve Ellis, *Chaucer at Large: The Poet in the Modern Imagination* (Minneapolis: University of Minnesota Press, 2000); Thomas A. Prendergast, *Chaucer's Dead Body: From Corpse to Corpus* (London and New York: Routledge, 2004); Candace Barrington, *American Chaucers* (New York: Palgrave Macmillan, 2007); Mary Catherine Davidson, *Medievalism, Multilingualism, and Chaucer* (New York: Palgrave Macmillan, 2009); Brantley L. Bryant, ed., *Geoffrey Chaucer Hath a Blog: Medieval Studies and New Media* (New York: Palgrave Macmillan, 2010); and Carolyn Dinshaw, *How Soon Is Now? Medieval Texts, Amateur Readers, and the Queerness of Time* (Durham, N.C.: Duke University Press, 2012). For the interrelationships between medievalism and postcolonial theory see Jeffrey Jerome Cohen, ed., *The Postcolonial Middle Ages* (New York: Palgrave Macmillan, 2000); Bruce Holsinger, 'Medieval Studies, Postcolonial Studies, and the Genealogies of Critique', *Speculum*, 77 (2002), 1195–227; and Kathleen Davis and Nadia Altschul, eds., *Medievalisms in the Postcolonial World: The Idea of 'The Middle Ages' Outside Europe* (Baltimore: Johns Hopkins University Press, 2009).

Index

Cambridge Introductions to...